John Knox

Fuzzy Logic and NeuroFuzzy Applications Explained

Constantin von Altrock

For book and bookstore information

http://www.prenhall.com
gopher to gopher.prenhall.com

Prentice Hall PTR
Englewood Cliffs, New Jersey 07632

Library of Congress Cataloging-in-Publication Data

Editorial/Production Supervision and Interior Design: Lisa Iarkowski
Interior "Fuzzy Logic Flag" Art: Gail Cockr-Bogusz
Acquisitions Editor: Bernard Goodwin
Manufacturing Manager: Alexis R. Heydt
Cover Design: Lundgren Graphics
Cover Illustration: Andreas Schiebel

The publisher offers discounts on this book when ordered in bulk quantities.
For more information, contact:

> Corporate Sales Department, PTR Prentice Hall, 113 Sylvan Avenue, Englewood Cliffs, NJ 07632
> Phone: 800-382-3419 or 201-592-2498, FAX: 201-592-2249, E-mail: dan_rush@prenhall.com

Printed in the United States of America

10 9 8 7 6 5 4 3 2 1

ISBN 0-13-368465-2

Prentice-Hall International (UK) Limited, London
Prentice-Hall of Australia Pty. Limited, Sydney
Prentice-Hall of Canada, Inc., Toronto
Prentice-Hall Hispanoamericana S.A., Mexico
Prentice-Hall of India Private Limited, New Delhi
Prentice-Hall of Japan, Inc., Tokyo
Simon & Schuster Asia Pte. Ltd., Singapore
Editora Prentice-Hall do Brasil, Ltda., Rio de Janeiro

Contents

Preface

In 1994, Japan exported products at a total of $35 billion that use fuzzy logic or NeuroFuzzy. The remarkable fact that an emerging key technology in Asia and Europe went unnoticed by the U.S. public until recently, combined with its unusual name and revolutionary concept, has lead to a controversial discussion among engineers. Many publications now deal with the theoretical background of fuzzy logic, its history, and how to program fuzzy logic algorithms.

In my book, I want to take a different approach. I will explain all elements of fuzzy logic system design using case studies of real-world applications. No formulas, no complex math, just everything you need for a hands-on start. Roll up your sleeves, and I will guide you step-by-step through fuzzy logic and NeuroFuzzy design on your PC. The disks included with this book contain a simulation-only version of professional fuzzy logic design software and software simulations of various technical processes. This lets you instantly design solutions without any programming.

The large number of case studies treated in this book illustrates the benefits of the technology in different application areas. This helps you to evaluate the potential of fuzzy logic in your own application work. Working with leading-edge development tools helps you get a practical start in just hours.

Constantin von Altrock
M.Sc.E.E., M.O.R.

Foreword

The past several years have witnessed a rapid growth in the number and variety of applications of fuzzy logic. The most visible applications are in the realms of consumer products, intelligent control, and industrial systems. Less visible, but of growing importance, are applications relating to data processing, fault diagnosis, man-machine interfaces, quality control, and decision-support systems. Although fuzzy logic has been and still is controversial to some extent, its successes are now too obvious to be denied.

What are the reasons for the rapid growth in the applications of fuzzy logic? How can fuzzy logic be applied to the conception and design of various types of products and systems? How can one learn to employ fuzzy logic techniques with a minimal investment in time and effort? What are the available software tools that can simplify and speed-up the design, analysis, and testing of fuzzy-logic-based systems? These are some of the basic questions which are posed and answered with authority and high expository skill in von Altrock's *Fuzzy Logic and NeuroFuzzy Applications Explained*.

Bypassing a discussion of the theoretical foundations of fuzzy logic, von Altrock goes directly to the key concepts and techniques which underlie its use. In essence, these are (a) the concept of a linguistic variable; and (b) what might be called the calculus of fuzzy if-then rules. In von Altrock's approach, these constructs form the basis for what he calls Fuzzy Technology Language (FTL). Basically, FTL is a hardware and vendor independent description language which provides the design engineer with powerful a and versatile tool, along with Inform's *fuzzy*TECH design software.

If I were asked to describe as succinctly as possible what fuzzy logic offers in the realm of systems analysis and design, I would answer: a methodology for computing with words. In this perspective, von Altrock's work may be viewed

as a very skillful, informative and up-to-date exposition of this methodology--
an exposition which is attuned to the needs of engineers and system designers.

One of the basic problems which arises in the design of fuzzy-logic-based
systems relates to the induction and tuning of rules through the observation of
input-output pairs. In many applications, this is accomplished through the use
of neural network techniques. The resulting NeuroFuzzy systems possess the capability to learn and adapt from experience. The design and analysis of Neuro-
Fuzzy systems is an important part of von Altrock's handbook.

The centerpiece of the book is a description of more than 30 case studies
of fuzzy logic applications which provide a unique insight into how fuzzy logic
systems are put together. There is no other book which does this. The case studies are the "real-life" experiences of companies that have successfully employed
fuzzy logic in their applications.

Fuzzy Logic and NeuroFuzzy Applications Explained is packed with information which is presented in a reader-friendly fashion. It is a must for anyone
who is interested in this analysis and design of fuzzy-logic-based systems. Von
Altrock deserves praise and congratulations for authoring an outstanding text
that has so much to offer.

Lotfi A. Zadeh
Berkeley, California

Fuzzy Logic in Five Minutes

Whether you have to tell your management in five minutes what fuzzy logic can do for your company or you would like to know in advance if fuzzy logic can be a solution to your problem, here are the most asked questions and answers.

What Is Fuzzy Logic?

Fuzzy logic is an innovative technology that enhances conventional system design with engineering expertise. Using fuzzy logic, you will circumvent the need for rigorous mathematical modeling. Fudge factors in your control system will be replaced by a self-explanatory linguistic description of the control strategy. See Section 2.3 for a simple example.

What Is Fuzzy Logic NOT?

Fuzzy logic is not rocket science. Although it is based on a complex mathematical body, its practical use is easy to learn. Use the case studies contained in this book and the software attached to get a first hands-on experience with fuzzy logic.

Can Fuzzy Logic Do Anything I Cannot Do Using Other Design Techniques?

Theoretically, you could have designed any fuzzy logic system using other design techniques. However, the effort of other design methods would have been overly complex in many cases. The case studies in Sections 5.2.2 and 5.3.3 are very good examples of this.

Is There Anything I Cannot Do with Fuzzy Logic?

Theoretically not. Fuzzy logic is a true extension of conventional logic, and fuzzy logic controllers are a true extension of linear control models. Hence, anything that was built using conventional design techniques can be built with fuzzy logic. However, in a number of cases, conventional solutions are simpler, faster, and more efficient. The key to successful use of fuzzy logic is clever combination with conventional techniques. See Section 5.1 for an overview.

Can I Verify a Fuzzy Logic System, and Can I Prove Stability for It?

Yes. A fuzzy logic system is a time-invariant and deterministic system. Hence, any verification and stability analysis method can be used with fuzzy logic, too. Section 6.4 treats stability analysis in more detail.

Fuzzy Logic Primer

The first section of this chapter gives a short history of fuzzy logic. For an extended history treatise, refer to [100] and [210]. Section 2.1 of this chapter will introduce the basic concepts of fuzzy logic, Section 2.2 its use in system design. If you are not interested in the history of fuzzy logic, just skip Section 2.1 and start with Section 2.2.

2.1 A Short History of Fuzzy Logic

The first publication on fuzzy logic, which also coined its name, dates back to 1965 [217]. It was published in the U.S. by Lotfi Zadeh, Professor of Systems Theory at the University of California, Berkeley. From then on, the history of fuzzy logic follows the pattern of many recent key technologies: invented in the U.S., engineered to perfection in Europe, and now mass-marketed in Japan.

When the concepts of fuzzy logic were first published in the U.S., they faced a lot of critics. One example from Zadeh's colleagues:

"… I would like to comment briefly on Prof. Zadeh's presentation. His proposals could be severely, ferociously, even brutally criticized from a technical point of view. This would be out of place here. But a blunt question remains: Is Zadeh presenting important ideas or is he indulging in wishful thinking? The most serious objection of 'fuzzification' of system analysis is that lack of methods of system analysis is **not** the principal scientific problem in the 'systems' field. **That** problem is one of developing basic concepts and deep insight into the nature of 'systems,' perhaps trying to find something akin to the 'laws' of Newton. In my opinion, Zadeh's suggestions have no chance to contribute to the solution of this basic problem... "

— R. E. Kalman (1972)

Even today, where hundreds of successful fuzzy logic applications have proved the value of this technology, some scientists still condemn the concept, as this more recent example shows:

"...Fuzzy Logic is based on fuzzy thinking. It fails to distinguish between the issues specifically addressed by the traditional methods of logic, definition and statistical decision-making..."

— Jon Konieki in *AI Expert* (1991)

Lotfi Zadeh credits these views to the "hammer principle." It says, if you have a hammer in your hand, and it's your only tool, everything starts to look like a nail.

2.1.1   First Industrial Applications in Europe

The first industrial applications of fuzzy logic were made after 1970 in Europe. At Queen Mary College in London, England, Ebrahim Mamdani used fuzzy logic to control a steam generator that he could not get under control with conventional techniques [12, 39]. At the RWTH University of Aachen, Germany, Hans Zimmermann used fuzzy logic for decision support systems. Other industrial applications such as the control of a cement kiln [84, 96] followed as a result of this initial work, but fuzzy logic could not get broad acceptance in industry. The few applications that used fuzzy logic hid the fact by circumscribing fuzzy logic with terms such as "multivalued logic" or "continuous logic" [106]. A survey on European applications before 1982 is contained in [173].

Starting around 1980, fuzzy logic gained more momentum in decision support and data analysis applications in Europe. A lot of the more advanced fuzzy logic technologies were developed in these applicational and research projects. Most developments were triggered by empirical research on how well fuzzy logic models the human decision and evaluation process [217]. Results of this work are described in Sections 3.1.1 and 5.1.1 of this book as well as in [102, 219, 220].

2.1.2   Japan Takes the Lead

Inspired by the first European fuzzy logic applications, the first Japanese companies started to use fuzzy logic in control engineering after 1980. Due to the poor computational performance of the first fuzzy logic algorithms on standard hardware, most applications looked into dedicated fuzzy logic hardware [205]. Some of the first fuzzy logic applications were a water treatment plant by Fuji Electric in 1983 and a subway system by Hitachi which opened in 1987 [208].

The success story of the initial applications raised a lot of interest in Japan. There were a number of reasons why fuzzy logic took off in Japan. First, Japanese engineers start with a simple solution and later tweak the most out of this system. Fuzzy logic supports the generation of a fast prototype and incremental optimization. Second, a fuzzy logic system always remains plain and simple to understand. The "intelligence" of a system is not buried in differential equations or source code. As Japanese engineers in general develop systems in a team where everybody wants to be able to understand the underlying behavior of the system, fuzzy logic delivers to them a more transparent means of system design. Also, due to the nature of their culture, Japanese engineers are not preoccupied with Boolean logic, nor has the Japanese language a negative connotation of the word "fuzzy."

Technological factors were only part of the reason fuzzy logic came to broad use in such a short time. Another reason is that the Japanese government joined forces with the big corporations to set up technology transfer programs. After the IFSA (International Fuzzy Systems Association) Japan Chapter was founded in 1985 to support research in the area, several new industry support circles were initiated:

- Japan Society for Fuzzy Theory and Systems (SOFT)
- Biomedical Fuzzy Systems Association (BMFSA)
- Laboratory for International Fuzzy Engineering Research (LIFE)
- Fuzzy Logic Systems Institute Iizuka (FLSI)
- Center for Promotion of Fuzzy Logic at TITech

As a result of this, fuzzy logic is now used in about any applicational area for intelligent control or data processing. Photo and video cameras use fuzzy logic to put photographer's expertise in their control. Mitsubishi announced the world's first car in which every control system is based on fuzzy logic, and most other Japanese car manufacturers use fuzzy logic in some of their components. In factory automation, Omron Corp. claims more than 350 patents, and fuzzy logic control optimizes many chemical and biological processes. See [18] for a summary.

2.1.3 Europe Chases Japan

Only five years ago, major European corporations realized that they had almost lost another key technology to the Japanese and started a major effort to promote fuzzy logic in their applications. Since then, more than 200 successful fuzzy logic mass market products have been launched in Europe. In addition, an uncounted number of industrial automation and process control applications have successfully used fuzzy logic. The fuzzy logic enhanced products include home appliances that realize major savings in energy and water consumption with no added product costs as well as many automotive applications. The industrial automation applications include chemical and biological process control, machinery equipment control, and intelligent sensors. For a summary of these applications, see [222].

Due to the big commercial success of these applications, fuzzy logic is now considered a "standard" design technique and has gained broad acceptance in the engineering community. One of the supporting factors was the advent of advanced fuzzy logic software design tools that support all development stages of a fuzzy logic design. Some of the fuzzy logic design tool software houses teamed up with major semiconductor and industrial automation equipment manufacturers to provide seamless development environments for most target hardware platforms [146, 201].

2.1.4 Fuzzy Logic in the U.S.

Now that fuzzy logic has made the trip from the U.S. to Japan via Europe, it's returning to the U.S. the same way. Recently, fuzzy logic gained a lot of interest in the U.S., especially among companies who are in heavy competition with both Asia and Europe. However, many argue whether this uphill battle can be won. I would argue yes, as there are many factors that count for the U.S. First, many applications done in Japan are with products for which U.S. manufacturers do not compete with the Japanese. As basically no major U.S. entertainment electronics manufacturer is left on the world market, the use of fuzzy logic in camcorders, cameras, and hifi is more a competitive factor among Japanese corporations themselves. In Europe, most applications are in industrial automation, mostly due to their very high labor costs. In other applicational areas, such as automotive engineering, the U.S. faces tough competition from both Europe and Japan. U.S. manufacturers in this area may be forced to use fuzzy logic design techniques soon.

This leaves some market segments open for U.S. corporations. For instance, fuzzy logic proved to be an excellent tool to build decision support systems, memory caches, and hard disk controllers, as well as compression algorithms for speech and video. Also, telecom applications such as echo cancellation, network routing, and speech recognition benefit from fuzzy logic. Combine this with the U.S. manufacturers' muscle in communication equipment, office automation, and computer software, and you can see that the U.S. can benefit from fuzzy logic technologies, although they picked them up late. Another factor is the strong research background in neural net technologies in the U.S. All fuzzy logic experts agree that the clever combination of neural network technologies and fuzzy logic will be the next logical step in developing the technology further.

2.2   Types of Uncertainty

This section will introduce you to the basic principles of fuzzy logic. Reading this section is essential to understand how fuzzy logic systems work. I will only introduce the standard methods here. Advanced fuzzy logic technologies are treated in Chapter 3 using case studies.

2.2.1   Mathematical Principles of Uncertainty

Many mathematical disciplines deal with the description of uncertainties, such as probability theory, information theory, and fuzzy set theory. It is most convenient to classify these by the type of uncertainty they treat. In this section, I will confine the discussion to only two types of uncertainty: stochastic and lexical. For a detailed treatise on different uncertainty theories, see [2, 155, 220].

Stochastic Uncertainty

Stochastic uncertainty deals with the uncertainty toward the occurrence of a certain event. Consider Statement 1.

Statement 1

The probability of hitting the target is 0.8.

The event itself—hitting the target—is well defined. Even a close shave wins no cigar. The uncertainty in this statement is whether the target is hit or not. This uncertainty is quantified by a degree of probability. In the case of Statement 1, the probability is 0.8. Statements like this can be processed and combined with other statements using stochastic methods, such as the Bayesian calculus of conditional probability.

Lexical Uncertainty

A different type of uncertainty lies in human languages, the so-called lexical uncertainty. This type of uncertainty deals with the imprecision that is inherent in most words humans use to evaluate concepts and derive conclusions. Consider words such as "tall men," "hot days," or "stable currencies," with no exact definitions underlying them. Whether a man is considered "tall" hinges on many factors. A child has a different concept of a "tall" man than an adult has. Also, the context and the background of a person making an evaluation play a role. Even for one single person, an exact definition of whether a man is considered "tall" does not exist. No law exists that determines the threshold above which a man is conceived "tall." This would not make sense anyhow, since a law that defines all men taller than 6' 4" to be "tall" would imply that a man of 6' 3" is not tall at all.

The science that deals with the way humans evaluate concepts and derive decisions is psycholinguistics. It has been proven that humans use words as "subjective categories" to classify figures such as "height," "temperature," and "inflation." Using these subjective categories, things in the real world are evaluated by the degree to which they satisfy the criteria.

Even though most concepts used are not precisely defined, humans can use them for quite complex evaluations and decisions that are based on many different factors. By using abstraction and thinking in analogies, a few sentences can describe complex contexts that would be very hard to model with mathematical precision. Consider Statement 2.

Statement 2
We will probably have a successful financial year.

At first glance, Statement 2 is very similar to Statement 1. However, there are significant differences. First, the event itself is not clearly defined.

For some companies, a successful financial year means that they defer bankruptcy; for others, it means to surpass last year's profit. Even for one company, no fixed threshold exists to define whether a fiscal year is considered successful or not. Hence, the concept of a "successful fiscal year" is a subjective category.

Another difference lies in the definition of expressing probability. While in Statement 1 the probability is expressed in a mathematical sense, Statement 2 does not quantify a probability. If someone expresses that a certain type of airplane probably has problems, the actual probability can well be lower than 10%, still justifying this judgment. If someone expresses that the food in a certain expensive restaurant is probably good, the actual probability can well be higher than 90%. Hence, the expression of probability in Statement 2 is a perceived probability, rather than a mathematically defined probability as in Statement 1. In Statement 2, the expression of probability is also a subjective category just like "tall men."

Modeling Linguistic Uncertainty

Statements using subjective categories, such as Statement 2, play a major role in the decision-making process of humans. Even though these statements do not have quantitative contents, humans can use them successfully for complex evaluations. In many cases, the uncertainty that lies in the definition of the words we use adds a certain flexibility. Consider, for example, the annual wage increase negotiations between unions and industry. Both want to achieve the same goal: an appropriate wage increase. The problem only starts when they have to express, in percentage, what they mean by "appropriate."

The flexibility that lies in the words and statements we employ is widely used in society. In most western societies, the legal system consists of a certain number of laws, each of which describes a different situation. For example, one law could express that theft of a car should be punished with two years of prison. Another law could define diminished responsibility. In one case in court, the judge now has to decide the exact number of days in prison for a thief who stole a car while under the influence with a blood alcohol level of 0.1%, who had a bad childhood, and was left by his spouse the day before. As a specific law does not exist for each case, the judge has to combine all applicable laws to derive a fair decision. This is only possible due to the flexibility in the definition of the words and statements used in each law.

2.2.2   Fuzzy Logic as Human Logic

The basic idea is simple: in reality, you cannot define a rule for each possible case. Exact rules (or laws) that cover the respective case perfectly can only be defined for a few distinct cases. These rules are discrete points in the continuum of possible cases and humans approximate between them. Hence, for a given situation, humans combine the rules that describe similar situations. This approximation is possible due to the flexibility in the definition of the words that constitute the rules. Likewise, abstraction and thinking in analogies are only rendered possible by the flexibility of "human logic."

To implement this human logic in engineering solutions, a mathematical model is required. Fuzzy logic has been developed as such a mathematical model. It allows the representation of human decision and evaluation processes in algorithmic form. There are limits to what fuzzy logic can do. The full scope of human thinking, fantasy, and creativity cannot be mimicked by fuzzy logic. However, fuzzy logic can derive a solution for a given case from rules that have been defined for similar cases. Thus, if you can describe the desired performance of a technical system for certain distinct cases by rules, fuzzy logic will effectively apply this knowledge to a solution.

2.2.3   Fuzzy Logic vs. Probability Theory

People working extensively with probability theory have especially denied the usefulness of fuzzy logic in applications. They claim that all kinds of uncertainty can be expressed with probability theory. Rather than embarking on a discussion of whether this is true or just another case of the previously cited "hammer principle," consider Example 1.

Example 1

"Patients suffering from hepatitis show in 60% of all cases high fever, in 45% of all cases a yellowish colored skin, and in 30% of all cases nausea."

If you find such a statement in a medical textbook, and you want to implement it in a system, it looks very easy at first glance. If you have a patient who suffers from high fever and nausea, but has normal colored, not yellowish, skin, you can compute the probability for a hepatitis infection using Bayesian calculus.

Although this looks very easy, the problem starts when you have to define what a "high fever" is. If you read medical books or ask doctors, you will not get an equivocal answer. Even if most doctors will agree that the threshold is at about 39°C (102°F), this does not mean that a patient with 101.9°F does not at all have a high fever while another patient with 102°F fully has a high fever.

If a threshold for "high fever" exists, the reverse must also exist. That is, a very precisely measured body temperature will result in a very precise diagnosis. If this were true, you could measure your body temperature up to the fifth significant figure and expect a doctor to tell you, just from this very precise information, from what disease you suffer. In contrast to this, a doctor will get a competent diagnosis not from the precision of a single parameter, but rather from evaluating many symptoms' parameters. Here, the precision of each parameter does not, for the most part, imply the quality of the result. If the doctor asks you whether you sweat at night, he is most likely not interested in the precise amount in ounces but rather a tendency.

As Example 1 illustrates, stochastic uncertainty and linguistic uncertainty are of different natures. Stochastic uncertainty deals with the uncertainty of whether a certain event will take place, and probability theory lets you model this. In contrast, lexical uncertainty deals with the uncertainty of the definition of the event itself. Probability theory cannot be used to model this because the combination of subjective categories in human decision processes does not follow its axioms.

2.2.4 A "Fuzzy" Set

Now, how can you model linguistic uncertainty adequately? If a doctor does not have a precise threshold in mind when evaluating whether a patient suffers from "high fever," how does it work? Psycholinguistic research has shown that a doctor would compare the patient with two "prototypes." On one side, the "perfect" high-fever patient, pale, sweating, shivering; on the other side, the "perfect" well-tempered patient who does not show any signs of fever at all. Comparing his patient's condition with these two extremes, a doctor evaluates where between the two his patient ranks.

How can this be mathematically modeled? Consider set theory, where you would first define the set of all patients with high fevers. Then you would define a mathematical function that indicates for each patient whether he is a member of this set or not. In conventional math, this indi-

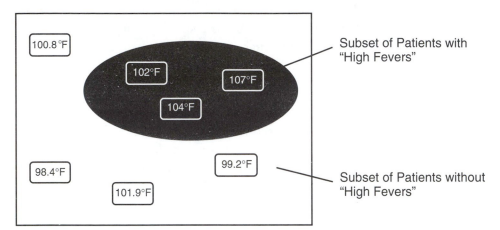

Figure 2.1   In conventional set theory, the set of "patients with high fevers" is defined exactly by 102°F.

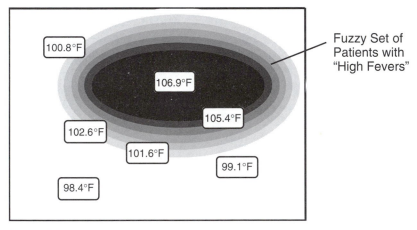

Figure 2.2   The "fuzzy" set of "patients with high fevers" also allows for elements that are "more-or-less" members of the set.

cator function has to uniquely identify each patient as member or nonmember of the set. Figure 2.1 gives an example of the set of "patients with high fevers" (black area), where the indicator function defines "high fever" as a temperature higher than 102°F.

As pointed out before, a doctor evaluates the degree to which his patient matches the prototype of a high fever patient. Figure 2.2 gives an eample of a set where certain elements can also be "more-or-less" members. The "shade of gray" indicates the degree to which the body temperature belongs to the set of high fever. This "shade of gray" which makes the black area in Figure 2.1 look "fuzzy" gave "fuzzy logic" its name.

In Figure 2.2, each body temperature is associated with a certain degree to which it matches the prototype for "high fever." This degree is called the "degree of membership" $\mu_{SF}(x)$ of the element $x \in X$ to the set "high fever" SF. The body temperature is called a "base variable" x with the universe X. The range of μ is from 0 to 1, representing absolutely no membership to the set and complete membership, respectively.

As a temperature of 94°F would have no membership at all, a temperature of 110°F would have complete membership. Temperatures between are members of the set only to a certain degree (Example 2).

Example 2

$\mu_{SF}(94°F) = 0$	$\mu_{SF}(100°F) = 0.1$	$\mu_{SF}(106°F) = 0.9$
$\mu_{SF}(96°F) = 0$	$\mu_{SF}(102°F) = 0.35$	$\mu_{SF}(108°F) = 1$
$\mu_{SF}(98°F) = 0$	$\mu_{SF}(104°F) = 0.65$	$\mu_{SF}(110°F) = 1$

The degree of membership can also be represented by a continuous function. Figure 2.3 plots such a membership function. Note, that a temperature of 102°F and a temperature of 101.9°F are evaluated differently, but just as a slight bit and not as a threshold. How to define membership functions for a certain application is treated in Section 4.1.

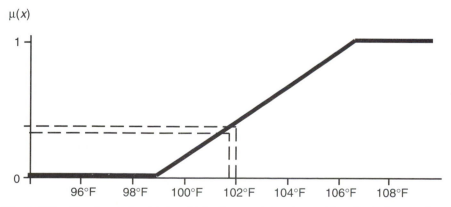

Figure 2.3   The degree $\mu_{SF}(x)$, to which a temperature x is considered to belong to the set of patients with "high fever" can be expressed as a continuous function.

Note, that fuzzy sets are a true generalization of conventional sets. The cases $\mu = 0$ and $\mu = 1$ of the conventional indicator function are just special cases of the fuzzy set. The use of fuzzy sets defined by membership functions in logical expressions is called "fuzzy logic." Here, the degree of membership in a set becomes the degree of truth of a statement. For example, the expression "the patient has a high fever" would be true to the degree of 0.65 for a temperature of 104°F.

The primary building block of any fuzzy logic system is the so-called linguistic variable. Here, multiple subjective categories describing the same context are combined. In the case of fever, not only high fever but also raised temperature, normal temperature, and low temperature exist. These are called "linguistic terms" and represent the possible values of a linguistic variable. Figure 2.4 plots the membership functions of all terms of the linguistic variable fever into the same graph.

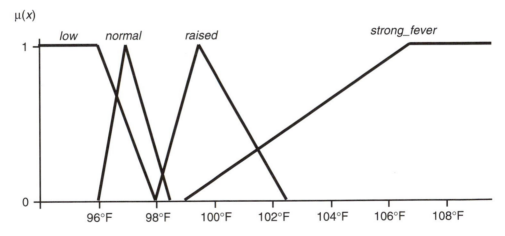

Figure 2.4   A linguistic variable translates real values into linguistic values.

This linguistic variable now allows for the translation of a measured body temperature, given in degrees Fahrenheit, into its linguistic description. For example, a body temperature of 100°F would be evaluated as "pretty much raised temperature, just slightly high fever." How to use this technology in engineering system design is treated in the next section.

2.3   Fuzzy Logic Technologies

In the past 30 years, a large number of methods using fuzzy sets have been developed. This book is restricted to the so-called rule-based fuzzy logic technologies. Nearly all recent fuzzy logic applications are based on this. This section will give a brief introduction to the basic technology of rule-based fuzzy logic systems using a case study in container crane control. More advanced fuzzy logic technologies are presented in Section 3.1.1 using a different case study. A detailed description of the fuzzy logic design methodology follows in Chapter 4.

2.3.1   Case Study: Container Crane Control

Container cranes are used to load and unload containers to and from ships in most harbors (Figure 2.5). They pick up single containers with flexible cables that are mounted at the crane head. The crane head moves on a horizontal track. When a container is picked up and the crane head starts to move, the container begins to sway (Figure 2.6). While sway is no problem during transportation, a swaying container cannot be released.

Figure 2.5   The control of a container crane using a human operator's expertise reveals a high potential for a fuzzy logic solution

Two trivial ways to solve this problem exist. One is to position the crane head exactly over the target position, and then just wait until the sway dampens to an acceptable level. On a non-windy day, this will eventually happen, but it takes by far too much time. A container ship has to be loaded and unloaded in minimum time for cost reasons. The other way is to pick up the container and just move so slowly that no sway ever occurs. This again works on a non-windy day, but takes far too much time. An alternative is to build container cranes where additional cables fix the position of the container during operation. Only very few cranes make use of this due to the much higher cost of the solution.

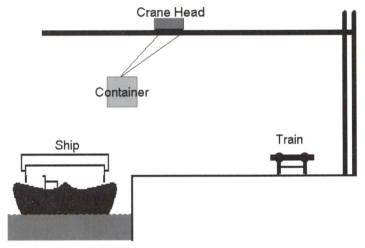

Figure 2.6   Since the container is linked to the crane head with a flexible cable, the container starts to sway when the crane moves. The fuzzy logic controller compensates for this sway using the human operator's experience (screen of the software simulation).

For these reasons, most container cranes use continuous speed control of the crane motor where a human operator controls the speed of the motor. The operator has to simultaneously compensate for the sway and make sure the target position is reached in time. This task is not easy, but a skilled operator is capable of achieving acceptable results.

Control Model Alternatives

Many engineers have tried to automate this control task in the past years. They have tried:

- Linear PID control
- Model-based control, and
- Fuzzy logic control

Conventional PID (proportional-integral-differential) control was not successful because the control task is nonlinear. Only when the container is close to the target, is sway minimization important. Other engineers have tried to derive a mathematical model of the crane to use in a model-based controller. They came up with a fifth-degree differential equation that describes the mechanical behavior. Although in theory this should work, it does not. The reasons for this are:

- The crane motor behavior is far less linear than assumed in the model.

- The crane head only moves with friction.

- Disturbances such as wind gusts cannot be included in the model.

A Linguistic Control Strategy

On the other hand, a human operator is capable of controlling a crane without differential equations. Chances are, if he knew how to use differential equations, he would not be a crane operator. The operator does not even use a cable-length sensor which any model-based solution would require. Once he has picked up the container, the operator starts the crane with medium motor power to see how the container sways. Depending on the reaction, he adjusts motor power to get the container a little behind the crane head. In this position, maximum speed can be reached with minimum sway. Getting closer to the target position, the operator reduces motor power or even applies negative power to brake. With that, the container gets a little ahead of the crane head until the container has almost reached target position. Then the motor power is increased so that the crane head is over target position and sway is zero. No differential equations are required for this, and disturbances and nonlinearities are compensated for by the operator's observation of the container's position.

The analysis of the operator's actions reveals that the operator uses some "rules of thumb" to describe his control strategy:

1   Start with medium power.

2   If you get started and you are still far away from target, adjust the motor power so that the container gets a little behind the crane head.

3   If you are closer to the target, reduce speed so the container gets a little ahead of the crane head.

4   When the container is very close to target position, power up the motor.

5   When the container is over the target and the sway is zero, stop the motor.

Implementing a Linguistic Control Strategy

To automate the control of this crane, sensors for the crane head position ("Distance") and the angle of the container sway ("Angle") are employed. Using these inputs to describe the current condition of the crane, the five rules of thumb can be translated to an "if-then" format:

1   IF Distance = far AND Angle = zero
      THEN Power = pos_medium

2 a   IF Distance = far AND Angle = neg_small
      THEN Power = pos_big

2 b   IF Distance = far AND Angle = neg_big
      THEN Power = pos_medium

3   IF Distance = medium AND Angle = neg_small
      THEN Power = neg_medium

4   IF Distance = close AND Angle = pos_small
      THEN Power = pos_medium

5   IF Distance = zero AND Angle = zero
      THEN Power = zero

Note that rule 2 has been translated into two rules to fit the if-then format.

If-then rules always describe the reaction to a certain situation as:

IF <situation> THEN <action>

In the case of the container crane, each situation is identified by two conditions. The first condition describes the value of Distance, the second the value of Angle. The conditions are combined by AND, representing the fact that both conditions have to be valid for the respective situation.

2.3.2   What Does Fuzzy Logic Bring to the Party?

Once you have set up a set of rules describing the desired behavior of a system, the question becomes, how can you implement these rules? First, consider using a programming language to code the "if-then" rules. The problem is that you have to define the words that the conditions of the rules use. However, exact definitions for these words do not exist. This is the same as with the definition of "high fever" discussed in Section 2.2. This is the reason you can use fuzzy logic to implement a linguistic control strategy. The following will show you, step by step, how you design a controller using fuzzy logic techniques.

Structure of a Fuzzy Logic Crane Controller

Figure 2.7 shows the complete structure of a fuzzy logic controller. First, all sensor signals have to be translated into linguistic variables. That is, a measured distance of 12 yards has to be translated to the linguistic value "still medium, just slightly far." This step is called "fuzzification" because it uses fuzzy sets for translating real variables into linguistic variables.

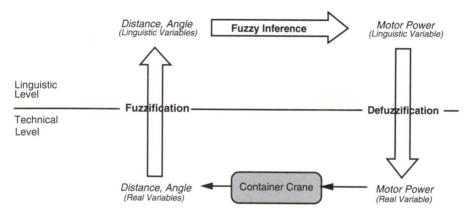

Figure 2.7   Structure of a fuzzy logic controller for the container crane. The fuzzy logic system consists of three steps: fuzzification, fuzzy inference, and defuzzification.

Once all input variable values are translated into respective linguistic variable values, the so-called fuzzy inference step evaluates the set of if-then rules that define system behavior. The result of this is again a linguistic value for the linguistic variable. For example, the linguistic result for Power could be "a little less than medium." The so-called defuzzification step translates this linguistic result into a real value that represents the power setting of the motor in kilowatts.

Fuzzification Using Linguistic Variables

Linguistic variables have to be defined for all variables used in the if-then rules. As described in Section 2.2, possible values of a linguistic variable are called terms or labels. The term definitions for the crane controller are shown in Example 3.

Example 3

Linguistic Variable	Possible Values (Terms)
1. Distance	$\in$ {far, medium, close, zero, too_far}
2. Angle	$\in$ {pos_big, pos_small, zero, neg_small, neg_big}
3. Power	$\in$ {pos_big, pos_medium, zero, neg_medium, neg_big}

For every linguistic variable, each term is defined by its membership function. Figures 2.8 and 2.9 show the definitions for the two input variables.

Consider a current situation of the crane, where Distance of the crane head to the target position is 12 yards, and the Angle of the container is +4°. Example 4 shows how the fuzzification is computed for this case.

Example 4

A Distance of 12 yards is a member in the fuzzy sets of the terms

far	to the degree of 0.1
medium	to the degree of 0.9
close	to the degree of 0
zero	to the degree of 0
too_far	to the degree of 0

An Angle of +4° is a member in the fuzzy sets of the terms

neg_big	to the degree of 0
neg_small	to the degree of 0
zero	to the degree of 0.2
pos_small	to the degree of 0.8
pos_big	to the degree of 0

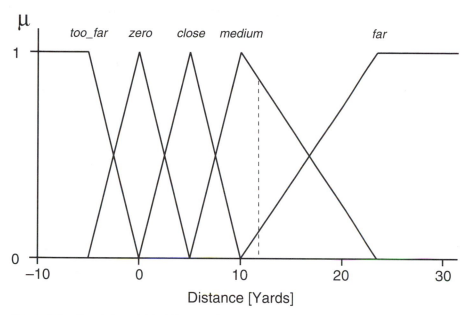

Figure 2.8   Linguistic variable "Distance" between crane head and target position.

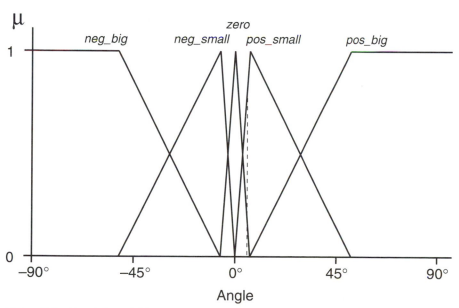

Figure 2.9   Linguistic variable "Angle" of the container to the crane head.

The Distance of 12 yards is translated into the linguistic variable value of {0.1, 0.9, 0, 0, 0}, which can be interpreted as "still medium, just slightly far." The Angle of +4° is translated into the linguistic value of {0, 0, 0.2, 0.8, 0}, which can be interpreted as "positive small, somewhat zero." How to define terms and membership functions is described in detail in Section 4.1.

Fuzzy Inference Using If-Then Rules

Now that all input variables have been converted to linguistic variable values, the fuzzy inference step can identify the rules that apply to the current situation and can compute the values of the output linguistic variable. Example 5 shows a subset of three rules.

Example 5

Rule 1	IF Distance = medium AND Angle = pos_small
	THEN Power = pos_medium
Rule 2	IF Distance = medium AND Angle = zero
	THEN Power = zero
Rule 3	IF Distance = far AND Angle = zero
	THEN Power = pos_medium

The computation of the fuzzy inference consists of two components:

- ■ Aggregation: computation of the IF part of the rules
- ■ Composition: computation of the THEN part of the rules

Aggregation

The IF part of rule 1 combines the two conditions "Distance = medium" and "Angle = pos_small." The IF part defines whether the rule is valid in the current situation or not. In conventional logic, the combination of the two conditions can be computed by the Boolean AND, shown in Table 2.1.

In the case of fuzzy logic, the Boolean AND cannot be used because it cannot cope with conditions that are more-or-less true. Hence, new operators had to be defined for fuzzy logic to represent logical connectives such as

Table 2.1   Boolean AND

A	B	A∧B
0	0	0
0	1	0
1	0	0
1	1	1

AND, OR, and NOT. The first set of operators that has been proposed [217] is given in Figure 2.10. These three operators are used in the majority of to-day's fuzzy logic applications.

AND:	$\mu_{A \wedge B} = \min\{\, \mu_A, \mu_B \,\}$
OR:	$\mu_{A \vee B} = \max\{\, \mu_A, \mu_B \,\}$
NOT:	$\mu_{\neg A} = 1 - \mu_A$

Figure 2.10   A set of fuzzy logic operators.

If you use the min operator to represent the logical AND, the IF parts of the rules of Example 5, using values from Example 4, can be computed as shown in Example 6. The results are the degrees of truth of the IF parts and indicate how adequate each rule is for the current situation.

Example 6

Rule 1	$\min\{\, 0.9; 0.8 \,\} = 0.8$
Rule 2	$\min\{\, 0.9; 0.2 \,\} = 0.2$
Rule 3	$\min\{\, 0.1; 0.2 \,\} = 0.1$

Composition

Each rule defines an action to be taken in the THEN part. The degree to which the action is valid is given by the adequateness of the rule to the cur-rent situation. This adequateness is computed by the aggregation as the de-gree of truth of the IF part. Hence, rule 1 results in the action "Power = pos_medium" to the degree 0.8, rule 2 in the action "Power = zero" to the degree 0.2, and rule 3 in the action "Power = pos_medium" to the degree 0.1. As both rules 1 and 3 result in the same action but with a different degree of truth, these results have to be combined before the defuzzification step.

In a fuzzy logic rule base, rules are defined alternatively: either rule A is true, OR rule B is true, OR rule C is true, OR…. Using the fuzzy logic operators as listed in Figure 2.10, the OR can mathematically be represented by the max operator. The final result of the fuzzy logic inference for the linguistic variable Power is shown in Example 7.

Example 7

For the linguistic variable Power, the fuzzy inference result is:

pos_big	to the degree of 0.0	
pos_medium	to the degree of 0.8	(= max{ 0.8; 0.1 })
zero	to the degree of 0.2	
neg_medium	to the degree of 0.0	
neg_big	to the degree of 0.0	

This fuzzy inference method is sometimes called MAX/MIN or MAX/PROD inference. Advanced inference methods and fuzzy logic operators are discussed in Section 5.3.4. Experience with the optimization of fuzzy logic systems has shown that it is necessary to associate weights to each rule. Section 6.2. describes how if-then rules and weights can be defined for a given application.

Defuzzification Using Linguistic Variables

At the end of the fuzzy inference, the result for Power is given as the value of a linguistic variable. To use it to set the motor power, it has to be translated into a real value. This step is called defuzzification. The relation between linguistic values and corresponding real values is always given by the membership function definitions. Figure 2.11 plots the membership functions for the linguistic variable "Power."

The result of the fuzzy inference given in Example 7 is both fuzzy and ambiguous as two different actions have non-zero truth degrees. How can two conflicting actions that are defined as fuzzy sets be combined to a "crisp" real-

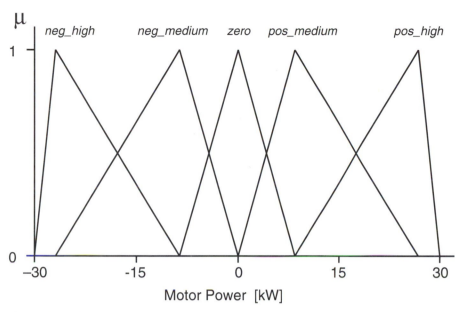

Figure 2.11   Linguistic variable "Power."

valued output for motor power? Consider how humans solve the problem of combining two fuzzy and conflicting actions in Example 8.

Example 8

Imagine yourself in an apartment building at 11 p.m. You would like to listen to some music, such as Wagner or Guns 'n' Roses, which requires some volume to be fun. On the other hand, your neighbors have already suffered quite a bit from your recent music sessions. Now, when you set the volume on your stereo, you have to combine these two conflicting and fuzzy goals into a crisp value, as only such a value can be set by the volume knob on your stereo.

To find a volume that compromises between the two goals, you could turn on the music and tune the volume until you balanced out the two goals.

As fuzzy logic mimics the human decision and evaluation process, a good defuzzification method should approximate this approach. Most defuzzification methods use a two-step approach for this. In the first step, a "typical" value is computed for each term in the linguistic variable. In the second step, the "best compromise" is determined by "balancing" out the results.

Compute the "Typical" Values

The most common approach to computing the typical value of each term is to find the maximum of the respective membership function. If the membership function has a maximizing interval, the median of the maximizing set is chosen. For the linguistic variable Power as shown in Figure 2.11, the computation of the typical values is illustrated in Figure 2.12. Here, the gray arrows point to the horizontal position of the typical values.

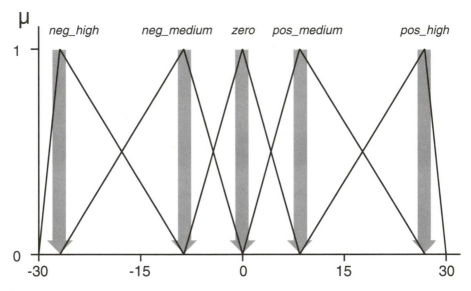

Figure 2.12   In the first step of defuzzification, the typical value for each term is computed as the maximum of the respective membership function.

Find the Best Compromise

In the second step, the best compromising crisp value for the linguistic result is computed. Figure 2.13 illustrates this step. At the horizontal position of the typical values, a "weight" of a size proportional to the degree to which the action is true is placed. The weights are shown as the heights of the black arrows over the gray arrows. The compromising crisp value is then determined by balancing the weights "on a pen tip." In the example, the position that balances the fuzzy inference result is at the position of 6.4 kilowatts. This value is considered the best compromise and is output to the motor.

This method of defuzzification is called "Center-of-Maximum" and is identical to the "Center-of-Gravity" method using singleton membership

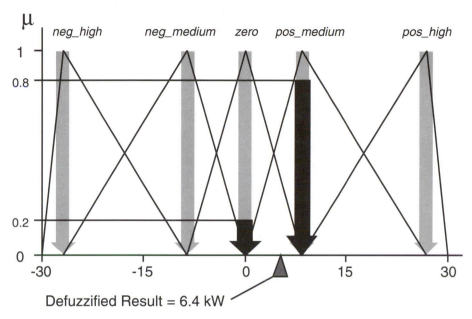

Figure 2.13   By balancing out the conflicting results, a crisp result is found.

functions. These defuzzification methods are used in most fuzzy logic implementations. Other defuzzification methods are introduced and compared in
Section 4.3.

3

Development Tools
for Fuzzy Systems

In principle, you can take the algorithm described in the previous chapter and implement a fuzzy logic system using whatever programming environment is available. However, this is not the state of the art. There are already a variety of software and hardware tools that significantly expedite the design of fuzzy logic systems. Most software tools provide extensive debugging and optimization features that make designing a fuzzy logic system a feast. Section 3.1 provides you with an overview on how software tools support fuzzy logic system design, and Section 3.2 treats the implementational alternatives on different industrial hardware platforms. If you are not interested in the design and implementation of fuzzy logic systems, skip this chapter.

3.1   Software Development Tools

An ideal software development tool for fuzzy logic should meet the following criteria:

- *Support of all development phases*
  (Design, Simulation, Optimization, Verification, Implementation)

- *Support of all target hardware platforms*
  (Microcontroller, Programmable Logic Controller, Personal Computer, Workstations, and Distributed Process Control Systems)

■ *Support of industry standard interfaces*
(MS-Windows user interface, standard fuzzy logic programming language support, DLL/DDE/OLE, and interface to control simulation software tools)

In this section, I will present the functionality of a fuzzy logic design tool, using the example of the *fuzzy*TECH® development system, which meets the listed criteria [114, 116, 119, 120]. The reason for selecting *fuzzy*–TECH as an example of a development system is that a simulation-only version of *fuzzy*TECH is provided on the attached disks. Note that the fundamental design steps are similar whether you program fuzzy logic systems in a conventional programming language or with other commercial tools.

Here, I present the components of *fuzzy*TECH in brief (a complete introduction is given in Section 7.1). Section 3.1.1 shows the visual design of a complete fuzzy logic system. Section 3.1.2 focuses on the various debugging techniques used for simulation, optimization, and verification. Section 3.1.3 introduces open programming languages for fuzzy logic systems. Different hardware implementations of fuzzy logic systems are discussed in Section 3.2.

3.1.1   Graphical Design

The hard way to implement a fuzzy logic system is to use a programming language and code the entire fuzzy logic system manually. This is a good exercise in programming, but delivers no deeper understanding of what fuzzy logic is. Also, any modification to the fuzzy logic system can cause major reprogramming.

Fuzzy Logic Precompiler

The second best way is to use a fuzzy logic precompiler. These precompilers basically translate a textual description of a fuzzy logic system into a standard programming language such as ANSI C. For example, there are precompilers that translate the fuzzy logic description language FTL (Fuzzy Technology Language) into ANSI C. For a description of FTL, refer to Section 3.2. Even though coding in FTL elevates design to a higher level, debugging a fuzzy logic design in a textual representation is difficult.

Visual Design Interfaces

The best and most efficient way to develop a fuzzy logic system is to use a visual design interface. Figure 3.1 shows an example of what such a visual

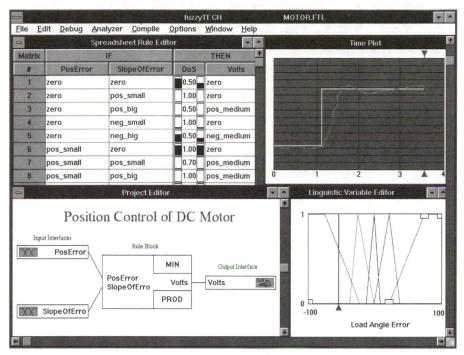

Figure 3.1   A visual design interface lets you develop an entire fuzzy logic system by "point-and-click."

user interface looks like. To store the designed project on disk, the tool uses the standard description format, FTL. Also, the tool reads in a system "hand-coded" in FTL and represents it graphically. Integrated code generators implement the current fuzzy logic system as C, assembly, or PLC (Programmable Logic Controller) code immediately from the graphical interface. For more details on the implementation of fuzzy logic systems on different target hardware platforms, refer to Section 3.2. The remainder of this section describes how to design a fuzzy logic system graphically.

Step 1: Structure of the System

The first step in a fuzzy logic system design is the definition of the system structure. Here, you define the inputs and outputs of the fuzzy logic system and how they should interact. Figure 3.2 shows this using the example of the anti-skid steering controller described in Section 5.3.4. The small blocks on the left side are the input interfaces. The input interfaces also contain the fuzzification of the input values. The icon on the left indicates the employed fuzzification method. The small blocks on the right side are the output inter-

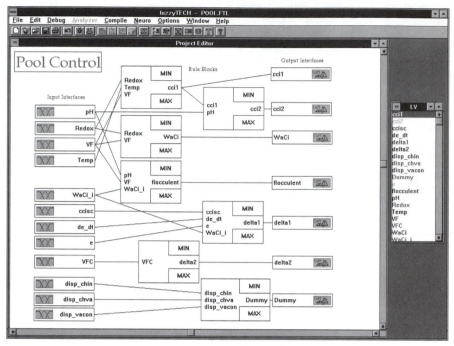

Figure 3.2   Visual design of the fuzzy logic system's structure in the Project Editor.

faces that contain the defuzzification method, respectively. For more information on how to select the appropriate fuzzification and defuzzification method, refer to Sections 2.3 and 6.1.

The larger blocks in the middle of the screen are the rule blocks. The rule blocks each contain an independent set of fuzzy logic rules. The text remarks illustrate the structure of the system. The Project Editor also lets you access the components of the fuzzy logic system. For example, a double click on the rule block opens an editor for the rules contained therein. To create a new object in the Project Editor, click on an empty area. For fuzzy logic systems running on distributed hardware, more than one Project Editor exists.

Step 2: Linguistic Variables and Membership functions

The next design step is to define the "vocabulary" of the system, that is, the linguistic variables. As linguistic variables are global to the fuzzy logic system, an LV window lists them by name. Double-clicking on an existing variable name or creating a new one invokes a graphical editor for the membership functions of the respective linguistic variables.

The most convenient way to design membership functions is the point-wise definition. Here, double-clicking in an empty space generates a new definition point. Clicking and dragging lets you move the definition points. Figure 3.3 shows such a pointwise definition. You can link the points by either straight lines or spline functions. For more details on the definition of membership functions, refer to Sections 2.3 and 6.1.

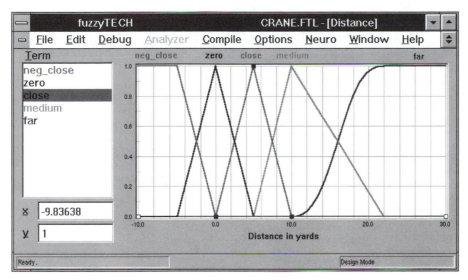

Figure 3.3   Visual design of membership functions of a linguistic variable in the Variable Editor.

Step 3: Fuzzy Logic Rule Blocks

The actual control strategy of a fuzzy logic system lies in the definition of the rules. Figure 3.4 shows three alternative ways to define and edit the rule blocks of a fuzzy logic system. For small rule blocks, the Spreadsheet Rule Editor is most convenient. Each row represents a rule, and the number in the left column is the rule number. The first row has three buttons. The Matrix button invokes the Matrix Rule Editor and the other two buttons, IF and THEN, title the if-part and then-part of the rules. Clicking on these buttons lets you change the inference methods. The second row contains buttons for each variable. Clicking on the buttons sorts the rule base with respect to the terms of the variable. The button DoS represents the weight of each rule, as *fuzzy*TECH uses the FAM extension of fuzzy logic rules. To modify any part of a rule, click on the respective element. This opens a pop-up window with

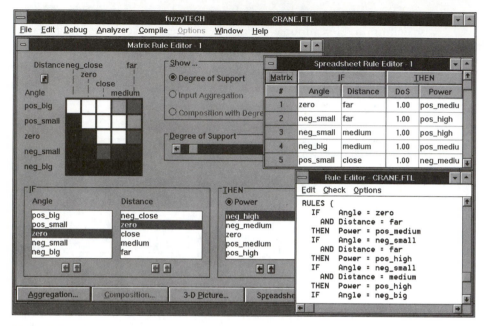

Figure 3.4 Alternative visual design of rules in the Matrix Rule Editor, the Spreadsheet Rule Editor, and in FTL text format.

the possible selections for the element. For a more detailed description on FAMs, refer to Section 4.2.

The Matrix Rule Editor provides a better overview of the rule block. The matrix always represents the relation between the rules in the base. It always shows how the rules define the relation between two variables. For each variable, a row or a column in the matrix represents a term, and the matrix elements represent a single rule. The shade of gray here indicates the weight of the rule. If more than two variables are defined in a rule block, the Matrix Rule Editor lists them in the lower part of the window. Here, an active term for the variables not shown in the matrix is selected. You can also define a fuzzy logic rule base as text using the FTL format as shown in Figure 3.4.

3.1.2   Debugging Modes for Simulation, Optimization, and Verification

The primary benefit of using a commercial fuzzy logic development tool is its comprehensive debugging support. Experience shows that more than

90% of the development time of fuzzy logic systems is spent in simulation, optimization, and verification. The tools support debugging modes such as:

- Interactive (lets you test system's reaction to inputs)

- fT-Link (links to process simulations)

- Serial Link (links to a simulation or a process by the COM port)

- DDE Link (links to any other software supporting DDE)

- File Recorder (processes data from a file)

- Connection (lets you connect to a running fuzzy logic system for tracing)

- Monitor (lets you monitor a fuzzy logic system running in real time)

- Online (lets you modify a fuzzy logic system in real time)

Interactive Debugging

Interactive debugging visualizes the entire fuzzy logic inference graphically. All the editors that you used for designing the system now display the computation. You see how the input values are fuzzified, which rules fire to what degree, and how defuzzification is computed (Figure 3.5). The most important factor here is that you can modify most parts of the system while you see how this affects the performance. If you move the definition point of a membership function, for instance, you see all the effects this has on the rules and the defuzzification.

Also, rules can be modified while a debug mode is active, and new rules can be added. The small bars next to the rule weight values in the DoS column indicate the input firing degrees (truth of the if-part) and the output firing degrees (truth of the then-part).

fT-Link and DDE-Link

For some applications, mathematical process simulations exist. They can be integrated with the fuzzy logic design tool so that the fuzzy logic inference can be monitored and modified in real time (Figure 3.6). Link debugging supports most standard programming languages as well as standard simulation software such as Mathlab/Simulink®, VisSim™, and Matrixx™.

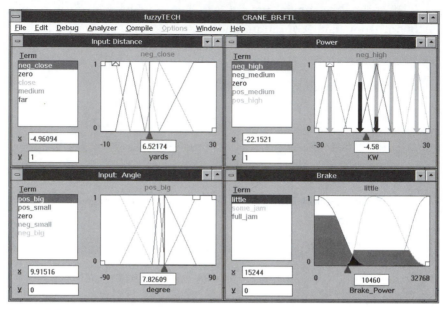

Figure 3.5 Interactive debugging lets you see the effects of all modifications immediately. The red lines with the arrow indicate the non-fuzzy inputs and outputs. Drag the arrows of the input variable to change its value. Move the definition points of the membership functions to optimize the system.

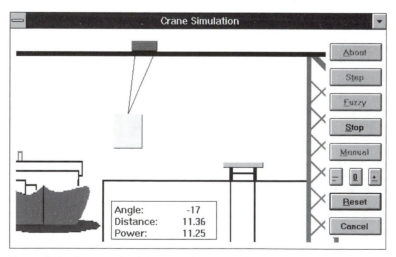

Figure 3.6 Process simulations can be written in any programming language and be linked to fuzzyTECH in Link Debug Mode.

Serial Link

In some cases, the simulation does not run on the same hardware as the fuzzy logic development system. Here, the serial link debug mode allows the entrance of the input variables of the fuzzy logic system by the serial port of the PC and return the output variables the same way. In principle, you can use the serial debug mode for real-time control, too. However, the response time of this is limited and undeterministic as the entire fuzzy logic computation runs on the PC. Also, any crash of the PC halts the control loop.

File Recorder

The file recorder mode lets you use process data that is recorded. A VCR-like control (Figure 3.7) lets you navigate through sets of input data from a file. This debug mode lets you understand and analyze the fuzzy logic system's reaction to a real process situation. Also, it supports "what-if" analyses.

■ A batch mode works similarly to the file recorder, but only writes the computed outputs of the fuzzy logic system on a second file. This is useful for the test of data analysis systems.

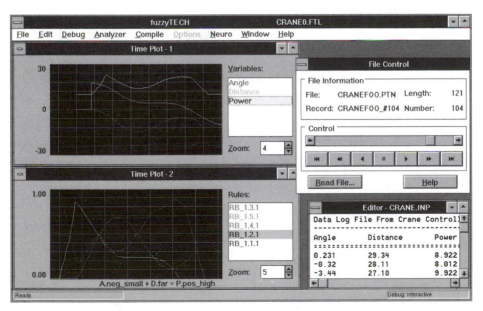

Figure 3.7   In file debug mode, a VCR-like control lets you navigate through pre-recorded process data.

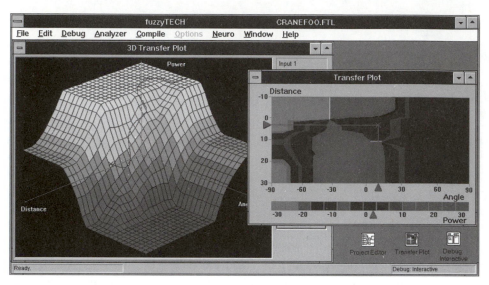

Figure 3.8   The 3D Plot.

Connection, Monitor, and Online Mode

All these modes allow a link to a fuzzy logic controller running on the target hardware. Refer to Sections 3.2.3 and 3.2.5 for details. In connection mode, you can only link to the running fuzzy logic system to configure, control, and upload traces made on the controller hardware. Monitor mode lets you also visualize the entire fuzzy logic inference flow, and online mode lets you modify the fuzzy logic system "on-the-fly."

Analyzers

To optimize, test, and verify your fuzzy logic design, a number of analyzers can help you. You can use all analyzers with most debug modes. Typical types of analyzers are:

- 3D Plot

- Transfer Plot

- Time Plot

- Statistics

The 3D Plot visualizes the transfer characteristics of a fuzzy logic system (Figure 3.8). The color and height of the contour plot indicates the value of the output variable. The plot shows linear regions, non-monotonous regions, and regions of instability, where no rules fire. When linked to a running system (online mode), to a simulation (fT-Link or DDE Link), or when browsing through files (file recorder), the current operational point can be traced. This allows one to detect superfluous and redundant rules.

The Time Plot (Figure 3.7) draws the value of selected variable values over time. The time plot also draws firing degrees of rules over time. Different time plots can show different variables on different time scales.

When linked to a running system (online), or a simulation (fT-Link), or browsing through files (file recorder), the statistics analyzers record how often each rule fires, and what the maximum and minimum firing degrees are. This lets you analyze the importance of the various rules in the rule base.

3.1.3   Fuzzy Logic Description Languages

To expedite the design of fuzzy logic systems, fuzzy programming languages have been created. These languages contain all the elements of a fuzzy logic system. Specific fuzzy compilers and precompilers translate this description into assembly code or into a programming language such as C.

Today, most designers use visual software design tools as presented in Section 3.1.1 rather than fuzzy programming languages. However, most software design tools use fuzzy programming languages such as a file format because they provide a hardware-independent system description. An open standard also supports custom extensions and the use of add-on tools from third-party suppliers.

In this section, I will use the example of FTL (Fuzzy Technology Language) which is supported by companies such as Intel, Texas Instruments, Microchip, Allen-Bradley, Foxboro, Siemens-HL, SGS-Thomson, and Klockner-Moeller. It is also supported by software tools such as *fuzzy*TECH. Figure 3.9 shows how FTL integrates various development tools into a workbench.

Definition of a Fuzzy Logic System in FTL

From a computer science viewpoint, the name "programming language" for description languages such as FTL is incorrect. They actually are definition formats as they do not contain loops or branches. FTL consists basically of two entities: objects and slots. Each object consists of an object name and an object body in "{}":

```
RULE {......}
```

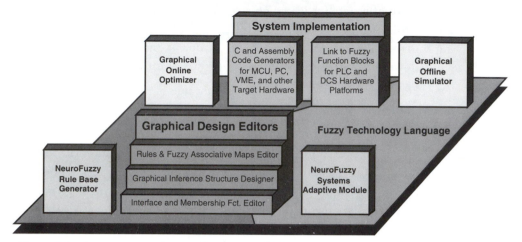

Figure 3.9   Fuzzy programming languages such as FTL provide an open interface to integrate various software design tools and enable the implementation on most target hardware platforms.

Within an object body, other objects and slots can be defined. A slot consists of a slot name to the left of an "=" and a value for this slot to the right:

```
POINTS = 10, 0, 4, 1, 2, 0;
```

There are defaults for most definitions, so even complex systems require only a few lines of code. Comments are put into "/*.....*/" marks. Extending FTL is simple, as FTL ignores the contents of unknown objects and slots. For example, there are fuzzy logic design tools for programmable logic controllers (PLCs) that support FTL and also contain objects for the PLC configuration and conventional ladder logic code.

For a complete description of FTL, refer to [116]. To illustrate how a fuzzy logic system is programmed in FTL, here is a commented listing of the crane controller of Section 2.3.

```
PROJECT {
  /* the project object contains a complete controller          */
  NAME = Crane_Controller;
    /* name is optional, if the FTL file only contains one project */
  MODEL {
    /* the model object contains the fuzzy logic system          */
    VARIABLE_SECTION {
      /* this object contains all linguistic variables           */
      LVAR {
        /* lvar contains one linguistic variable definition      */
        NAME    = Angle;
        LVRANGE = MIN(-90),MAX(90);
        TERM {
```

```
                        /* each term object contains one term and mbf definition*/
                        TERMNAME = pos_big;
                        POINTS = (-90,0), (10,0), (60,1), (90,1);
                        /* the slot points defines piecewise linear membership
                           function as (x,y) coordinates                      */
                    }
                    TERM {
                        TERMNAME = pos_small;
                        POINTS = (-90,0), (0,0), (10,1), 60,0), (90,0);
                    }
                    TERM {
                        TERMNAME = zero;
                        POINTS = (-90,0),(-10,0),(0,1),(10,0),(90,0);
                    }
                    TERM {
                        TERMNAME = neg_small;
                        POINTS = (-90,0),(-60,0),(-10,1),(0,0),(90,0);
                    }
                    TERM {
                        TERMNAME = neg_big;
                        POINTS = (-90, 1), (-60, 1), (-10, 0), (90, 0);
                    }
                }
            }
            LVAR {
                NAME    = Distance;
                LVRANGE = MIN(-10), MAX(40);
                TERM {
                    TERMNAME = too_far;
                    POINTS = (-10, 1), (0, 1), (0, 0), (40, 0);
                }
                TERM {
                    TERMNAME = zero;
                    POINTS = (-10,0),(-5,0),(0,1),(5,0),(40,0);
                }
                TERM {
                    TERMNAME = nah;
                    POINTS = (-10,0), (0,0), (5,1), (10,0), (40,0);
                }
                TERM {
                    TERMNAME = medium;
                    POINTS =(-10,0),(5,0),(5,1),(15,1),(24,0),(40,0);
                }
                TERM {
                    TERMNAME = far;
                    POINTS = (-10, 0), (15, 0), (24, 1), (40, 1);
                }
            }
            LVAR {
                NAME    = Power;
                LVRANGE = MIN(-30), MAX(30);
                TERM {
                    TERMNAME = neg_big;
                    POINTS = (-30,0),(-27,1),(-8,0),(30,0);
```

```
      }
      TERM {
        TERMNAME = neg_medium;
        POINTS = (-30,0),(-27,0),(-8,1),(0,0),(30,0);
      }
      TERM {
        TERMNAME = zero;
        POINTS = (-30,0),(-8,0),(0,1),(8,0),(30,0);
      }
      TERM {
        TERMNAME = pos_medium;
        POINTS = (-30,0),(0,0),(8,1),(27,0),(30,0);
      }
      TERM {
        TERMNAME = pos_big;
        POINTS = (-30,0),(8,0),(27,1),(30,0);
      }
    }
}
OBJECT_SECTION {
  /* the object section contains all structural elements of a
     fuzzy logic system, such as interfaces and rule blocks    */
  INTERFACE {
    INPUT = (Angle, CMBF);
    /* the slot input defines an input interface, the input
       variable name, and the fuzzification method            */
  }
  INTERFACE {
    INPUT = (Distance, CMBF);
  }
  INTERFACE {
    OUTPUT = (Power, COM);
  }
  RULEBLOCK {
   /* a rule block object contains the definition of its input
      and output variable as well as its rules                */
    INPUT = Angle, Distance;
    OUTPUT = Power;
    RULES {
      IF Distance = far AND Angle = zero
        THEN Power = pos_medium;
      IF Distance = far AND Angle = neg_small
        THEN Power = pos_big;
      IF Distance = medium AND Angle = neg_small
        THEN Power = pos_big;
      IF Distance = medium AND Angle = neg_big
        THEN Power = pos_medium;
      IF Distance = nah AND Angle = pos_small
        THEN Power = neg_medium;
      IF Distance = nah AND Angle = zero
        THEN Power = zero;
      IF Distance = nah AND Angle = neg_small
        THEN Power = pos_medium;
```

```
            IF Distance = zero AND Angle = pos_small
              THEN Power = neg_medium;
            IF Distance = zero AND Angle = zero
              THEN Power = zero;
          }
        }
      }
    }
}
```

If you use a software tool to generate an FTL file graphically, more objects and slots exist that describe position and default values of the objects, data types of the variables, and many other parameters.

3.2   Hardware Platforms for Fuzzy Logic Systems

Fuzzy logic is a universal technology; its applications range over the entire spectrum of electronic control. Thus, target hardware platforms are as diverse. Today's tools enable you to implement fuzzy logic systems on almost any target hardware, ranging from low-cost 8-bit microcontrollers that have only a few bytes of RAM and a few hundred bytes of ROM up to distributed process control systems that use multiple 64-bit RISC processors. In this section, I will introduce you to the technology and tools required for fuzzy logic implementations on various hardware platforms. Section 3.2.1 presents dedicated processors for fuzzy logic (FCUs), Section 3.2.2 describes implementation on standard microcontrollers (MCUs), and Section 3.2.4 covers workstations and PC as the target hardware platform. For industrial automation and process control, Section 3.2.3 shows special implementational techniques for programmable logic controllers (PLCs), and Section 3.2.5 for distributed process control systems (DCSs).

3.2.1   Dedicated Fuzzy Processors

In 1980, a software implementation of a fuzzy logic system required about one second of computing time on a standard 8-bit MCU. For most closed-loop control applications, this is way too slow. For these reasons, some chip designers developed dedicated hardware for fuzzy logic. I will present the history of fuzzy processors and point out what the applicational areas are for them.

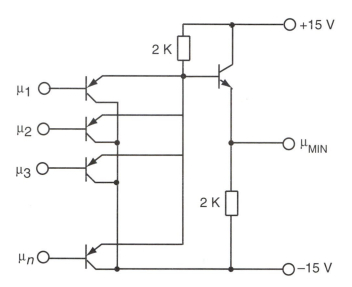

Figure 3.10   Renaissance of analog computing. The first fuzzy processor uses analog fuzzy gates. The schematic shows a fuzzy AND, implemented as minimum. The output voltage μ_{MIN} is the minimum of the input voltages μ_1–μ_n.

First Generation: Analog Fuzzy Processors

The first implementation of a fuzzy processor came from Japan in 1980 [205]. Analogous to discrete logic implementations, the fuzzy processor uses "fuzzy logic gates" as shown in Figure 3.10. In this circuit, signal voltages in the range from –5 to +5 volts express membership degrees from $\mu = 0$ to $\mu = 1$. This keeps the circuit in the linear range. By integrating this fuzzy gate, the temperature drifts of the transistors' U_{BE} compensate each other. Hence, fuzzy processors based on this technology achieve an accuracy in the 0.1% range and switch times in the nanosecond range. Since, in most fuzzy logic systems, not more than about five of these gates follow each other, this technology has some advantages:

■ It is faster than any standard computer processing fuzzy logic.

■ The integration complexity is much less than in any other hardware implementation of fuzzy logic.

■ The electromagnetic compatibility (EMC) is much higher than any other hardware implementation of fuzzy logic.

In spite of these advantages, analog fuzzy processors never found their way out of the labs. The main reason for this lies in the lack of programmability. Each modification of a fuzzy rule or membership function required a change of hardware. Many attempts were made to overcome these shortcomings. For example, the bipolar solution was replaced by a CMOS current mirror technique and additional elements that enabled programming were added [206]. Still, these architectures never became commercially successful, although research work in this area is still active [128].

A possible application area for analog fuzzy processors today could be a high-volume product with analog inputs and outputs where the fuzzy logic system does not require modification. Here, the analog solution is a fast and low-cost alternative to general-purpose microcontrollers.

Second Generation: Digital Fuzzy Processors

The second generation of fuzzy processors was developed from the experience with the first generation. However, the name "digital fuzzy processor" seems to be a paradox. Either something is digital (i.e., two-valued), or something is fuzzy (i.e., continuous). The solution is simple. Digital fuzzy processors are digital processors where the conventional instruction set is replaced by a fuzzy logic instruction set. Some of these digital fuzzy processors also contain architecture optimizations for fuzzy logic, such as hardware ALU functions for fuzzification, rule inference, and defuzzification.

Second-generation fuzzy processors only supported fuzzy logic computation. This made a host microcontroller that handles peripherals, I/O, preprocessing, and conventional code modules necessary. The fuzzy processor connects to the host MCU by either dual ported RAM (DPRAM) or a serial communication (Figure 3.11).

Figure 3.12 shows the computational layers of such a two-chip solution. The Interface Code layer fetches the inputs of the fuzzy logic system and preprocesses them. Then, the host MCU writes the input variables to the fuzzy logic system in the DPRAM and triggers the fuzzy processor. After computing the fuzzy logic system, the fuzzy processor writes back the output variables in the DPRAM, informing the host MCU by interrupt. The host MCU uses these output variables to drive its periphery. The layer FL system contains the description of the fuzzy logic system (i.e., the membership function definitions, the rules, etc.).

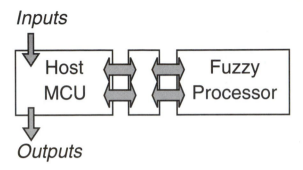

Figure 3.11   Digital fuzzy processors of the second generation can only compute fuzzy logic. For handling the peripherals, preprocessing, and other computational tasks, they need a conventional microcontroller as host.

In contrast to analog fuzzy processors, digital fuzzy processors made their way out of the labs about five years ago. About a dozen different digital fuzzy processor chips are commercially available at this time. However, they are not yet used in many industrial applications. This is mostly due to the fact that a two-chip solution is both expensive and difficult to design. If you use DPRAM (dual-ported RAM) for the communication, you even wind up with a three-chip solution. Also, the speed benefit of using a fuzzy processor declines when you add the overhead of communication with the host MCU. In addition, programming inter-processor communication between the host MCU and the fuzzy processor is complicated, and requires code and interrupt channels on the host MCU.

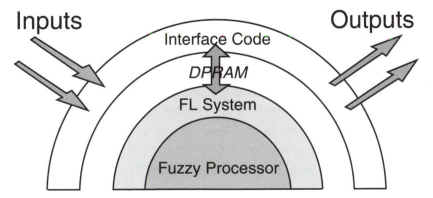

Figure 3.12   Computation layers of a fuzzy logic system implemented with a fuzzy processor linked to a host microcontroller.

Third Generation: Integrated Fuzzy Processors

Now a third generation of fuzzy processors is about to hit the market: integrated fuzzy processors. They overcome the deficiencies of the second generation by integrating the fuzzy processor functionality within standard microcontrollers.

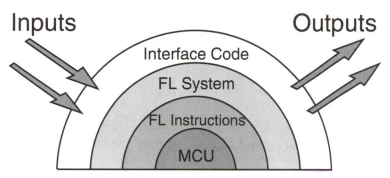

Figure 3.13   An integrated fuzzy processor provides the functionality to process a fuzzy logic system on the same chip with the microcontroller.

The functionality to process fuzzy logic systems can be implemented in different ways. Some semiconductor manufacturers integrate complete fuzzy logic coprocessor units on the same chip with a microcontroller (Figure 3.13). This has the advantage that the fuzzy logic coprocessor and the MCU can work simultaneously. The communication overhead is much smaller compared to the two-chip solution because the fuzzy logic coprocessor can use the same registers for the exchange of data. The other advantage is that such a modification is easy for modular MCU architectures, since the fuzzy logic coprocessor links just like another macrocell or memory area. However, the added silicon area required is quite large, as the fuzzy logic coprocessor has to implement standard ALU (arithmetic logic unit) functionality of the MCU required for the fuzzy logic computation.

A different solution is to enhance the instruction set of a standard MCU. The easiest way is to just extend the microcode and use the same ALU architecture. This speeds up fuzzy logic computation up to three times, depending on the MCU architecture. The microcode extension also compacts the code of a fuzzy logic system about two times, depending on the size of the fuzzy logic system. To accelerate the computation of fuzzy logic systems more, the ALU also needs extensions. Such extensions are hardware-supported fuzzification of standard MBFs, rule inference instructions, and hardware-supported CoM defuzzification. Some of these instructions are also useful for general-purpose. For example, a MAC instruction (multiply and accumulate) expedites both CoM and digital signal processing. The advantage of an instruction extension is that a standard ALU already contains many of the instructions needed for the fuzzy logic computation. Hence, the silicon area required for the execution of a certain fuzzy logic computation is smaller compared to the integration of a fuzzy logic coprocessor. The disadvantage of extending the ALU is that it makes redesign of the ALU necessary.

The integration of a fuzzy logic coprocessor as a macrocell to an existing modular MCU is already offered by a number of silicon manufacturers. The reason is that such an extension does not require redesign of the MCU. The ALU and instruction extension has greater potential in the long run, since it delivers a better performance-price ratio. However, only new microcontroller designs will feature it.

3.2.2   Standard Microcontrollers and Microprocessors

I mentioned at the beginning of Section 3.2.1 that the computation of a fuzzy logic system requires about one second on a standard 8-bit MCU using the algorithms that were available 15 years ago. While back then one group of developers went into dedicated hardware to expedite the computation of fuzzy logic systems, the other group made the effort of optimizing the fuzzy logic algorithm itself. The second path proved very successful: the computation of the same fuzzy logic system now requires only about one millisecond on a standard 8-bit MCU.

Fuzzy Logic Compilers

Today's fuzzy logic compiler generates assembly or C code either from fuzzy logic programming languages such as FTL or directly from the graphical design environment [114]. The degree of code optimization usually surpasses manual coding. This is because the fuzzy logic compiler analyzes the structure of the fuzzy logic system at compile time and prestructures it. This eliminates unnecessary computational steps during runtime.

Take a fuzzy logic system with 1000 rules. During compilation, the fuzzy logic compiler partitions the rule base into subsets. Each of these subsets contain rules that only fire if the input variables are within a certain interval.

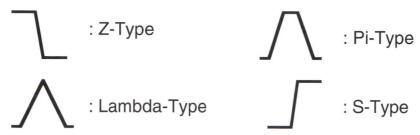

Figure 3.14   Standard membership functions.

These intervals are subsets of the universe of the variables. Typically, each of the subsets contains about 1/20 of the total rule set. The generated code automatically checks which subsets of the rule base can fire for any input condition at runtime. Of a rule set containing 1000 rules, this typically leaves only about 100 rules that could fire at all. Then the runtime code identifies all dominated rules, that is, rules which have no influence on the result. This may leave only 20 rules that have to be computed for a 1000-rule fuzzy logic system. These types of optimization are the key to achieving very high fuzzy logic computation performance on standard microcontrollers.

If you code your fuzzy logic system manually, you need to repeat this entire analysis any time you change the fuzzy logic system. The effort this takes is prohibitive. In addition, an optimizing fuzzy logic compiler optimizes not only rule inference, but also all steps of the fuzzy logic computation. Let me now sketch out some of the principles used in these compilers.

Fast Fuzzification of Standard MBFs

If you use standard MBFs, as shown in Figure 3.14 an optimized algorithm for fuzzification exists. Figure 3.15 illustrates this for a Π-type membership function. The generated code represents each membership function by four values. Since the membership degrees of point 1 and point 2 are always $\mu = 0$ and $\mu = 1$, respectively, the code only stores the base value of the two points. In addition to the two points, the code also stores the slopes. This allows for the computation of the fuzzification in the following way:

```
MBF_DEFINITION := (Point_1, Slope_1, Point_2, Slope_2)
CASE Input OF
  - Area 1: Membership = 0
  - Area 2: Membership = min{1, (Input-Point_1)*Slope_1}
  - Area 3: Membership = max{0, 1-(Input-Point_2)*Slope_2}
```

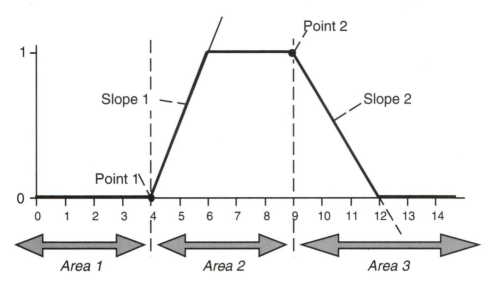

Figure 3.15   Fast fuzzification. Only four values must be stored for each membership function. Compilation of the slopes during compilation makes the generated code faster.

For example, let the input value be 10. Fuzzification using 8-bit resolution computes as (μ=1 equals FFh):

```
MBF_DEFINITION := (04h, 70h, 09h, 55h)
```

The letter "h" behind a value indicates a hexadecimal representation. The input value of 10 (0Ah) lies in area 3:

```
=> Membership = max{0, (FFh-(0Ah-09h)* 55h)}
              = max{0, AAh} = AAh
```

This fuzzification algorithm is very fast since the necessary computing operations are only comparisons, subtraction, and a maximum of one multiplication per membership function. The computationally intensive division is not necessary. On low-cost microcontrollers without a hardware multiplier/divider, this fast fuzzification can be up to five times faster than using the four definition points of the Π-type membership function directly.

Note that there is a possible problem related to the limited resolution of the value representing the slopes. If you represent the slopes as 8-bit integers, you cannot represent slopes smaller than 1 or a non-integer slope. In this case, the fuzzy logic compiler must automatically select a different range to minimize rounding errors [144].

Fuzzy Logic Inference

If you use the minimum operator for aggregation, just one invalid condition in the if-part of the rule deactivates the entire rule. If the fuzzy logic compiler prestructures the rule base in such a way that the generated code can identify the invalid rules after fuzzification, fuzzy logic inference becomes much faster.

Figure 3.16 shows the work. Only rules where all input variable terms are true to a nonzero degree can influence the result of the fuzzy logic inference. The example in Figure 3.16, with two input variables, contains 49 rules. However, only six rules actually fire. A rule of thumb is that the compression factor you can achieve with this method ranges from 1:5 for small rule bases to 1:50 for large rule bases.

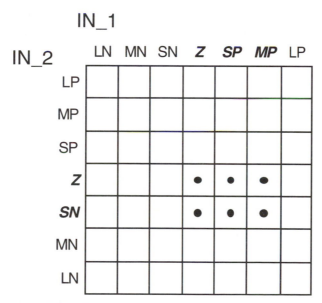

Figure 3.16   Expediting the fuzzy logic inference. Only terms *Z*, *SP*, and *MP* are non-zero for input variable IN_1. Only terms *Z* and *SN* are non-zero for input variable IN_2. Using the minimum operator for the aggregation of the two variables, only the marked "•" rules must be computed.

Further optimization is possible. Using the FAM inference, the result of the rule comes from multiplying the degree of validity of the precondition (if-part) of the rule with the DoS (degree of support) of the rule. Since many rules may have the same conclusion (then-part), the maximum of all firing rules with the same conclusion is taken. Once this maximum becomes 1 during computation, no further rule with this conclusion must be computed as it can have no effect on the final result. But even if the maximum is not yet 1, computation of rules can be skipped. This is the case if the DoS of a rule is smaller than the current maximum. These rules also can have no effect on the result of the fuzzy logic inference.

Defuzzification

Optimization of the defuzzification depends on the method used:

- *Mean-of-Maximum (MoM)*
  The mean of maximum method selects the most typical value of the term that is most valid as output value. As fuzzy logic compilers compute the most typical values at compile time, the remaining computation in the generated code is limited to comparisons. This is very fast anyway, leaving no need for optimization.

- *Center-of-Area (CoA)*
  This should not be used due to possible implausibilities (refer to Section 6.3). The accurate computation by numerical integration is computationally very intensive and rarely implemented. If you use singleton membership functions for the output variable, the CoA defuzzification is exactly the same as CoM defuzzification. An approximation of the CoA defuzzification, used by some fuzzy logic compilers and fuzzy processors, is to compute the areas under the membership functions at compile time. This is the same as a CoM defuzzification where the terms are weighted.

- *Center-of-Maximum (CoM)*
  CoM defuzzification is computationally more intensive than the MoM defuzzification. This is due to the fact that it requires a division that is slow on low-cost microcontrollers. If the resolution of the fuzzy logic system is 8-bit and the output variable has 8 terms, defuzzification requires 16 8-bit-by-8-bit multiplications and one 19-bit-by-11-bit division. This division consumes far more computing resources on microcontrollers with no hardware multiplier/divider. Fuzzy logic compilers structure inference and defuzzification in such a way that this defuzzification reduces to a 16-bit-by-8-bit division [literature reference to N.N., *fuzzy*TECH Online Edition Manual].

Comparison of Fuzzy Logic Computing Performance

In the past, fuzzy logic specialists have tried to quantify fuzzy logic computing performance on different target hardware by MFLIPS (million fuzzy logic inferences per second) or similar measures [202]. Since the measures for computing performance only cover parts of the fuzzy logic computation, they do not give meaningful information on total system performance. For these reasons, standard benchmark suites that contain complete fuzzy logic systems have been defined [113] and published. These benchmark systems stem from real applications that represent typical configurations.

Benchmark 0: Positioning Controller

This is a simple fuzzy logic control system similar to the crane controller from Section 2.3, which has two input variables, one output variable, and seven rules. Each input variable has three terms; the output variable has five terms.

Benchmark 1: Fuzzy-PI Controller

This is a fuzzy logic controller type often used in temperature or motor control. It has two input variables, one output variable, and 20 rules. Each linguistic variable has five terms. Section 5.1 treats the fuzzy-PI controller in more detail.

Benchmark 2: Weighted Fuzzy-PI Controller

This is the same as Benchmark 1, but uses weighted (FAM) rules.

Benchmark 3: State Estimator for Fuzzy-ABS

Many applications use fuzzy logic for state estimation. This system stems from a state estimator of a fuzzy ABS (anti-lock braking system), similar to the one presented in Section 5.3.1. It has three input variables, one output variable, and 80 FAM (weighted) rules. The input variables have three, four, and six terms; the output variable has five terms.

Benchmark 4: Research System

This is the largest published fuzzy logic system that runs on a microcontroller/microprocessor platform. It stems from the research project of intervehicle dynamics control treated in Section 5.3.4. It has eight input variables, four output variables, and 500 FAM (weighted) rules. Each linguistic variable has seven terms.

This set of benchmarks covers a fair amount of the spectrum of implemented fuzy logic systems, from a very simple to a highly complex controller. The FTL source files of these benchmarks are included in the software accompanying this book.

Computation Time Comparison

Figure 3.17 compares the computing times of the four fuzzy logic benchmarks for different types of microcontrollers:

- A typical low-cost 8-bit microcontroller (8-bit MCU). Computational resolution of the fuzzy logic system is 8-bit.

- A high-performance 8-bit microcontroller with internal 16-bit resolution (8/16-bit MCU). Computational resolution of the fuzzy logic system is 8-bit.

- A typical 16-bit microcontroller (16-bit MCU). Computational resolution of the fuzzy logic system is 16-bit.

- The fastest commercially available fuzzy logic processor today (high-end fuzzy processor). Computational resolution of the fuzzy logic system is 8-bit.

For the code generation, fuzzy logic compilers were used to generate assembly code optimized for the microcontroller used.

Typical loop times of control systems are:

- 10–1000 seconds: Biological Processes

- 1–100 seconds: Chemical Industry

- 0.1–1 seconds: Large Mechanical Systems, Appliances

- 10–100 milliseconds: Small Mechanical Systems

- 1–10 milliseconds: Automotive Engineering (ABS, Engine Control)

- 0.1–1 milliseconds: Hard Disk Drives, Motor Control

The comparison shows that even a low-cost 8-bit microcontroller can run most real-time fuzzy logic control applications. The performance of 16-bit microcontrollers allows the implementation of complex systems that compute in less than a millisecond. Note that in most applications, the fuzzy logic system is only a fraction of the total solution. Hence, total loop time will be longer.

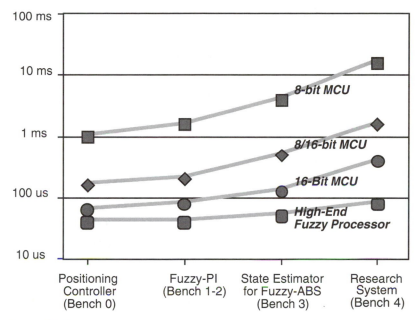

Figure 3.17 Comparison of computation times for fuzzy logic systems on different microcontrollers with today's fastest commercially available 8-bit fuzzy processor for different system sizes [113]. Note the logarithmic scale for computation time.

Fuzzy Processor Performance

From a performance point of view, even the fastest fuzzy processor today is not much faster than a microcontroller or DSP [19]. Even if faster fuzzy processors become available, a software solution on a microcontroller will be sufficient and most cost effective for the vast majority of control applications. Two areas remain where it is beneficial to use a fuzzy processor:

■ If a low-cost 8-bit MCU with an integrated fuzzy processor can do the job of a 16-bit MCU, it may be the cheaper solution.

■ In non-control applications. Most control systems react slower than a millisecond. This is because they involve mechanical, thermodynamic, or electrical time constants that rarely surpass the millisecond threshold. However, in non-control applications, such as database search, voice compression and recognition, video compression and such, these time constants do not exist, and much faster fuzzy processors can find their potential.

Code Size Comparison

Figure 3.18 compares the RAM and ROM requirements of the four fuzzy logic benchmark systems. Due to the 16-bit computational resolution of the 16-bit microcontrollers, their RAM requirement for intermediate results grows slightly larger with the system size. Note that the fuzzy logic system uses most of the RAM only during computation. Before and after the computation, this RAM is available for other purposes.

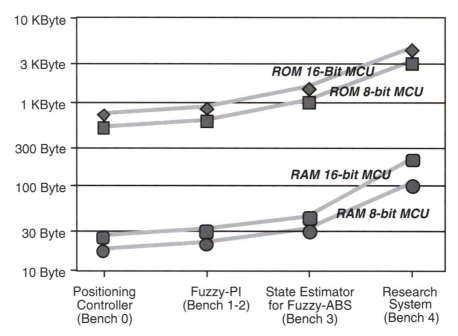

Figure 3.18 Comparison of ROM and RAM requirements for fuzzy logic systems on different microcontrollers [113]. Note the logarithmic scale for RAM/ROM sizes.

Debugging of Embedded Systems

Most of this section has dealt with the implementation of a fuzzy logic system as optimized assembly code. Another important issue is the debugging technology for embedded systems. Since fuzzy logic systems are best optimized on a running process, some fuzzy logic development software systems support real-time remote cross-debugging (RTRCD).

To use RTRCD in an embedded systems design, you link the RTRCD module to the generated assembly code. This RTRCD module communicates with the software development tool on the PC by a standard serial cable. With that, the PC visualizes the entire fuzzy logic inference graphically (Figure 3.19). Also, you can modify rule weights and membership functions without halting the system [115].

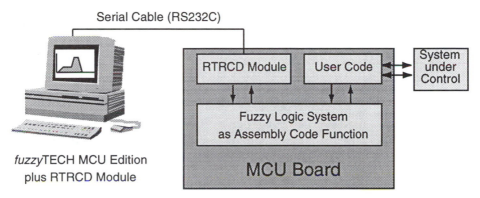

Figure 3.19   A real-time remote cross debugger (RTRCD) supports visualization of the fuzzy logic inference and system modifications "on-the-fly."

The RTRCD technique provides partial functionality of the online technique presented in Section 3.1.2. Due to the limited computational resources of microcontrollers, RTRCD does not support any structural modifications of the system without recompiling. RTRCD only allows rule weight and membership function modifications.

3.2.3   Programmable Logic Controller (PLC)

Programmable Logic Controllers (PLCs) are a common hardware platform in industrial automation and process control. PLCs have standard interfaces to sensors and actors, are rugged for an industrial environment, and support standard field buses. Most PLCs use specialized programming languages such as ladder logic, a semi-graphical way to represent a control algorithm.

Some PLCs offer high-level language programming in structured programming languages such as C. For these PLCs you can use a fuzzy logic precompiler that generates the system as C code and implement the code on the PLC. For most closed-loop control applications in industrial automation, however, "on-the-fly" modifications without halting the system significantly expedite development (Figure 3.20).

Not all PLCs support programming in C. Small PLCs only support ladder diagrams, instruction lists, structured text, function block diagrams, or se-

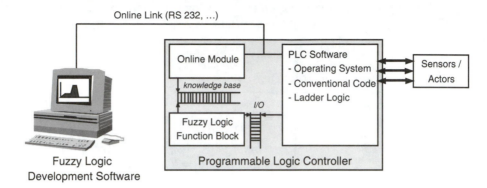

Figure 3.20   The online technique lets you visualize and modify the running fuzzy logic system "on-the-fly" on PLC hardware.

quential function charts conforming to the international norm IEC1131. For some of these PLCs, fuzzy logic function blocks exist [60, 117].

To develop a system using the fuzzy logic function blocks, you do not need to generate any code. First, you design the basic structure of the fuzzy logic system on the PC using the fuzzy logic development software. Then you link the PC to the PLC and download the fuzzy logic system as parameter blocks for the fuzzy logic function block. After that, the online mode allows for visualization and modifications "on-the-fly." The advantage of using fuzzy logic function blocks over the implementation of C code is that neither code generation, compilation, nor integration effort is necessary.

3.2.4   Fuzzy Logic Implementation on Workstation and PC

There are quite a few applications for which the PC or the workstation not only is the development platform but also the target hardware platform: first, when a workstation or PC control processes directly by plug-in peripheral boards; second, for applications such as quality control systems, data analysis systems, and nontechnical applications, where mostly PCs and workstations are used.

Compared to implementations on microcontrollers, PC and workstations have much higher computing performance and lower performance for input/output periphery. Also, microcontrollers have RAM/ROM resources in the kilobyte area, while PCs and workstations usually have megabytes of RAM. Hence, code optimization is not nearly as much of an issue as with microcontroller implementations.

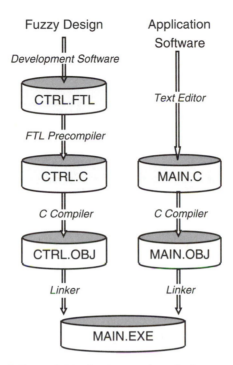

Figure 3.21   Implementation of a fuzzy logic system on PC or workstation.

To implement a fuzzy logic system on a PC or workstation (Figure 3.21), you first develop the fuzzy logic system using a fuzzy logic software tool. A C precompiler then generates a C source file (CTRL.C) from the FTL format (CTRL.FTL). This C source file contains one single function definition that contains the entire fuzzy logic computation. Various compiler options let you optimize the code for your applications' needs.

The most comfortable way to integrate this code in your application is to call this fuzzy logic function with all input and output variables as function parameters. For that, you write your application software in a linkable programming language, for example, in C (MAIN.C). This code first performs the preprocessing of the input variables for the fuzzy logic system. Then this code calls the fuzzy logic function. This function generated by the fuzzy logic compiler contains the entire fuzzy logic algorithm in source code. After the fuzzy logic system is computed, the code in MAIN.C performs postprocessing of the output variables.

To integrate the code, you compile all C source files to object files (CTRL.OBJ, MAIN.OBJ) and link them to an executable program.

3.2.5   Fuzzy Logic on Distributed Process Control Systems

Control of large plants, for example, in steel or chemical processing, often employs distributed process control systems (DCS). In DCSs, bus systems connect individual control processors (CPs) that drive sensors and actors. The control algorithms, PIDs or others, run on these control processors. An application processor (AP) supervises the CPs and tunes the control algorithms running on them. High-resolution screens connected to the AP visualize the process and let the operators modify systems parameters.

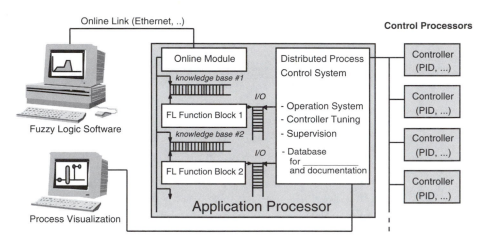

Figure 3.22   Integration of a fuzzy logic component in a DCS.

In process control, PID controllers work very well in keeping single parameters of a process, such as temperatures, flows, and pressures, at a constant level. However, PID controllers cannot control the operating point of the entire process, as this is a multivariable control problem. Many applications showed the successful use of fuzzy logic for this (see also Figure 5.13). Refer to Section 5.1 on how to combine fuzzy logic with conventional PID controllers. Section 5.4. presents case studies of fuzzy logic applications in chemical industry.

The integration of fuzzy logic in an existing DCS is shown in Figure 3.22. Since the fuzzy logic system outputs the set values for the PID controller running on the CPs, the fuzzy logic function blocks run on the AP. The AP allows for the integration of the online module and the fuzzy logic function blocks in C code. The online module communicates with the PC or workstation on which the fuzzy logic development software runs. It enables the visualization of the entire fuzzy logic inference and "on-the-fly" modifications [118].

4

NeuroFuzzy
Technologies

To enhance fuzzy logic systems with learning capabilities, you can integrate neural net technologies. The combination of fuzzy logic and neural net technology is called "NeuroFuzzy" and combines the advantages of the two technologies. Section 4.1 introduces you to the basic principles of neural nets, and Section 4.2 shows the combination of neural nets with fuzzy logic.

4.1 Neural Net Basics

The imitation of human minds in machines has inspired scientists for the last century. About 50 years ago, researchers created the first electronic hardware models of nerve cells. Since then, a large scientific community works on new mathematical models and training algorithms. Today, so-called neural nets get most of the interest in this domain. Neural nets use a number of simple computational units called "neurons," of which each tries to imitate the behavior of a single human brain cell. In the following, I refer to the brain as a "biological neural net" and to implementations on computers as "neural nets." Figure 4.1 shows the basic structure of such a neural net.

Each neuron in a neural net processes the incoming inputs to an output. The output is then linked to other neurons. Some of the neurons form the interface of the neural net. The neural net shown in Figure 4.1 has a layer for the input signals and one for the output signals. The information enters the neural net at the input layer. All layers of the neural net process these signals through the net until they reach the output layer.

63

Input Signal   Output Signal

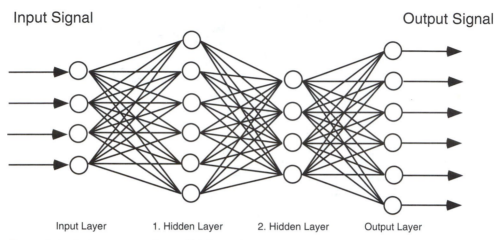

Input Layer   1. Hidden Layer   2. Hidden Layer   Output Layer

Figure 4.1   Basic structure of an artificial neural net.

The objective of a neural net is to process the information in a way that is previously trained. Training uses either sample data sets of inputs and corresponding outputs or a teacher who rates the performance of the neural net. For this training, neural nets use so-called learning algorithms. Upon creation, a neural net is dumb and does not exhibit any behavior at all. The learning algorithm then modifies the individual neurons of the net and the weight of their connections in such a way that the behavior of the net reflects the desired one.

4.1.1   How to Mimic Human Nerve Cells

Researchers in the area of neural nets have analyzed various models of human brain cells. In the following, I will only describe the one most commonly used in industrial applications. For a detailed introduction to neural nets, refer to [7, 53, 94, 195].

The human brain contains about 10^{11} nerve cells with about 10^{14} connections to each other. Figure 4.2 shows the simplified scheme of such a human neuron. The cell itself contains a kernel, and the outside is an electical membrane. Each neuron has an activation level, which ranges between a maximum and a minimum. Hence, in contrast to Boolean logic, more than two values exist.

To increase or decrease the activation of this neuron by other neurons, so-called synapses exist. These synapses carry the activation level from a sending neuron to a receiving neuron. If the synapse is an excitatory one, the activation level from the sending neuron increases the activation of the receiving neuron. If the synapse is an inhibiting one, the activation from the sending

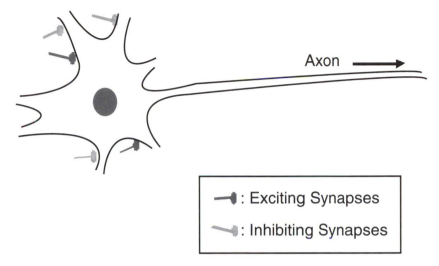

Figure 4.2   Simplified scheme of a human neuron.

neuron decreases the activation of the receiving neuron. Synapses differ not only in whether they excite or inhibit the receiving neuron, but also in the amount of this effect (synaptic strength). The output of each neuron is transferred by the so-called axon, which ends in as much as 10,000 synapses influencing other neurons.

Can Neural Nets Copy Human Thinking?

This is the simple neuron model that underlies most of today's neural net applications. Note that this model is only a very coarse approximation of reality. You cannot exactly model even one single human neuron; it is beyond the ability of humans to model. Hence, every work based on this simple neuron model is unable to exactly copy the human brain. It is rather an "inspiration" by nature than a "copy" of it. However, many successful applications using this technique prove the benefit of neural nets based on the simple neuron model.

Simple Mathematical Model of a Neuron

Various mathematical models are based on this simple neuron concept. Figure 4.3 shows the most common one. First, the so-called propagation function combines all inputs X_i that stem from the sending neurons. The means of combination is a weighted sum, where the weights w_i represent the synaptic strength. Exciting synapses have positive weights, inhibiting synapses have negative weights. To express a background activation level of the neuron, an offset (bias) Θ is added to the weighted sum.

The so-called activation function computes the output signal Y of the neuron from the activation level f. For this, the activation function is of the sigmoid type as plotted in the lower right box of Figure 4.3.

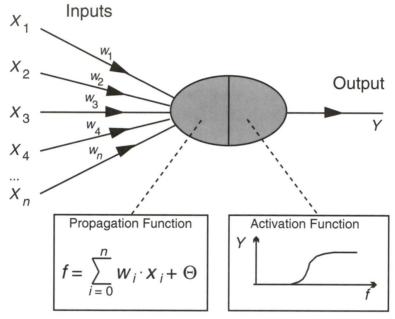

Figure 4.3 Simple mathematical model of a neuron. All inputs are combined by weighted sum (propagation function). Then the activation level of the neuron is computed by the activation function. The activation level is also the output signal.

4.1.2   Training Neural Nets

There are a multitude of ways to build a neural net. They differ in their topology and the learning methods they employ. This section describes learning methods for neural nets based on the simple layer-type neural nets shown in Figure 4.1.

Learning Phase and Working Phase

The first step in designing a neural net solution is teaching the desired behavior. This is called the learning phase. Here, you can either use sample data sets or a "teacher." A teacher is either a mathematical function or a person who rates the quality of the neural net performance. Since neural nets are mostly used for complex applications where no good mathematical models exist, and rating the performance of a neural net is hard in most applications, most applications use sample data training.

After completion of learning, the neural net is ready to use. This is called the working phase. As a result of the training, the neural net will output values similar to those in the sample data sets when the input values match one of the training samples. For input values in between, it approximates output values. In the working phase, the behavior of the neural net is deterministic. That is, for every combination of input values, the output value will always be the same. During the working phase, the neural net does not learn. This is important in most technical applications to ensure that the system never drifts to hazardous behavior.

Pavlov's Dogs

So, how do you teach a neural net? Basically, it works like Pavlov's dogs. More than one hundred years ago, the researcher Pavlov experimented with dogs. When he showed the dogs food, the dogs salivated. He also installed bells in the dogs' cages. When he rang the bell, the dogs did not salivate, as they saw no link between the bell and the food. Then he trained the dogs by always letting the bell ring when he presented the dogs food. After a while, the dogs also salivated when just the bell rang and he showed no food.

Figure 4.4 shows how the simple neuron model can represent the Pavlov dog. There are two input neurons: one represents the fact that the dog sees food, the other one the fact that the bell rings. Both input neurons have links to the output neuron. These links are the synapses. The thickness of the lines represents synapse weights. Before learning, the dog only reacts to the food and not the bell. Hence, the line from the left input neuron to the output neuron is thick, while the line from the right input neuron to the output neuron is very thin.

The Hebbian Learning Rule

Constantly letting the bell ring when food is presented creates an association between the bell and the food. Hence, the right line also becomes

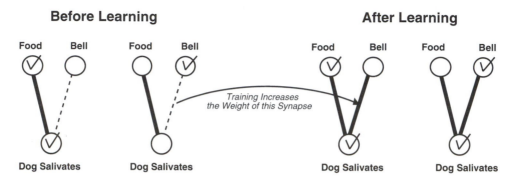

Figure 4.4   Principle of the Pavlov dog experiment. Before learning, the dogs salivate only when Pavlov shows them food. They ignore the bell. After they learn that the bell is linked to food, the dogs also salivate, but only when the bell rings.

thicker—the synapse weight increases. From these experiments, a researcher by the name of Hebb deduced the following learning rule [52]:

> Increase weight to active input neuron, if the output of this neuron should be active; decrease weight to active input neuron, if the output of this neuron should be inactive.

This rule, called the Hebbian rule, is the forerunner of all learning rules, including today's most used neural net learning algorithm, the so-called error back propagation algorithm. This algorithm first applies the input values of a sample data set to be trained at the inputs of the neural net and computes the outputs. Then it compares the outputs of the neural net with the given output value of the example and computes the error. This error is used to analyze which synaptic weight it shall modify to reduce the error for this example. The algorithm repeats these steps with every data set until the average error gets below a predefined threshold. Note that this iterative approach normally cannot reduce the error for all data sets to zero. This is, because in most applications, the sample data sets are not completely unambiguous.

4.2 Combining Neural and Fuzzy

The key benefit of fuzzy logic is that it lets you describe desired system behavior with simple "if-then" relations. In many applications, this gets you a simpler solution in less design time. In addition, you can use all available engineering know-how to optimize the system performance directly.

While this is certainly the beauty of fuzzy logic, at the same time it is a major limitation. In many applications, knowledge that describes desired system behavior is contained in data sets. Here, the designer has to derive the "if-then" rules from the data sets manually, which requires a major effort with large data sets.

When data sets contain knowledge about the system to be designed, a neural net promises a solution because it can train itself from the data sets. However, only a few commercial applications of neural nets exist. This is in contrast to fuzzy logic, which is a very common design technique in Asia and Europe.

The sparse use of neural nets in applications is due to a number of things. First, neural net solutions remain a "black box." You can neither interpret what causes a certain behavior nor modify a neural net manually to change to a certain desired behavior. Second, neural nets require prohibitive computational effort for most mass-market products. Third, selection of the appropriate net model and setting the parameters of the learning algorithm is still a "black art" and requires much experience. Of these three reasons, the lack of an easy way to verify and optimize a neural net solution is probably the mayor limitation.

Simply put, both neural nets and fuzzy logic are powerful design techniques that have strengths and weaknesses. Neural nets can learn from data sets, while fuzzy logic solutions are easy to verify and optimize. If you look at these properties in a portfolio (Table 4.1), it becomes obvious that a clever combination of the two technologies delivers the best of both worlds. Combine the explicit knowledge representation of fuzzy logic with the learning power of neural nets, and you get NeuroFuzzy.

Table 4.1   Strengths and Weaknesses of Neural Nets and Fuzzy Logic

	Neural Nets	**Fuzzy Logic**
Knowledge Representation	Implicit, the system cannot be easily interpreted or modified (−)	Explicit, verification and optimization is easy and efficient (+++)
Trainability	Trains itself by learning data sets (+++)	None, you have to define everything explicitly (−)

4.2.1   Training Fuzzy Logic Systems with NeuroFuzzy

Many alternative ways of integrating neural nets and fuzzy logic have been proposed in the scientific literature [203]. Very few have already been successfully applied in industrial applications. In this book, I will focus on methods that have been developed as an extension of the work of Zedeh, Zimmermann, and Kosko, and are used by companies such as Inform, Intel, Texas Instruments, Microchip, Foxboro, and Allen-Bradley [119].

Learning by Error Back Propagation

The first artificial neural net implementation dates back over 50 years ago. Since then, most research has dealt with learning techniques and algorithms. One major milestone in the development of neural net technology was the invention of the so-called error back propagation algorithm about 10 years ago.

The error back propagation algorithm soon became the standard for most neural net implementation due to its high training performance [138]. First, it selects one of the examples of the training data set. Second, it computes the neural net output values for the current training example's inputs. Third, it compares these output values to the desired output value of the training example. Finally, the difference, called error, determines which neuron in the net shall be modified and how. The mathematical mapping of the error back into the neurons of the net is called error back propagation.

If the error back propagation algorithm is so powerful, why not use it to train fuzzy logic systems too? Alas, this is not straightforward. To determine which neuron has what influence, the error back propagation algorithm mathematically differentiates the transfer functions of the neurons. One problem here is that the standard fuzzy logic inference cannot be differentiated because it uses mathematical operations such as minimum and maximum.

To solve these problems, some NeuroFuzzy development tools use extended fuzzy logic inference methods. The most common approach is to use so-called fuzzy associative memories (FAMs). In a simple implementation, a FAM is a fuzzy logic rule with an associated weight. A mathematical framework exists that maps FAMs to neurons in a neural net (Figure 4.5). This enables the use of a modified error back propagation algorithm with fuzzy logic. For more details on the math behind this technology, refer to [84, 116, 119]. As a user of NeuroFuzzy software tools, you do not need to worry about the details of the algo-

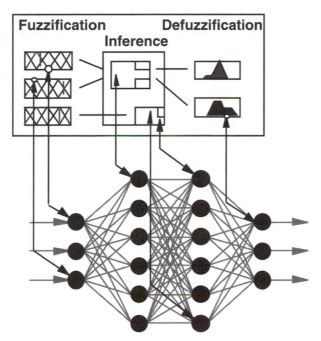

Figure 4.5   NeuroFuzzy technologies map a neural net to a fuzzy logic system. This enables powerful neural net learning algorithms with fuzzy logic system design.

rithm. Today's NeuroFuzzy software tools work as an "intelligent" assistant to your design. They help you to generate and optimize membership functions as well as rule bases from sample data. The next section gives you an overview on the design steps you take when you use NeuroFuzzy tools.

4.2.2   Development Steps of NeuroFuzzy Systems

To illustrate the design steps of a NeuroFuzzy system, I will return to the example of the development software tool, *fuzzy*TECH, used in Section 3.1. The *fuzzy*TECH software can be found among the software accompanying this book.

Step 1: Obtain Training Data

When you start with a NeuroFuzzy design, the first step is to obtain the data sets that represent the desired system behavior. Each data set gives sample output values for a combination of input variables.

For example, if you want to build a system that estimates the type of a water vessel just from its underwater sound, you may use a Fourier transformation and filter windows to get signal intensity information on certain frequency ranges. These intensities are the input variables of the fuzzy logic system. Now, you conduct experiments where you record the sound of different known water vessels under varying conditions and compute the intensities. Table 4.2 shows an example of the resulting data set.

Table 4.2   Training Data for a Neurofuzzy System

F1	F2	F3	F4	F5	Vessel Type
0.012	0.001	0.441	0.218	0.815	1
0.135	0.517	0.941	0.600	0.095	2
0.037	0.060	0.451	0.193	0.774	1
0.234	0.957	0.219	0.020	0.031	3
0.187	0.412	0.802	0.701	0.130	2
...					

Vessel Types: 1 = Small, 2 = Medium, 3 = Large.

Columns F1–F5 are the input variables of the fuzzy logic system; the column Vessel Type is the output variable. Each row represents an experiment. The intensity values in the F1–F5 columns are the result of the Fourier transformation. In the experiment, you know which vessel caused the sound spectrum and enter it in the Vessel Type column.

Step 2: Creating a Fuzzy Logic System

The NeuroFuzzy training process starts with an initial fuzzy logic system. If you have not set up an initial fuzzy logic system yet, the Fuzzy Design Wizard can automatically set one up for you. The Fuzzy Design Wizard analyzes the data sets and proposes a system definition. You can either accept this definition or modify it before the Fuzzy Design Wizard creates a fuzzy logic system for this sample data set.

If you already have any idea of how the rules or the membership functions should look, you can manually create an initial system. The NeuroFuzzy learning can either start from the default rules that the Fuzzy Design Wizard created or from any other fuzzy logic system. For the vessel classification example, you may know from experience that the sound of large ships has high intensity in the low frequency range and not in the high frequency range. Hence, you could use the following rules in your initial system:

IF F2=high AND F4=low AND F5=low THEN VesselType=3
IF F1=high AND F4=medium THEN VesselType=3

The advantage of coming up with such initial rules is that it enhances the speed and performance of the learning process. Any piece of information that you can put in the initial system out of experience, the NeuroFuzzy algorithm must not extract from training data. This is a very important fact, since poor data quality is the reason neural net training most often fails. Neuro-Fuzzy allows the use of information from multiple sources: designer's experience and sample data.

Step 3: Define the NeuroFuzzy Learning

In this step, you select the parts of the system that the NeuroFuzzy Module may modify. This is a major advantage over learning in a neural net in which the entire system is always trained, since it lets you better control the learning process. Especially when you use NeuroFuzzy to optimize an existing fuzzy logic system, you can exclude parts of the system from learning. For example, if you are confident that parts of the system already work fine with the fuzzy logic system, exclude them from learning, and the training becomes much faster. Also, if you have data sets representing different aspects of system behavior, you may direct the NeuroFuzzy Module to learn different parts of the system from different data sets.

If you have defined rules from experience as part of your initial fuzzy logic system, you can also open them for learning. This is useful if you are not completely confident that the rules or membership functions you defined are correct.

Now you can select the learning method. The learning method defines how the errors between the results computed by the current fuzzy logic systems, and the desired output values will cause modification of the rules and the membership functions. The NeuroFuzzy Module of *fuzzy*TECH automatically selects the best method for the given data set as the default; however, you can manually select one of the predefined learning methods or define your own. There are learning methods that either only train membership functions or train rules. Others determine during training whether they should train a membership function or a rule next.

To optimize the performance, you can parameterize the learning method. Two parameters are most important. One is the learn rate for rules, the other one the learn rate for membership functions. These parameters define how strongly the NeuroFuzzy algorithm modifies a rule or a membership function in each learning step. The NeuroFuzzy Module automatically selects default values for these parameters; however, you may change these values. Increase the values if you either have a simple system to learn or if you start learning from a system completely created by the Fuzzy Design Wizard. Decrease the values if you have a complex system and many sample data sets. Increasing the values speeds up training, but, in some cases, values that are too high will keep the system from converging.

Most NeuroFuzzy training algorithms train one of the data sets at a time. Here, you need to define in what sequence the examples shall be used for training. You achieve high training performance when using sequential selection. However, for some training data sets, the sequential selection may direct training in a loop. An example of such a data set is one with a non-arbitrary sequence, where the examples are in a certain sequence or somehow structured. Here, random selection will give better results.

Step 4: Training Phase

When you start training, all graphical editors show how the NeuroFuzzy Module modifies rules and membership functions. You can interrupt the training at any time, either for system analysis or to carry out manual modifications. You can continue the training with the current or a different data set at any time. Also, you may set termination conditions if you do not want to control the training progress manually.

Step 5: Optimization and Verification

The result of NeuroFuzzy training is a normal fuzzy logic system. Hence, you can use all the analyzers and simulation tools of the fuzzy logic software development tool shown in Section 3.1. After systems verification, you may implement the solution on target hardware, as described in Section 3.2.

One advantage of NeuroFuzzy over a neural net solution is that the generated code is much more efficient. Computing a fuzzy logic system trained by NeruoFuzzy on a microcontroller or a PC may require as little as 0.1 milliseconds and as little as 1 KB of memory. This is orders of magnitude faster and more compact than a neural net solution for the same applications. Hence, you can use NeuroFuzzy solutions in most real-time applications.

4.2.3   Learning the Exclusive OR

Lets look at this now using a the case study of a digital exclusive or (XOR). Researchers in the neural net area use the XOR to demonstrate the capability of a neural training algorithm to learn a nonlinear behavior.

Training Data for the XOR

The desired performance of an XOR is the data table of its possible inputs with the respective outputs (Table 4.3). The inputs of the XOR are X and Y, and the output is Z. The data sets are the four possible combinations of input variables.

Table 4.3   Sample Data Set
for the XOR

X	Y	Z
0	0	0
0	1	1
1	0	1
1	1	0

To train the XOR, you have to first set up an initial fuzzy logic system. Figure 4.6 shows the structure of the fuzzy logic system that the Fuzzy Design Wizard of *fuzzy*TECH generated from the sample data. The linguistic variables for the input variables and output variable are identical, and each contains two membership functions. These membership functions represent the linguistic terms "true" and "false" (Figure 4.7). The Fuzzy Design Wizard also created a rule set that contains every possible rule. All rules have the degree of support of 0 (Figure 4.8).

To supervise the learning progress, you can watch the modifications of the rule base and the membership functions interactively in the respective editors. Alternatively, you can use the analyzers to see the input/output characteristics of the system during modification. Figure 4.9 shows the transfer plot for the initial fuzzy logic system. Since all rules have a degree of support of

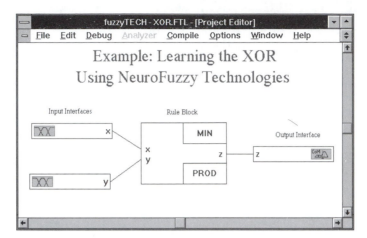

Figure 4.6   Structure of the initial fuzzy logic system generated by the Fuzzy Design Wizard of fuzzyTECH from the sample data.

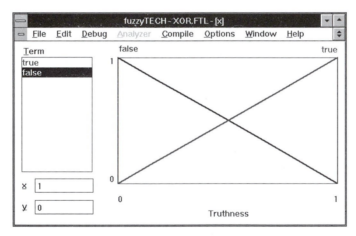

Figure 4.7   Definition of the linguistic variables *x*, *y*, and *z*. They contain two membership functions, one for "true" and one for "false."

zero, the value of the output variable is always 0.5, the default value for the output variable.

Figure 4.10 shows the four training samples in the cube that represent the input/output transfer space. Figure 4.11 shows the transfer plot after some training steps. You can see how the NeuroFuzzy algorithm "bends" the transfer surface to fit the samples.

After training, the fuzzy logic system has completely learned to represent the four samples. Also, the fuzzy logic system approximates the space be-

fuzzyTECH - XOR.FTL - [Spreadsheet Rule Editor]				
File Edit Debug Analyzer Compile Options Window				

Matrix	IF		THEN	
#	x	y	DoS	z
1	false	false	0.00	false
2	false	false	0.00	true
3	false	true	0.00	false
4	false	true	0.00	true
5	true	false	0.00	false
6	true	false	0.00	true
7	true	true	0.00	false
8	true	true	0.00	true

Figure 4.8 The Fuzzy Design Wizard created all possible rules with a degree of support of 0. The NeuroFuzzy training algorithm will increase the degree of support for all rules that represent the sample data.

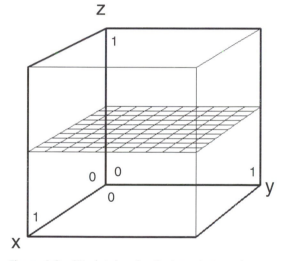

Figure 4.9 3D plot showing the input/output characteristics of the initial fuzzy logic system. The horizontal axis plots the two input variables x and y, the vertical axis plots the output variable z. For the initial fuzzy logic system, the output is 0.5 constant.

tween the samples, as shown in Figure 4.12. The training time for this system is about 0.1 second on a 486-class PC. Larger systems, however, may require much longer training times. The training time becomes longer as the number of input/output variables and training samples increase. Alas, there is no rule that can tell you how long training will take.

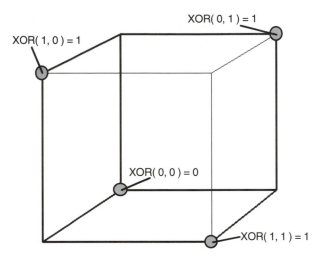

Figure 4.10 The training examples are the four possible combinations of the input variable values of the digital XOR. They are located at corners of the cube.

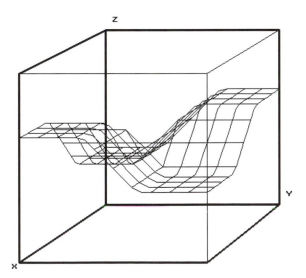

Figure 4.11 This 3D plot shows the input/output characteristic after the first learning steps. The NeuroFuzzy training algorithm bends the transfer surface so that it fits the training samples.

In the case of the XOR, NeuroFuzzy training succeeded with a final error of 0. That is, the fuzzy logic system represents all samples perfectly. This is not the normal case. First, the XOR example is very simple and academic.

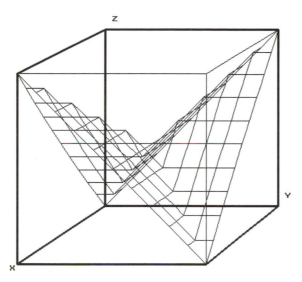

Figure 4.12   Result of the NeuroFuzzy training. The fuzzy logic system represents all four training samples and approximates an output for the space between the samples.

Who wants to train digital logic to a (continuous) fuzzy logic system? Second, the training data quality was perfect and the samples were unambiguous, free of artifacts, consistent, and complete.

For real world applications, this is never the case. Experience of both neural net and NeuroFuzzy users indicates that the most crucial factor of the design is quality of the sample data. An additional problem is that the quality of a given set of training data is hard to judge before using it. Both neural nets and NeuroFuzzy never guarantee a solution. However, if they got you half the way with training, with NeuroFuzzy you can continue the design manually with fuzzy logic.

4.2.4   NeuroFuzzy vs. Other Adaptive Technologies

Compared to other adaptive techniques, NeuroFuzzy has got some advantages:

■ Because you start with a prestructured system, the degrees of freedom for learning are limited. Experience shows that in many applications the quantization of input and output variables by membership functions and the structure of the information flow in the system already contain much of the information that a neural net would have to derive from the sample data sets.

■ You can use any knowledge of the system under design right from the start. In most applications, a few things are perfectly clear. Using NeuroFuzzy, you can implement all this knowledge in the initial fuzzy logic system.

■ You can exclude parts of the system from training. For example, this is necessary in applications where some rules contain knowledge that is essential to the safe operation of a plant.

■ You can always interpret the result or current stage of the NeuroFuzzy training as it consists of self-explanatory fuzzy logic rules and linguistic variables.

■ You can manually optimize the result of a NeuroFuzzy training.

■ You can train the system interactively. After any manual correction or modification, you can start training over with the same or other sample data sets.

■ The resulting fuzzy logic system of NeuroFuzzy training is faster and more compact on most target hardware platforms as opposed to a neural net implementation.

On the other hand, there are a few disadvantages of NeuroFuzzy compared with other adaptive techniques. First, there is much more experience with neural nets after extensive research for 50 years. NeuroFuzzy, in contrast, is still a "young" technology that came from practitioners rather than researchers. Second, NeuroFuzzy training features fewer degrees of freedom for the learning algorithm when compared to a neural net. In engineering, this is an advantage rather than a drawback. However, in applications where no knowledge of the system's structure exists, but where there are massive amounts of data, NeuroFuzzy may not deliver a solution at all.

5

Case Studies
of Industrial Applications

Fuzzy logic enables system design based on human experience. NeuroFuzzy enhances this by generating fuzzy logic systems from sample data. Such technologies are beneficial for a very large spectrum of applications. Hence, successful fuzzy logic applications range from closed-loop control to data analysis and decision support.

In this book, I will only show case studies of closed-loop control applications and data analysis solutions. Most successful applications of fuzzy logic do not replace conventional control techniques, but rather use a clever combination of both. Section 5.1 presents different ways to combine fuzzy logic and conventional control approaches. The remainder of this chapter concentrates on different applicational areas. Section 5.2 covers appliances, Section 5.3 automotive engineering, and Section 5.4 industrial automation and process control. Section 5.5 deals with fuzzy data analysis applications and Section 5.6 presents selected industrial fuzzy logic and NeuroFuzzy applications in other areas.

5.1   Combining Fuzzy Logic with Conventional Control Methods

Many different ways exist to use fuzzy logic in closed-loop control. The most simple structure is to use the sensor signals from the process as the inputs to the fuzzy logic system and the outputs of the fuzzy logic system to drive the actors of the process. Figure 5.1 shows the outline of such a control loop. Here, set values can be either external inputs, as drawn, or part of the fuzzy logic rule base.

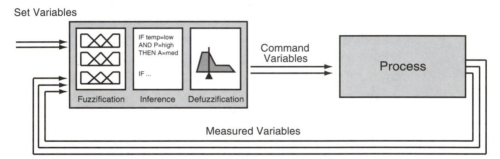

Figure 5.1   In a simple fuzzy logic controller, the outputs of the process (measured variables) are the inputs of the fuzzy logic system, the outputs of the fuzzy logic system (command variables) are the inputs of the process under control.

This "pure" fuzzy logic control is more the exception than the rule. Most of the time, the fuzzy logic controller output proceeds into a conventional controller rather than driving an actor in the process directly. The so-called fuzzy-PI controller shown in Figure 5.2 uses the error signal and its derivative as inputs. These inputs correspond to the P (proportional) and D (differential) signal of a conventional PID controller. As the output of the fuzzy logic controller proceeds to an integrator, the resulting characteristic of the controller is PI (the I stands for integral). This is why it is called a "fuzzy-PI" controller. In contrast to a conventional PI controller, the fuzzy-PI controller is nonlinear, and linguistic rules express the control strategy rather than gains. Another combination of fuzzy logic and conventional control is widely used. Figure 5.3 shows the case where the fuzzy logic controller outputs the set values for PID controllers.

The benefit of the fuzzy-PI controller is that it does not have an operating point. The rules evaluate the difference between the measured value and

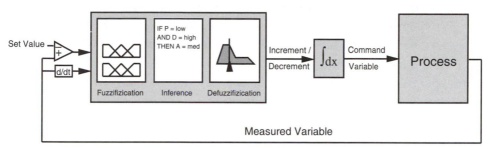

Figure 5.2   The fuzzy-PI controller uses the error signal and its derivative as inputs. The output of the fuzzy logic controller proceeds into an integrator.

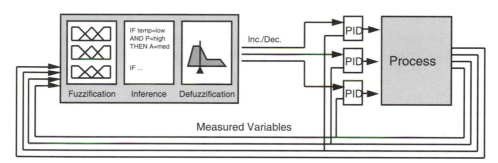

Figure 5.3   Using a fuzzy logic controller to determine the set values for underlying PID control loops.

the set value, and the tendency of this difference to determine whether to increment or decrement the control variable of the process. The absolute value of the command variable has no influence. This is similar to a person who controls the temperature of his shower. He evaluates the difference of the temperature from the desired one and decides whether to increase or decrease the flow of hot or cold water. The actual position of the mixer knob is of no relevance. Due to the time lag between turning the knob and the resulting temperature change, the person will also take the tendency of temperature error into account. If it is slightly too cold, but the temperature is increasing, the person will probably leave the mixer knob unchanged and wait until the temperature becomes constant.

Many applications, such as temperature and motor control, use fuzzy-PI controllers. The advantage over a conventional PI controller is that it can implement nonlinear control strategies and that it uses linguistic rules. The shower example exhibits this nonlinearity. If the temperature is way too cold, the increment will be strong, regardless of its tendency. Only if the temperature error is small is the tendency taken into account. Also, the sign of the temperature error plays a role; first, because the discomfort of the person under the shower is not symmetric (much too hot is more dangerous than much too cold), and second, because of different pressures in the water tubes, the control characteristic is neither linear nor symmetric.

Another advantage of the fuzzy-PI controller is it that is easy to extend. For example, in most houses, the withdrawal of large quantities of hot water in other places in the house will cause the shower temperature to drop. The controller can only respond to the temperature drop, not avoid it. If, however, there is a sensor that measures the amount of hot water withdrawn at other places in the house, this could be another input to the fuzzy logic controller. Expressing the knowledge of the effect of water withdrawal in the fuzzy logic rules, the controller can react even before a temperature error occurs. Such extended fuzzy-PI controllers are used quite often in the chemical industry for robust temperature and flow control.

Figure 5.3 shows a controller structure often used in the chemical industry and process technology. In these applications, PID controllers work very well in keeping single parameters of a process, such as temperatures, flows, or pressures, at a constant level. However, a PID controller cannot control the operating point of the entire process, because this is a multivariable control problem. Hence, either human operators supervise the operation or a model-based controller for automatic operation must be built. For most applications, the process is too complex to be modeled adequately or the required mathematical modeling task requires a laborious effort. The benefit of using a fuzzy logic controller instead is that the knowledge of the operators in supervising the process often forms a fuzzy logic rule base with much less effort.

In some applications, preprocessing of the measured variables of the process is necessary (Figure 5.4). For example, such preprocessing can be statistical analysis, filtering, or a Fourier transformation. Often, such applications are not closed-loop applications but are used for off-line analysis.

In all of the examples shown so far, the conventional control techniques only do preprocessing and postprocessing of the fuzzy logic system. The next examples show how to integrate fuzzy logic and conventional techniques more closely. Figure 5.5 shows how a fuzzy logic system interprets the process reaction and tunes the P, I, and D parameters of a PID controller. For example, the fuzzy

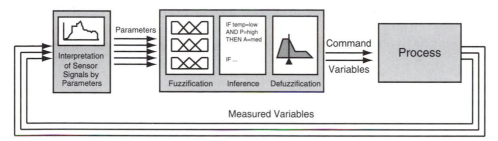

Figure 5.4   Some applications require preprocessing of the process signals.

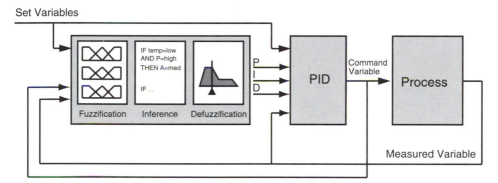

Figure 5.5   Adaptation of P, I, and D parameters by a fuzzy logic system.

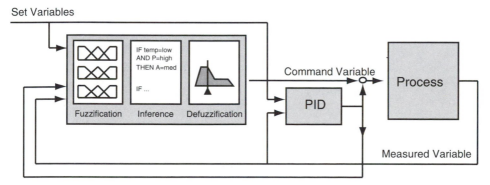

Figure 5.6   Intervention of a fuzzy logic system to a PID controller output.

logic system can detect hunting of the PID controller and correct the parameters accordingly [194]. Processes that change their characteristics over time benefit most from this technique. Also, successful applications of fuzzy logic systems for the auto-tuning of PID controllers exist [140].

Figure 5.6 shows another combination of a fuzzy logic system and a PID controller. Here, the fuzzy logic system and the PID controller work in parallel. Its outputs are added, but the output of the fuzzy logic system is zero in normal operating conditions, letting the PID controller do the job. Only if the fuzzy logic system detects abnormal operating conditions, such as strong disturbances does it intervene.

5.2   Intelligent Solutions for Appliances

Fuzzy Logic is an innovative technology that enables the implementation of intelligent functions in embedded systems. One of its advantages is that even complicated functions and adaptive control loops can be implemented with the limited resources of low-cost 8-bit microcontrollers. This section will study methodologies, tools, and code speed/size requirements of three case studies.

The first case study shows how existing products can be enhanced with new, intelligent functions (Section 5.2.1). In home air conditioners, the enhancement of the thermostat by fuzzy logic control techniques allows for better adaptation to the requirements of the user. This results in a higher comfort level. Also, detection of low-load situations yields energy savings.

The second case study covers the replacement of sensors with fuzzy logic state estimators (Section 5.2.2). In the example of a central heating system control, a $35 outdoor temperature sensor and its installation were replaced. Comparisons show that the fuzzy logic solution better adapts to high and low heat demand periods, thus yielding higher comfort and energy savings at the same time. This system is now in production in Germany (350,000 units per year).

The third case study focuses on combining neural net techniques with fuzzy logic (Section 5.2.3). For laundry load detection in washing machines, NeuroFuzzy was used to generate a fuzzy logic system from experimental data. The results of washing experiments, evaluated by experts, form this sample database. The introduction of the resulting fuzzy logic laundry load detector saves an average 20% of water and energy. This system is now in production in Germany (400,000 units per year).

5.2.1   Energy-Saving AC Control Using Fuzzy Logic

One major consumer of the total energy produced in the world is the heating and cooling of homes and office buildings. Hence, increasing the efficiency of these systems has a great effect on energy savings. These savings can be realized either through constructional improvements, such as better insulation and more efficient heating/cooling systems, or by using more intelligent control strategies for the operation of these devices. This case study focuses on the application of fuzzy logic control techniques in air conditioning systems.

Fuzzy logic allows for the formulation of a technical control strategy using elements of everyday language. In this application, fuzzy logic was used to design a control strategy that adapts to the individual user's needs, thereby achieving both a higher comfort level and reduced energy consumption at the same time. By using fuzzy logic development software, the entire system, containing both conventional code for signal preprocessing and the fuzzy logic system, can be implemented on a standard 8-bit microcontroller. Using fuzzy logic on such a low-cost hardware platform enables this solution to be implemented in most air conditioning systems.

Fuzzy Logic in Air Conditioning Control

Quite a few air conditioning systems already use fuzzy logic control. In 1990, Mitsubishi introduced their first line of fuzzy-logic-controlled home air conditioners. Also, industrial air conditioning systems in Japan have used fuzzy logic [170] since 1990. Four years later, most Korean, Taiwanese, and European air conditioning manufacturers also use fuzzy logic as a standard control technique [74, 165, 193]. There are different incentives to use fuzzy logic:

■ Industrial AC systems use fuzzy logic to minimize energy consumption. The fuzzy logic controller optimizes the set values for heater, cooler, and humidifier depending on the current load state [170].

■ Car AC systems use fuzzy logic to estimate the temperatures at the head of the driver from multiple indirect sensors.

■ Home AC systems are much simpler. They do not contain a humidifier and can only either cool or heat at a given time. They use fuzzy logic for robust temperature control.

Air Conditioning Control Thermostats

The application discussed in this case study falls more into the third category. Each AC system has a thermostat that measures the room temperature and compares it with the temperature that is set on the dial. Figure 5.7 shows the principle of such a thermostat.

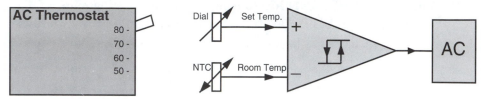

Figure 5.7 A conventional thermostat compares room temperature with set temperature to turn AC on and off.

The thermostat compares the set temperature dialed by the user with the actual room temperature. To minimize the number of starts for the AC, a hysteresis is used. Both mechanical and electronic designs are used for this. Figure 5.7 shows the principle of an electronic analog AC controller.

Intelligent Fuzzy Logic Thermostat

This method works well to maintain a certain temperature level in a room. However, the actual room temperature does not always correspond with the subjective temperature of the people in the room. A certain comfort level is reached with different room temperatures, depending on a number of conditions:

- During the day, the temperature may be higher than during the night.

- The same room temperature is perceived to be warmer if the sun is shining.

Empirical analysis on how people adjust the temperature dial on their air conditioners has shown even more:

- Someone who turns down the set temperature significantly wants a large cooling effect. Because of this, most people tend to turn the temperature dial lower than necessary. Usually, they forget to turn the temperature dial up again when the proper temperature is reached, and the room is cooled more than necessary. Before this is corrected, the increased cooling wastes energy.

- Someone who turns down the AC just a little bit is not interested in a quick response, but in accurate temperature. Reacting too much to this can cause the air conditioning to overshoot the desired room temperature.

■ If someone changes the temperature very often, the control should respond exactly and carefully.

■ If room temperature changes a lot (due to doors or windows being opened or closed throughout the day, for example), the control should respond sensibly.

The objective in this case study is to design an "intelligent" thermostat that "understands" both different environmental conditions and the current needs of the user. Knowledge of different situations such as those described in the list above must be implemented by the thermostat. Since this kind of knowledge is hard to model mathematically as well as to code in a conventional algorithm, fuzzy logic has been used for implementation.

Figure 5.8 shows the scheme of the "intelligent thermostat." To measure the brightness in the room, an LDR photo sensor is added. The fuzzy logic system corrects the signal before the threshold unit and sets its hysteresis. The fuzzy logic system uses four input variables:

1   *Difference between set temperature and room temperature (Temp_Error)*
    When the difference between set temperature and room temperature is very large, the fuzzy logic system increases the signal so the desired temperature is reached faster (rules 5 and 6 in Figure 5.10). At the same time, the hysteresis is set to large, so disturbances do not cause unnecessary on/off switches.

2   *Time differentiated set temperature (dTemp_by_dt)*
    The set temperature signal is differentiated with a time constant of 30 minutes. The fuzzy logic system uses this signal to understand when the user wants the AC to cool down a room quickly (rule 3 in Figure 5.9). Also, the hysteresis is set large, so disturbances do not interrupt the cooling process. As this signal is a differentiated signal, it disappears after some time if the user does not modify the dial any more.

3   *Number of set temperature changes (Changes)*
    This input signal is used to identify a user who tries to set the room temperature very precisely (rule 4 in Figure 5.9). To satisfy such a user, the hysteresis is set to small. This variable counts each time the user moves the dial. Every six hours this variable is counted down until 0 is reached.

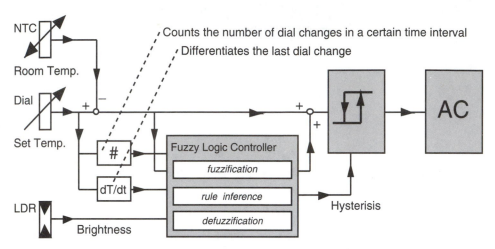

Figure 5.8 A conventional thermostat compares room temperature with set temperature to turn the AC on and off.

4 *Brightness in the room (Brightness)*

If direct sunlight hits the room, the set temperature is automatically reduced (rule 2 in Figure 5.9). During the day or when lights are on in the room, the set temperature is slightly increased (rule 1 in Figure 5.9) and the hysteresis is set to small.

Implementation of a Fuzzy Logic Control Strategy

Figure 5.9 shows part of the rule base that defines the strategy of the system. This spreadsheet representation is appropriate for small rule bases. Each row represents a rule. The left part of the screen under the [IF] button shows all input variables of the rule block; the right part under the [THEN] button shows all output variables. The column [DoS] that is displayed for each output variable allows for the association of a weight to this conclusion. This enables fine-tuning of the fuzzy logic system during optimization.

Figure 5.10 shows the structure of the fuzzy logic system as designed with the *fuzzy*TECH development system [116]. All input variables have three terms with standard membership functions. The output variable "Correction" has five terms and uses Center-of-Maximum defuzzification. The output variable "Hysteresis" has three terms and also uses Center-of-Maximum defuzzification.

Matrix	IF				THEN		THEN	
Utilities	Temp_Error	dTemp_dt	Changes	Brightness	DoS	Correction	DoS	Hysterisis
1				medium	1.00	warmer	1.00	small
2				high	1.00	cooler		
3		negative			1.00	much_cool	1.00	large
4			frequent				1.00	small
5	too_cold				1.00	warmer	1.00	large
6	too_warm				1.00	cooler	1.00	large
7	OK	zero			1.00	zero	1.00	small
8								

Figure 5.9   The fuzzy logic rules represent the knowledge that the thermostat uses to correct the set temperature and the hysteresis.

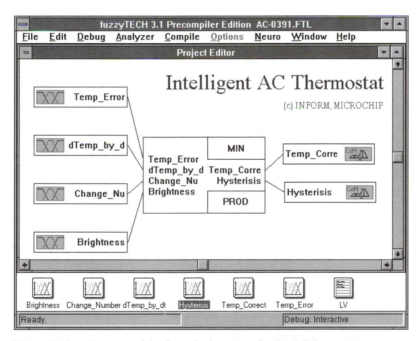

Figure 5.10   Structure of the fuzzy logic system for the AC thermostat.

Integration on a Standard Microcontroller

The entire fuzzy logic system requires less than 1 KB ROM and 40 bytes of RAM space on a standard 8-bit microcontroller using the *fuzzy*TECH code generators [113]. The non-fuzzy code to link to the sensors, preprocessing of the sensor signals, and driving the relay also require less than 1 KB ROM. Since the RAM space used for the fuzzy logic system can be used for other code while the fuzzy inference is not being computed, no additional RAM is required.

Simulation Results and Comparison

The fuzzy logic system has been tested using data that has been recorded in rooms of different buildings under various conditions. This test data has been preprocessed using the spreadsheet software MS-Excel™. To test the performance of the fuzzy logic solution, *fuzzy*TECH's Excel-link has been used [116]. It allows for MS-Excel cells to be linked to fuzzy logic input and output variables. As this link is dynamic, the fuzzy logic system can be monitored and modified using the *fuzzy*TECH analyzers and editors while browsing through the data sets.

Analysis of the fuzzy logic controller performance shows that the fuzzy logic thermostat detected situations where less cooling effort sufficed. In an average residential house, the average energy consumption was reduced by 3.5%. At the same time, the comfort level was increased, since, depending on the situation, the fuzzy logic thermostat reduced the room temperature by 5°F more than the conventional thermostat.

The fuzzy logic thermostat does not require any modification of the AC itself. Hence, by replacing existing temperature controllers, even old ACs can be upgraded. By also controlling the ventilation, an even better performance could be reached in a more sophisticated design.

5.2.2 Adaptive Heating System Control

To maximize both energy efficiency and comfort of a private home heating system, fuzzy logic control has been used by a German company in a new generation of furnace controllers [58, 118]. The fuzzy logic controller ensures optimal adaptation to changing customer heating demands while using one sensor less than the former generation. Both the fuzzy logic controller and the conventional control system were implemented on the same standard 8-bit microcontroller.

European Heating Systems

Most European houses are equipped with a centralized heating system that uses a furnace for diesel-type fuel to heat a water supply (boiler). From this boiler, the hot water is distributed by a pipe system to individual radiators in the rooms of the house. To meet the changing heat demands, the temperature of the furnace-heated water must constantly be adjusted in relation to the outdoor temperature (heat characteristic). To measure the outdoor temperature, a sensor is installed at the outside of the house. Figure 5.11 depicts the basic structure of such a system.

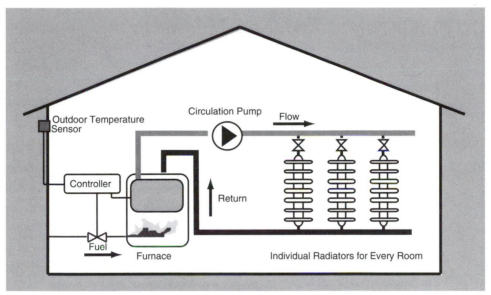

Figure 5.11   Scheme of a centralized heating system.

The basic structure of a controller for this system is shown in Figure 5.12. The control loop itself follows an on-off pattern. If the water temperature in the boiler drops to 2° Kelvin below the set temperature, the fuel valve opens and the ignition system starts the burning process. When the water temperature in the boiler rises to 2° Kelvin above the set temperature, the fuel valve closes. This on-off control strategy involving hysteresis minimizes the number of starts while assuring that the boiler temperature remains within the desired tolerance.

Although the structure of this control loop is quite simple, the determination of the appropriate set boiler temperature is not. The maximum heat dissipation of the room radiators depends on the temperature of the incoming water (approximately the boiler temperature). Therefore, the set point for the water temperature in the boiler must never be set so low that it cannot warm the house when necessary. On the other hand, an excessively high setting of

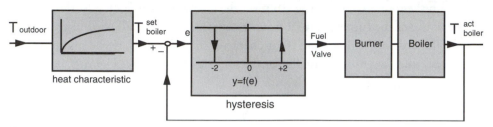

Figure 5.12   Block scheme of the conventional furnace controller.

the boiler temperature would result in energy loss in both the furnace and the piping system. Thus, the boiler temperature needs to be carefully set to ensure both user comfort and energy efficiency.

In the 1950s, the German Electrical Engineering Society (VDE) defined a procedure for this. The assumption is that the maximum amount of heat required by the house depends on the outdoor temperature ($T_{outdoor}$). A parametric function $T^{set}_{boiler} = f(T_{outdoor})$ adjusts the set boiler temperature in relation to the outside temperature. This function is also called the "heat characteristic." The parameters of this function are the insulation coefficient of the house and a so-called "comfort parameter." The physical model of this is one in which the maximum amount of available heat equals the amount of heat disposed by the house plus some excess energy to compensate for occasional door and window opening.

The assumption, that the amount of energy a heating system has to deliver is largely outdoor-temperature-dependent, was true back in those days when most houses had only poor thermal insulation. Today, this is obsolete. Due to rising energy costs and environmental concerns, modern houses are built with greatly improved insulation. Therefore, the outdoor temperature only poorly reflects the required energy amount. Other factors, such as ventilation, door/window openings, and personal lifestyle, have to be considered as well.

Estimation of Heat Demand by Fuzzy Logic

Two approaches for determining the appropriate set boiler temperature for a well-insulated house exist:

- Extensive use of sensors (i.e., temperature sensors in every room) and use of a mathematical model of the house

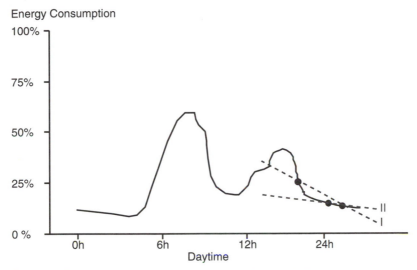

Figure 5.13   Actual energy consumption of the house (draft).

■ Definition of engineering heuristics to determine the set boiler temperature based on a knowledge-based evaluation of existing sensor data

Since the use of extensive sensors is expensive and developing a comprehensive mathematical model is of overwhelming complexity, the second approach has been chosen for realizing the new generation of heating system controllers.

The most important criterion about individual customer heat demand patterns comes from the actual energy consumption curve of the house, which is measured by the on/off ratio of the burner. An example of such a curve is given in Figure 5.13. From this curve, four describing parameters are derived:

■ Current energy consumption, indicating current load

■ Medium-term tendency (I), indicating heating-up and heating-down phases

■ Short-term tendency (II), indicating disturbances like door/window openings

■ Yesterday's average energy consumption, indicating the general situation and heating level in the house.

These parameters were used to heuristically form rules for the determination of the appropriate set boiler temperature. To allow for the formulation of plausibility rules (such as "temperatures below 30° Fahrenheit are rare in August"), the appropriate average outdoor temperature for that season is also a system input parameter. These curves are plotted in Figure 5.14. Since the average temperature curves are given in a look-up-table, no outdoor temperature needs to be measured. Hence, the outdoor temperature sensor can be eliminated.

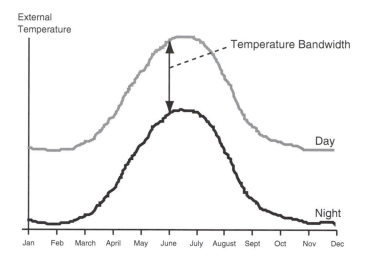

Figure 5.14   Average outside temperatures in Munich.

The structure of the new furnace controller is shown in Figure 5.15. The fuzzy controller uses a total of five inputs, four of which are derived from the energy consumption curve using conventional digital filtering techniques; the fifth is the average outdoor temperature. This input comes from a look-up-table within the system clock. The output of the fuzzy system represents the estimated heat requirement of the house and corresponds to the $T_{outdoor}$ value in the conventional controller (Figure 5.12).

Design of the Fuzzy Logic Rule Base

The objective of the fuzzy controller is to estimate the actual heat requirement of the house. For this, if-then rules were defined to express the engineering heuristics of this parameter estimation:

IF   current_energy_consumption IS low

AND   medium_term_tendency IS increasing

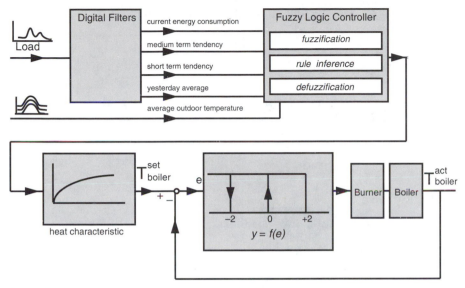

Figure 5.15   Schematics of the new furnace controller.

AND   short_term_tendency IS decreasing

AND   yesterday_average IS medium

AND   average_outside_temperature IS very_low

THEN   estimated_heat_requirement IS medium_high

In total, 405 rules were defined for the parameter estimation. To develop and optimize such a large system efficiently, *fuzzy*TECH's matrix representation was used [181]. This technique enables rule bases to be viewed and defined graphically rather than in text form. Figure 5.16 shows a screen shot of such a rule matrix. In this representation, all linguistic labels of two selected linguistic variables (established heating requirement and yesterday's average energy consumption) are displayed. All other variables (such as medium-term tendency) are kept one term. The matrix may be browsed to show the entire rule base by selecting other terms for these variables.

Within the matrix, a white square indicates a plausible rule, whereas a black square indicates an implausible rule (not existent in the rule base). For instance, the highlighted rule (the matrix element with the small frame) in Figure 5.16 is valid. Its textual representation (in the lower part of the window) can be read as:

IF   medium_term_tendency IS stable

AND   yesterday_avg IS medium

THEN   est._heat_req. IS medium.

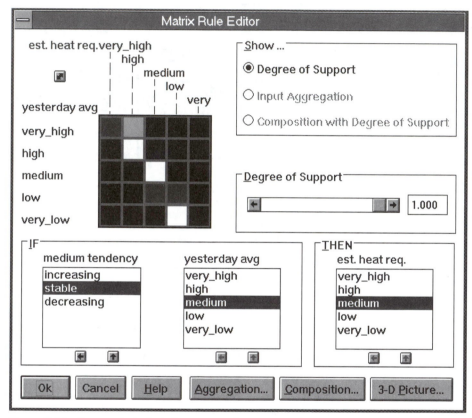

Figure 5.16   Screen shot of rule base as matrix representation.

For the formulation of these if-then rules, an initial system prototype was built. During system optimization, however, it became apparent that some rules were more important than others and that mere rule addition/deletion was too inexact a system-tuning method. Thus, the inference strategy had to be extended to allow rules to be associated with a "degree of support." Such a degree of support is a number between 0 and 1 that expresses the individual importance of each rule with respect to all other rules. The degree of support for each rule is indicated in the matrix by a gray-shaded square. This allows for the expression of rules like:

IF   medium_term_tendency IS stable

AND   yesterday_avg IS very_high

THEN   est_heat_req IS rather high and slightly very_high

This rule is represented as the two gray elements in the first row of the matrix in Figure 5.16.

The inference method used to represent individual degrees of support is based on approximate reasoning and fuzzy associative map (FAM) techniques. After fuzzification, all rule premises are calculated using the minimum operator for the representation of the linguistic AND, and the maximum operator for the representation of the linguistic OR. Next, the premise's degree of validity is weighted with the individual degree of support of the rule, resulting in the degree of truth for the conclusion. In the third step, all conclusions are combined using the maximum operator. The result of this is a fuzzy set. The Center-of-Maximum method is used for defuzzification.

The entire structure of the fuzzy controller is shown in Figure 5.17. In this screen shot, the large block in the middle represents the previously described rule base, while the small blocks represent input and output interfaces. The icons show the fuzzification/defuzzification methods used in the respective interfaces.

Implementation and Optimization

After completion of the design of the fuzzy controller structure and the definition of linguistic variables, membership functions, and rules, the system was compiled to the assembly language of the target microcontroller. With this technology, the fuzzy controller uses only 2 KB ROM on a standard 8-bit microcontroller. Once the fuzzy controller had been linked to the entire furnace controller code, the system was optimized.

To achieve the most efficient system optimization, *fuzzy*TECH's RTRCD Module was used, and the target hardware based on an 8-bit microcontroller was connected to the developer's PC. The RTRCD technique allows for the graphical visualization of the information flow while the system is running. All fuzzification, defuzzification and rule inference steps can be graphically cross-debugged in real-time. In addition, the fuzzy controller can be modified and optimized "on-the-fly" during run-time using the graphical editors (Figure 5.18) [180, 181].

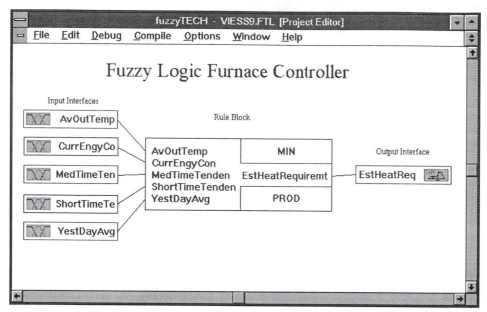

Figure 5.17   Structure of the fuzzy logic furnace controller.

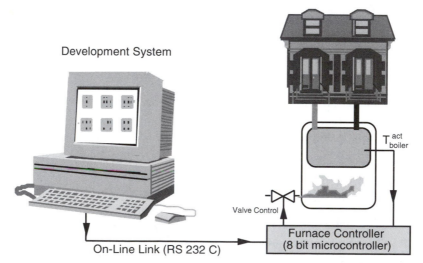

Figure 5.18   Optimization using the "online" technique allows for cross-debugging and "on-the-fly" modifications.

During optimization, the fuzzy logic controller was connected to a real heating system. This enabled the optimization of the system robustness against process disturbances such as:

■ Preparation of hot water, e.g., for a bath tub

■ Opening of windows

■ Extended departure, e.g., for vacation

Evaluation of the Fuzzy Logic System

To evaluate system performance, both the conventional controller and the fuzzy controller were connected to a test house, and varying load conditions were applied. Figure 5.19 shows the performance over a period of 48 hours. Three graphs were plotted:

■ Optimal boiler temperature (calculated from the external/internal house condition)

■ Set boiler temperature, as determined by the conventional controller (from outdoor temperature)

■ Set boiler temperature, as determined by the fuzzy logic controller

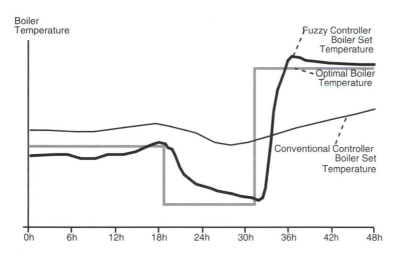

Figure 5.19 Comparative performance test (scheme).

The result of the comparative performance tests showed that the fuzzy controller was highly responsive to the actual heat requirement of the house. It was very responsive to sudden heat demand changes like the return of house inhabitants from vacation. Besides this, the elimination of the outdoor temperature sensor saved about $35 in production costs and even more in installation costs that average $120. By setting the set boiler temperature below the level typically set by a conventional controller in low-load periods, the fuzzy controller saves energy. Long-term studies collecting statistical data for quantifying exactly how much energy per house could be saved annually are currently under way. In addition, the two knobs parameterizing the heat characteristic (see Figure 5.12) for the individual house used by conventional heating systems, are not necessary with the fuzzy logic controller anymore. This makes the use of the heating system easier, since setting the parameters of the heating curves requires an expertise most home owners do not have.

This new generation of fuzzy logic heating controller achieves:

- Improved energy efficiency, since the fuzzy controller reduces heat production at low heat demand periods

- Improved comfort, due to the detection of sudden heat demand peaks

- Easy setup, since the heat characteristic does not need to be parameterized manually

- Savings in both production and installation cost

Taking into account the benefits of introducing engineering heuristics formulated with fuzzy logic, the price was rather low. In the product, the added expense of the fuzzy logic controller was only 2 KB of ROM space of the microcontroller. Using matrix rule representation and RTRCD technology, the optimization of a complex fuzzy logic system containing 405 rules was done efficiently.

5.2.3   NeuroFuzzy Signal Analysis in Washing Machines

In some applications, the knowledge about the system solution is contained in sample data. In these cases, NeuroFuzzy is the method of choice. The following case study is a good example to show the potential of Neuro-Fuzzy technologies. The German home appliance manufacturer AEG used the *fuzzy*TECH NeuroFuzzy Module to design an environment-friendly washing machine. The NeuroFuzzy system analyzes the signal of an existing sensor to estimate laundry volume and type. This information is used to optimize the washing program. In an average home, this saves about 20% water and energy [151].

European Washing Machines

Washing machines in Europe are different from those used in the U.S. and the Far East (Figure 5.20). The washing process is much more complicated and takes about 2 hours. On the other hand, water consumption is much lower. Typical water consumption ranges from 50 to 60 liters (13–18 gallons). White laundry, such as underwear, tableware, and bed sheets, is washed at temperatures up to 95°C (203°F). Hence, washing machines do not use the hot water from the tap but rather heat the water electrically.

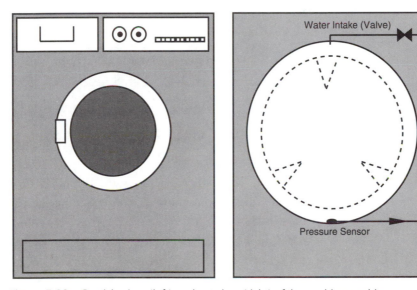

Figure 5.20   Outside view (left) and cut view (right) of the washing machine.

The complex washing process consists of multiple wash, enzymatic process, bleach, rinse, and spin steps. To control this, today's washing machines use microcontroller hardware and multiple sensors such as:

■ Tachometer for the drum spin

■ Analog pressure sensor for the water level (Figure 5.20, left)

■ Digital sensor to detect strong unevenness during spinning

■ Digital sensor to detect excessive foam

To determine an optimal washing program, actual laundry load (type and volume) of the washing machine must be known. Sensors that could measure these parameters directly are expensive and unreliable. Hence, AEG wanted to design a system that estimates the actual laundry load using only the existing sensors.

Water Absorption Curves

Figure 5.21 plots the pressure sensor signal over time. The plot starts when the water intake valve first opens.

- The water intake valve opens at T_0. At T_1, the water level reached set value. This duration does not depend much on the laundry load since the laundry in the non-rotating drum does not absorb much water.

- At T_1, the drum starts to rotate in a specific rhythm, causing the laundry to absorb water. Since the weight of the laundry is held by the drum, the water pressure measured by the sensor decreases. At a later time T_2, the new pressure is stored by the microcontroller and the difference to the pressure at T_1 gives an indication of the absorption speed.

- At T_3, the current water pressure is stored again. It gives an indication of the absorption volume, as the laundry is mostly saturated at this time. At T_3, the water valve is opened again to fill up the water level to the set point.

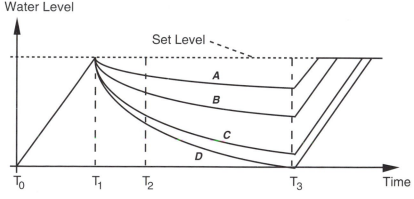

Figure 5.21   Water level in the drum of the washing machine during initial water intake. By interpreting the curves, estimation of laundry type and volume is possible.

As there is no mathematical model of the relation of the water absorption curves to the laundry load, AEG decided to use fuzzy logic to design a solution based on the knowledge of their washing experts. Figure 5.22 shows the structure of the fuzzy logic system that estimates the water requirement in

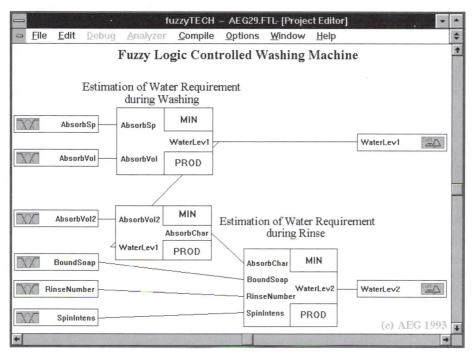

Figure 5.22   The multilevel fuzzy logic system interprets the water intake function and determines the amount of water to be used in the subsequent washing steps. Also, the rest of the washing program is optimized according to the laundry load.

washing and rinse steps. The input variables of the fuzzy logic system stem from the water absorption curve.

The upper fuzzy logic rule block estimates the water requirement during washing (WaterLev1) from absorption speed (AbsorbSp) and absorption volume (AbsorbVol). Both of these input variables are calculated from the water absorption curve. The two lower fuzzy logic rule blocks estimate the water requirement during rinse (WaterLev2). Inputs to the intermediate rule block are the water requirement during washing as determined by the upper rule block and total absorption volume. These are combined to describe the total absorption characteristic (AbsorbChar). This variable is not an output of the fuzzy logic system, only one input for the lower fuzzy logic rule block.

The lower rule block estimates the water requirement during the rinse step (WaterLev2). Other inputs are the ratio of the bonded soap, the number of rinse steps given by the selected washing program, and the selected intensity of the spin step. All membership functions are of standard type (Z, Lambda, S) and the defuzzification employs the Center-of-Maximum (CoM) method.

Fuzzy Logic vs. NeuroFuzzy

The approach of interpreting the water absorption curve to estimate the laundry load was new to AEG, and hence, not much engineering "know-how" on the interpretation of the curves existed among the washing experts. As engineering "know-how" of the application is essential to build a solution with fuzzy logic, AEG's first attempt to find a satisfying set of fuzzy logic rules failed.

On the other hand, AEG had already recorded water absorption curves for various known laundry loads. The optimal water requirement for these laundry loads could easily be determined by the washing experts. Using these experimental results as training examples, AEG's next try was to use Neuro-Fuzzy training [119]. Figure 5.23 shows some of the sample data used for training of the upper fuzzy logic rule block. The left column (Laundry load) lists the materials used for this washing experiment, and the next two columns (Water absorption speed and Water absorption volume) give parameters from the measured water absorption curve. AEG showed the washing experts the first columns with the actual known load and asked them to recommend the optimum water requirement for this load.

The NeuroFuzzy training used the right column as the desired output and the middle two columns as the respective inputs. The training cannot use the left column since the actual load is not known to the washing machine during operation. The aim is that after training, the fuzzy logic system trained by the NeuroFuzzy Module responds with the appropriate water level recommendation determined from the actual values of the input variables [119].

Laundry load	Water absorption speed	Water absorption volume	Water requirement in subsequent washing steps (expert recommendation)
4 kg Wool / 1 kg Cotton	0.67	2.44	3.5
3 kg Wool / 1 kg Cotton	0.61	2.10	3.1
2 kg Wool / 2kg Cotton	0.62	1.99	2.8
	...	...	...

Figure 5.23 The sample data for the NeuroFuzzy training has been gained through extensive washing experiments. In each experiment, different laundry types and volumes were used. For each experiment, the washing expert gave his recommendation for the amount of water to be used in subsequent washing steps.

The NeuroFuzzy learning process created 159 rules in the fuzzy logic system shown in Figure 5.22. The solution was capable of estimating the water requirement with a maximum difference from the optimum value of ±0.35 liters (0.09 gallons). In an average home, this saves about 20% in water consumption. As most of the electricity used by Euopean washing machines is used to heat up water, an energy savings of 20% results as well. The fuzzy logic system that the NeuroFuzzy learning process generated was implemented on a standard 8-bit microcontroller.

5.2.4   Fuzzy Logic Controlled Microwave Clothes Dryer

Microwave clothes dryers provide faster results with less electrical energy. However, the control of such devices is much more complicated compared to conventional clothes dryers. Because the control problem is multiparametral and nonlinear, traditional control techniques do not perform well in this application. Defining a closed-loop mathematical description of the operation of a microwave dryer is an intractable task at best.

For these reasons, Honeywell Corporation employed a fuzzy logic controller [126]. The test device was a traditional dryer configuration using a horizontally rotating drum with paddles and a front access door. The design included three 1.8-kW magnetrons which provide microwave energy, and electric resistive elements, which provide up to 5 kW of thermal energy. The dryer is equipped with an outlet temperature sensor and a humidity sensor. These sensor signals and user inputs form the five input variables of the fuzzy logic system. Figure 5.24 shows the structure of the fuzzy logic controller. The input variables of the fuzzy logic system are:

- *Durability*
  The durability of the clothing is entered by the user and ranges from "delicate" to "sturdy"

- *Load*
  The load of the dryer is measured by an integrated sensor

- *DeltaHumid*
  Time derivative of the humidity in the dryer

- *DeltaTemp*
  Time derivative of the outlet temperature

■ *TimeEnergy*

The user enters his preference between a fast or energy-efficient drying process.

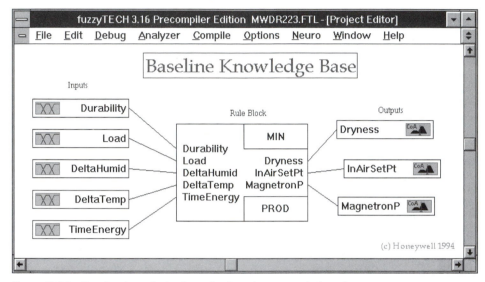

Figure 5.24 Baseline knowledge base for the microwave clothes dryer.

The fuzzy logic controller comprises three functions. First, it determines the actual dryness of the laundry (Dryness). This output variable determines completion of the drying process. The second output variable is the inlet air set point (InAirSetPt). A subsequent (nonfuzzy) controller uses this set point information to keep this air temperature using the resistive heating elements. The third output variable is the magnetron power (MagnetronP), which controls the microwave power. While the first output variable is continuously updated during the drying process, the second and third output variables are only computed once and remain constant at this level throughout the drying process.

The rule base implements the designer's experience in drying control. For example, if the clothing is still wet, the following rule applies:

IF DeltaHumid = slow AND DeltaTemp = slow
THEN Dryness = wet

The output variable, inlet air temperature set point (InAirSetPt), is set at the start of a dry cycle. The input variable's durability of the clothing (Durability) and the time/energy trade-off (TimeEnergy) information are used to calculate this output. If the clothing is more durable, it can withstand a higher inlet temperature set by the rule base which will shorten the drying time. Less durable clothing will have to be dried at a lower inlet temperature set point, lengthening the drying time.

If the user wants to conserve energy, a lower set point for the inlet temperature is set by the rule base. This requires more drying time. If the user wants to conserve time, a higher set point for the inlet air temperature is set by the rule base, requiring more energy. An example rule of how a very hot inlet air temperature set point is arrived at is:

IF Durability = sturdy AND TimeEnergy = mintime
THEN InAirSetPt = very_hot

Another example rule shows how a lukewarm inlet air temperature set point is arrived at by simply having delicate clothing in the dryer:

IF Durability = verydelicate AND TimeEnergy = mintime
THEN InAirSetPt = lukewarm

The third output variable, magnetron power set point, is also set at the start of a dry cycle. The durability and time/energy trade-off information set by the user will be used here as well. As the durability of the clothing increases, so does the allowable maximum magnetron power level.

If the user wants to conserve energy, less magnetron power is set by the rule base. However, this will require more drying time. If the user wants to conserve time, a higher magnetron power level is set by the knowledge base. This, however, requires more energy. An example rule of how a medium magnetron power level is concluded by the rule base is:

IF Durability = verydelicate AND Load = heavy
THEN MagnetronP = medium

In the cited application, more general fuzzy logic rule bases were developed too. To evaluate the performance of the fuzzy logic controller, Honeywell used performance measures for energy efficiency, ability to detect dry clothing, and the effect on clothing in the dryer. Initial tests show that the fuzzy logic approach delivers much more flexible and accurate control although no quantitative analysis was available at the time of this printing. Another observation Honeywell made was that the translation of the designer's expertise into a system solution had been much easier and quicker compared to similar design projects involving conventional design techniques.

5.3   Applications in the Automotive Industry

One of the areas in which fuzzy logic is a common design technology is the automotive industry. In Japan, Germany, and France, cars with fuzzy-logic-controlled components are already quite common. The reasons are many. First, control systems in cars are complex and involve multiple parameters. Second, the optimization of most systems is based on engineering expertise rather than mathematical models. "Good handling," "Fahrvergnügen," and "riding comfort" are optimization goals that cannot be defined mathematically. Third, automotive engineering is very competitive on an international scale. A technology that proves it can provide a competitive advantage is soon commonly used. This section shows case studies of fuzzy logic applications in the automotive industry. The applications are anti-lock braking (Section 5.3.1), engine control (Section 5.3.2), and automatic transmission (Section 5.3.3). The case study of an anti-skid steering system in Section 5.3.4 illustrates an innovative solution in intervehicle dynamics control that fuzzy logic makes possible.

5.3.1   Anti-Lock Braking Systems with Fuzzy Logic

In 1947, Boeing Corporation developed the first anti-lock braking system for airplanes as a mechanical system. Today, electro-mechanical anti-lock braking systems (ABSs) come as standard equipment with most cars. They use electronic sensors that measure the speed of every wheel and microcontrollers to control the fluid pressure for the brake cylinders. Mathematical models for the braking system of a car do exist, but the interaction of the braking system with the car and the road is by far too complex to model adequately. Hence, today's anti-lock braking systems contain the engineering knowledge of years of testing in different roads and climates.

Fuzzy Anti-Lock Braking Systems in Production

Fuzzy logic is a very efficient technology to put engineering knowledge right into a technical solution. Hence, it is no surprise that many applications with anti-lock braking systems are already on the market. Currently, Nissan and Mitsubishi already ship cars with fuzzy ABS. Honda, Mazda, Hyundai, BMW, Mercedes-Benz, Bosch, and Peugeot are working on solutions.

Another reason anti-lock braking systems benefit from fuzzy logic is the high computational efficiency of its implementation. In an ABS, the control loop time is about 5 milliseconds. Within this interval, the microcontrollers must fetch all sensor data, preprocess it, compute the ABS algorithm, drive the bypass valves for the brake fluid, and conduct the test routines. Hence, any additional functions must be very computationally efficient. Most ABS systems use a16-bit microcontroller, which can compute a medium size fuzzy logic system in about 1/2-millisecond using only about 2 KB of ROM space.

Adapting the ABS to the Road Surface

The implementations of fuzzy logic ABSs are very different [88, 6]. The implementation of Nippondenso [99] that I now present as a case study exhibits an intelligent combination of conventional techniques with fuzzy logic. First, let's discuss some basics of the braking process.

If a wheel rotates exactly as fast as the speed of the car, the wheel has no braking effect at all. If a wheel does not rotate at all, it is blocked. This braking situation has two disadvantages. First, a car with blocking wheels is hard or even impossible to steer. Second, the brake effect with blocking wheels is not optimal. The point of optimum brake effect is between these two extremes.

The speed difference between the car and the wheel during braking is called "slack." Its definition is

$$s = (V_{Car} - V_{Wheel})/ V_{Car}$$

where s: slack, always between 0 (no braking) and 1 (blocking)

V_{Car}: velocity of the car

V_{Wheel}: velocity of the wheel

Figure 5.25 plots the relation between brake effect and slack for different road surfaces. For $s = 0$, the speed of the wheel equals the speed of the car. In the case of $s = 1$, the wheel blocks completely. The curves show that the optimum brake effect lies between these two extremes. However, the point of maximum brake effect depends on the type of road. Table 5.1 lists typical values.

Estimation of Road Surface Using Fuzzy Logic

A conventional anti-lock braking system controls the bypass valves of the brake fluid so that the slack equals a set value. Most manufacturers program this set value to a slack of 0.1, as this is a good compromise value for all road conditions. As Figures 5.25 and Table 5.1 show, this set value is not optimal for every road type. By knowing the road type, the braking effect could be enhanced further.

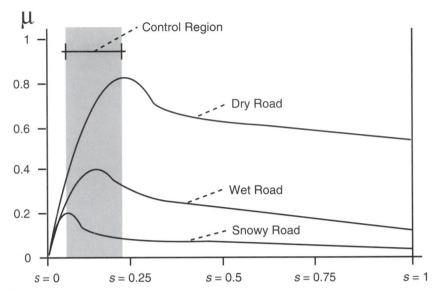

Figure 5.25   Plot of brake effect over the wheel slack for dry, wet, and snowy road surfaces (μ: friction coefficient, measure of brake effect).

Table 5.1   Slack Value for Maximum Brake Effect
Depending on Type of Road

Road Condition	Optimum Slack
Dry	0.2
Slippery or wet asphalt	0.12
Ice or snow	0.05

The problem is how to know what the road type is. Asking the driver to push a button on the dashboard before an emergency brake is not feasible. An alternative is the use of sensors. Many companies have evaluated different types of sensors. The result is that sensors which deliver good road surface identification are not robust enough and too expensive.

The idea behind the cited fuzzy logic application is simple. Consider sitting in your own car equipped with a standard ABS. After driving at a known speed you would jam the brake pedal, so the ABS starts to work. Even if you did not know what the road surface was like, you could now make a good guess just from the reaction of the car. Now, if you can estimate the road surface just from the car's reaction, why not implement this in the ABS using fuzzy logic?

This is just what Nippondenso did. When the ABS first detects blocking of a wheel, it starts to control the brake fluid valves so that each wheel rotates with a slack of 0.1. The fuzzy logic system then evaluates the reaction of the car to the braking and estimates the current road surface. Considering this estimation, the ABS then corrects the set value for the slack so that it achieves the best braking effect.

The fuzzy logic system only uses input data that stems from the existing sensors of the ABS. Such input variables are deceleration and speed of the car, deceleration and speed of the wheels, and hydraulic pressure of the brake fluid. These input variables are an indirect indicator of the current operation point of the braking system (Figure 5.25) and its behavior over time. Experiments showed that a first prototype with just six fuzzy logic rules already improved performance significantly. One of the test tracks alternated from snowy to wet. Here, the fuzzy logic ABS detected the change in road condition even during braking.

Other Applications of Fuzzy Logic in ABS

Due to the fierce competition in this area, most manufacturers are reluctant to publish any details about the technologies they use. The cited application only shows results from an experimental fuzzy logic system. The details about the final product are not published.

Also, some companies worry about the negative connotation of the word "fuzzy." Because it implies "imprecision" and "inexactness," manufacturers are afraid drivers might think of a "fuzzy ABS" as something inferior or unstable. Others are threatened by the scenario that a clever lawyer might be able to win a lawsuit against them by suggesting to a laymen's jury that a fuzzy logic ABS is something hazardous. In Japan, where an appreciation for ambiguity lies in the culture, "fuzzy" does not have any negative connotation. In contrast, it is considered an advantage, as it is known to enable intelligent systems such as the cited application. Hence, companies are proud of its use and even use it in advertising.

In Germany, for example, the situation is different. Here, the concepts of fuzziness and engineering masterpiece do not fit together in the public perception. Hence, most manufacturers who use fuzzy logic in ABS actually hide the fact. After all, a fuzzy logic system is only a segment of assembly code in a microcontroller, once implemented. Who could tell that this code implements fuzzy logic? Some engineers already talk about "hidden fuzzy logic" because of the reluctance of some manufacturers to admits its use.

Stability of a Fuzzy ABS

Some engineers, especially those who went to a well-reputed engineering school, argue the stability of fuzzy logic systems. For a detailed discussion on stability analysis of fuzzy logic systems, refer to Section 6.4. In the case of the fuzzy ABS shown, stability is not an issue. The conventional ABS was considered to be stable for any slack value in the interval from 0.05 to 0.25. Hence, a fuzzy logic road surface estimator that only tunes this value to the optimum cannot make this system unstable. Of course, nobody has proved the stability of the underlying conventional ABS because no comprehensive mathematical model for the interaction of skidding cars with different road surfaces exists.

5.3.2   Engine Control with Fuzzy Logic

The control of car and truck engines becomes increasingly more complex due to raised emission standards and constant striving for higher fuel efficiency. Twenty years ago, control systems were mechanical (carburetor, distributor, and breaker contact). Now, microcontroller-based systems control fuel injection and ignition point. Since the control strategy for an engine depends strongly on the current operating point (revolutions, momentum, temperature, etc.), linear control models, such as PIDs, are not suitable. On the other hand, no mathematical model that describes the complete behavior of an engine exists. Because of this, most engine controllers use a look-up-table to represent the control strategy. The look-up-table is generated from the results of extensive testing and engineering experience.

The generation of such a look-up-table, however, is only suitable for three dimensions (two inputs, one output). Also, the generation and interpretation of these look-up-tables is difficult and considered a "black art" among engineers. Hence, replacing these look-up-tables is a potential application for fuzzy logic. Alas, most manufacturers are unwilling to publish any details on their fuzzy logic engine control solution. This is due to the fact that the rules of the fuzzy logic system make the entire engine control knowledge of the company completely transparent. Hence, manufacturers are afraid that their competitors could learn too much about the solution by disassembling the fuzzy logic rules.

Identification of Driving Condition

The case study of an engine control system by NOK and Nissan [75] illustrates the benefits of using fuzzy logic. Figure 5.26 sketches the components of the engine controller, which contains three fuzzy logic modules. The basic idea of the system is that it first identifies the operational condition of the engine by the linguistic variable "Situation," which has the following linguistic terms:

linguistic variable Situation {

Term 1:   *Start*

Control strategy is that the cold engine runs smooth–ignition is timed early and the mix is fat;

Term 2:   *Idle*

Control ignition timing and fuel injection depending on engine temperature to ensure that the engine runs smooth;

Term 3:   *Normal drive, low or medium load*

Maximize fuel efficiency by meager mix, watch knocking;

Term 4:   *Normal drive, high load*

Fat mix and early ignition to maximize performance—the only constraint is the permitted emission maximum;

Term 5:   *Coasting*

Fuel cut-off, depending on situation;

Term 6:   *Acceleration*

Depending on the load, fattening of the mix

}

The determination of the linguistic variable "Situation" is a state estimation of the operating point. As "Situation" is a linguistic variable, more than one term can be valid at the same time. This allows for expressing combinations of the operational points defined by the terms. Hence, a possible value of "Situation" could be {0.8; 0; 1; 0; 0; 0.3}. Linguistically, this value represents the driving condition *engine started just a short while ago, normal drive condition at medium or low load, slightly accelerating.* From this operation point identification, the individual fuzzy logic modules control injection, fuel cut-off, and ignition.

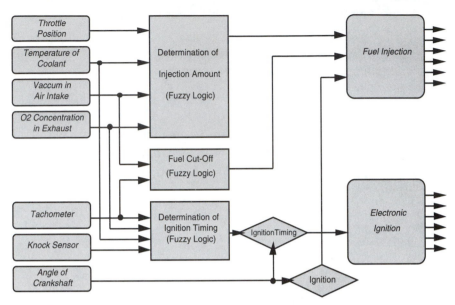

Figure 5.26   Modules of the fuzzy logic engine controller of NOK.

Similar to the ABS systems described in the previous section, engine control requires a very short loop time. Some systems are as fast as one millisecond for an entire control loop. For this, some manufacturers design the system using fuzzy logic, but then translate it into a look-up-table for faster processing. Even though a look-up-table is very fast to compute, the memory requirements may be prohibitive. A look-up-table with two inputs and one output, all 8-bit resolution, already requires 64 Kbytes of ROM. Restricting the resolution of the input variables to 6 bits each, the look-up-table still requires 4 Kbytes. A look-up-table with three inputs and one output, all 6-bit resolution, would require 1/4 Mbyte. Some engineers tried to implement a look-up-table with a very limited resolution and use an interpolation algorithm. Comparison shows, however, that the interpolation requires about as much computing time as the fuzzy logic system itself [113].

Another published application of fuzzy logic in engine control is an idle control unit by Ford Motor Corporation [40].

5.3.3   Adaptive 5-Speed Automatic Transmission

When the first three-speed automatic transmissions appeared on the market about 30 years ago, the engine power of most cars was just sufficient to keep the car in pace with traffic. The necessity of getting maximum momentum from the engine determined the shift points for the gears. Now, when most car engines can deliver much more power than necessary to keep the car in pace with traffic, automatic transmission systems have up to five speeds, and fuel efficiency is an important issue, the control has become much more complex.

The greater engine power and five speeds from which to choose give the automatic transmission system a much higher degree of freedom. Driving at 35 m.p.h. (56 km/h), a three-speed automatic transmission has no choice but to select the second gear. A five-speed automatic transmission with a powerful engine could select the second gear if maximum acceleration is required, the third gear if only a little acceleration is needed, and the fourth gear for cruising.

Acceleration vs. Fuel Efficiency

Unfortunately, the goal for the control strategy is a dilemma. For maximum fuel efficiency, you must select the next higher gear as early as possible. For maximum performance, you shift to the next higher gear later. If you have a manual transmission, you can choose the strategy depending on traffic conditions. An automatic transmission gearbox has no understanding of the traffic conditions and the driver's wishes.

In this section, I will show how intelligent control techniques can enhance automatic transmissions. As this intelligent control technique is based on experience and engineering knowledge rather than on mathematical models, fuzzy logic proves to be an efficient technology for implementation. I will use existing applications as case studies. In 1991, Nissan introduced fuzzy-logic-controlled automatic five-speed transmission systems [65, 158]. Honda followed one year later [141], and General Motors first introduced its solution with its 1993 Saturn. Nissan also holds a patent for a fuzzy logic automatic transmission system [80]. In Europe, Siemens Corporation of Germany has developed a fuzzy logic automatic transmission system using just 29 rules [200].

The task for the fuzzy logic system in these applications is similar:

■ Avoid "nervous" shifting back and forth on winding or hilly roads.

■ Understand whether the driver wants economical or sporty performance.

■ Avoid unnecessary "overdrive," if shifting to the next lower gear does not deliver more acceleration.

Figure 5.27 shows a typical situation on a winding road. While a driver with a manual transmission would remain in fourth gear, a 5-speed automatic transmission shifts between fourth and fifth gears.

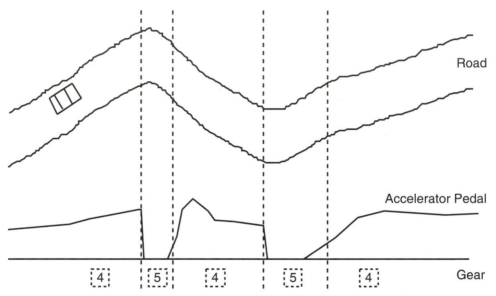

Figure 5.27 A 5-speed automatic transmission with fixed shift points always switches between fourth and fifth gear on a winding road. A driver with a manual transmission would leave it in fourth gear.

The fuzzy logic controller in the automatic transmission evaluates more than just the current speed of the car. It also analyzes how the driver accelerates and brakes. To detect the condition of a winding road, for instance, the fuzzy logic controller looks at the number of accelerator pedal changes within a certain period. Figure 5.28 shows the definition of the linguistic variable "Accelerator pedal changes." Also, the variance of the accelerator pedal changes is an input to the fuzzy logic controller.

Some of the rules that estimate the driving condition from these input variables are:

- Many pedal changes within a certain period indicate a fast and winding road

- Few pedal changes within a certain period indicate a freeway

- Many pedal changes within a certain period and very high variance of the pedal changes indicate a slow and winding road

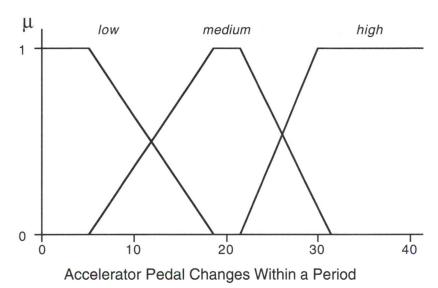

Figure 5.28   Classification of driving condition using a linguistic variable. The variable linguistically interprets the accelerator pedal changes within a certain period.

■ Medium variance of the pedal changes indicates a fast and winding road

■ Low variance of the pedal changes indicates a freeway

An interesting aspect of this application is that it uses the driver as the actual sensor for the driving condition. The fuzzy logic controller detects the driving condition by interpreting the driver's reaction and then adapts the car's performance accordingly. This more than meets the definition of an intelligent control system. The technical system tries to understand whether the human is satisfied with its performance. If not, the technical system adapts itself to suit the needs of the human who uses it.

"Intelligent" Automatic Transmissions

Another example of an automatic transmission system, currently under development in Germany, shows adaptiveness to the user even better. The following situation is typical if the driver is not satisfied with the acceleration of a car. The driver pushes down the accelerator pedal and within two seconds, he pushes the pedal down a little bit more. This is the subconscious reaction to unsatisfactory acceleration. Most drivers do not even consciously realize that they want the car to accelerate faster. If the automatic transmission system is capable of detecting this, it could move the shift points higher to deliver more acceleration. The opposite case is similar. If the automatic transmission detects that the driver accelerates very carefully and then slows down long before red lights, chances are that the driver wants high fuel efficiency.

Why Fuzzy Logic?

The question remains, can you only implement these intelligent functions with fuzzy logic? The answer is you can certainly use other techniques to implement these control strategies, but fuzzy logic may be more efficient:

- Intelligent control strategies stem from experience and experiments rather than from mathematical models. Hence, a linguistic formulation is much faster.

- Intelligent control strategies mostly involve a large number of inputs. Most of the inputs are only relevant for some specific condition. Using fuzzy logic, this input is only considered in the relevant rules. This keeps even complex systems transparent.

- Intelligent control strategies implemented in mass-market products have to be implemented very cost-efficiently. Compared to conventional solutions, fuzzy logic is often much more comp–utationally and code space efficient.

5.3.4   Anti-Skid Steering Systems

Active stability control systems in cars have a long history. The first generation, anti-locking brakes (ABSs), improved braking performance by reducing the amount of brake pressure to that which the road can take. This avoids sliding and results in shorter braking distances. The second generation, traction control systems, do essentially the same thing—improve acceleration. If a car accelerates to the point of skidding, the traction system detects the excess acceleration and adjusts it to return the car to a manageable speed. The result is maximum safe acceleration and reduced tire wear. The next logical step, after skid-controlled braking and skid-controlled acceleration, is skid-controlled steering. Such an anti-skid steering system (ASS) reduces the steering angle to the amount the road can take. By that, it optimizes the steering action and avoids sliding. A sliding car is very hard to restabilize, especially for drivers not used to it.

Though an ASS makes a lot of sense from a technical point of view, such a system will be hard to market. For an ABS, one can prove that its performance is never inferior to a traditional brake system. For an ASS, this is very hard to prove. Also, it may be difficult to sell cars that in emergency situations "take over the steering." Even ABS initially faced a long period of rejection by customers, because drivers felt uneasy about a system inhibiting their braking action. For these reasons, it may take a long time before ASS systems will be implemented in production cars. All findings shown in this section stem from a research project of a German car manufacturer [180]. As this system is one of the most complex embedded systems using fuzzy logic, it shows the potential of the technology well.

The Test Vehicle

Real experiments were conducted with a modified Audi sedan and on a 20" model car (Figure 5.29). In the following, I will only present the results derived from the model car experiments. A one-horsepower electric motor powers the car, giving the model proportionately the same power-to-weight ratio as a race car. This allows skidding and sliding experiments in extreme situations at high speeds. On a dry surface, the car reaches a velocity of 20 m.p.h. in 3.5 seconds with a top speed of 50 m.p.h. The speed for most experiments ranges from 20 to 30 m.p.h. Each wheel features individual suspension and has a separate shock absorber. The car is equipped with disk brakes and a lockable differential [180].

The controller of the car uses the motherboard of a 12-MHz notebook 286-PC connected to an interface board that drives actors and sensors. The actors are the power steering servo, disk brake servo, and pulse-width-modulated motor control. The sensors are three ultrasound distance sensors for track guidance (Figure 5.30) and infrared sensors in every wheel for speed. The control loop time, from reading in sensor signals to set the values for the actors, is 10 milliseconds.

To measure the dynamic state of the car, such as skidding and sliding, the infrared sensors measure the individual speed of all four wheels. Evaluating wheel speed differences, the fuzzy logic system interprets the current situation. Three ultrasound sensors mounted in a fixed direction measure the distance to the next obstacle in front and on the left and right. This enables autonomous operation of the car. Intentionally, low-cost ultrasound sensors have been used in this study instead of CCD cameras and picture recognition techniques to prove that inexpensive sensors work just as well as more expensive ones with a fuzzy logic control strategy.

Figure 5.29   Model car for high-speed driving experiments.

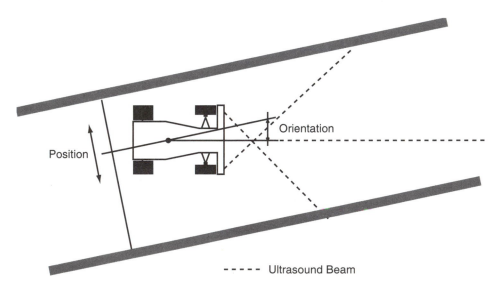

Figure 5.30   Three ultrasound sensors guide the car on the race track.

Figure 5.31 shows the example of an experiment involving the model car. The obstacle (block) is placed right after the curve, so that the ultrasound sensors of the car will "see" the obstacle too late. To avoid hitting the obstacle, the car must choose a very rapid turn. To optimize the steering effect, the anti-skid controller has to reduce the desired steering angle to the maximum the road can take, to avoid both sliding and hitting the obstacle.

Model-Based Solution vs. Fuzzy Logic Control

In theory, you can build a mechanical model for the car and derive a mathematical model with differential equations from it to implement a model-based controller. In reality, the complexity of this approach would be overwhelming and the resulting controller would be very hard to tune. Here is a good reason for using fuzzy logic: race car drivers can perform this control task very well without solving differential equations. Hence, there must be an alternative way to design anti-skid steering control. This alternative way is to represent the driving strategy through engineering heuristics.

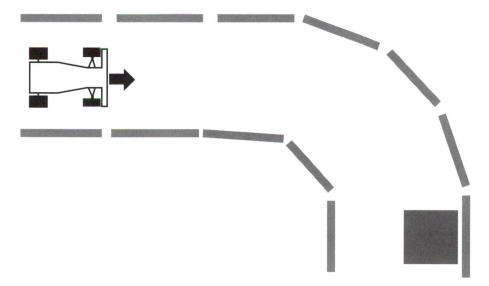

Figure 5.31   Example of an experiment. The ultrasound sensors of the car will detect the obstacle placed right after the curve very late, making a quick turn necessary.

Though there are multiple ways of implementing engineering heuristics, fuzzy logic has proven to be very effective, due to the following reasons:

- ■ You can often formulate engineering heuristics as "if-then" causalities. The "if" part usually represents a certain state of a process, while the "then" part represents the action to be taken in this case.

■ In contrast to other methods of expressing "if-then" causalities, such as expert systems, the computation in a fuzzy logic system is quantitative rather than symbolic. In a fuzzy logic system, you use a few rules to express hypothetical situations, and then the fuzzy logic algorithm makes decisions for the actual situations. A conventional expert system, in contrast, would need a rule for every possible situation.

■ In a fuzzy logic system, every element is self-explanatory. Linguistic variables are very close to the human representation of continuous concepts. Fuzzy inference and fuzzy operators combine these concepts very much the way humans do.

■ Fuzzy logic is nonlinear and multiparametric by nature. Thus, it can better cope with complex control problems that are nonlinear and involve multiple parameters.

■ Fuzzy logic can be efficiently implemented in embedded control applications. Even on a standard microcontroller, a fuzzy logic system can outperform a comparable conventional solution in both code size and computing speed.

Design and Implementation of a Fuzzy Logic Controller

Figure 5.32 shows the first version of a fuzzy logic controller for the car. The objective of this controller was autonomous guidance of the car on the track at slow speed, where no skidding and sliding occurs. In the figure, the lower rule block uses the distances measured by the three ultrasound sensors to determine the steering angle. The upper rule block implements a simple speed control by using the distance to the next obstacle measured by the front ultrasound sensor and the speed of one front wheel only. Due to the slow speeds, no skidding or sliding occurs. Hence, all wheel speeds are the same, and using only one speed sensor suffices. The first version contains about 200 rules and took only a few hours to implement.

The second version of a fuzzy logic controller for the car implements a more complex fuzzy logic system for dynamic stability control. It includes anti-lock braking, traction, and anti-skid steering control (Figure 5.33). This 600-rule fuzzy logic controller has two stages of fuzzy logic inference. The first stage, represented by the three left rule blocks, estimates the state variables of the dynamic situation of the car from sensor data. The two lower rule blocks

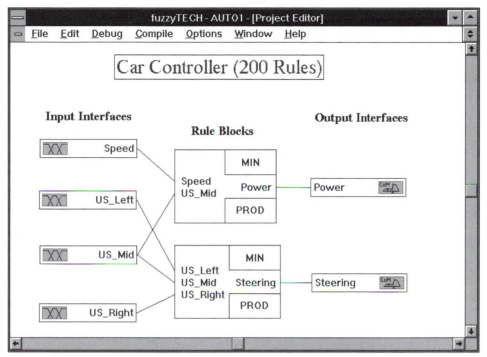

Figure 5.32   First version with 200 rules in two rule blocks. The four left boxes indicate input interfaces for the sensors, the two right boxes indicate output interfaces for the actors, and the two large boxes in the middle represent fuzzy logic rule blocks.

estimate skidding and sliding state from speed sensor signals, while the upper rule block estimates position and orientation state of the car on the test track. Note that the output variables of the left three rule blocks are linguistic rather than numerical. An estimated state of the car, therefore, could be: "the position is a little to the left, while the orientation is strongly to the right, and the car skids over the left front wheel."

The second stage, represented by the three right rule blocks, uses this state variable estimation to determine the best control action for the current situation. The upper rule block determines the steering angle, the middle one the engine power to be applied, and the lower one controls the brake. Such a two-stage control strategy parallels human behavior, which first analyzes the situation and then determines an action. Also, this allows efficient optimization, since the total of 600 rules is structured in six rule blocks. These rule blocks can be designed and optimized independently.

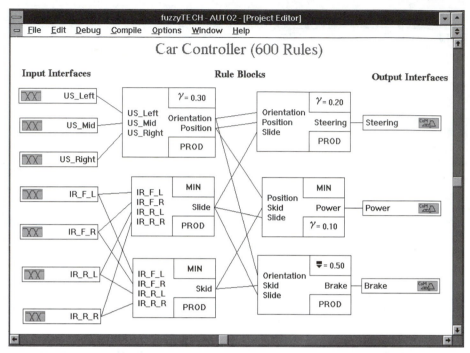

Figure 5.33 Second version of the fuzzy logic controller. The controller uses advanced fuzzy logic design technologies and contains a total of 600 rules.

The first version of the controller with 200 rules was only able to guide the car for autonomous cruise (Figure 5.32). The second version with 600 rules also succeeded in dynamically stabilizing the car's cruise with anti-locking brakes, traction control, and anti-skid steering. However, this second version required a much longer design time before the results were completely satisfactory. It also used advanced fuzzy logic technologies, such as FAM inference [119] and the Gamma aggregational operator [217].

Online Development

The development of the fuzzy logic system used the *fuzzy*TECH Online Edition [116]. After the graphical definition of the system structure (Figures 5.32 and 5.33), the linguistic variables and the rule blocks, the compiler of *fuzzy*TECH generates the system as C code. This code was compiled and implemented on the microprocessor mounted on the car. Figure 5.34 shows how the running fuzzy logic system was modified "on-the-fly" for optimization. The fuzzy logic code is separated into two segments. One contains all "static" code, that is, code that does not need to be changed for system modifications. The other one contains all "dynamic" code, that is, the code containing the membership functions of the linguistic variables, the inference structure, and the rules. The "dynamic" segment is mirrored, with only one of the segments active at a time. With this, the parser, linked to the development PC via a communications manager, can modify the inactive code segment. After each modification, the inactive dynamic code segment becomes the active one, and vice versa. This allows for modifications on the running system without halting or compiling. At the same time, the entire inference flow inside the fuzzy logic controller is graphically visualized on the PC, since the communications manager on the target system also transfers all real-time data.

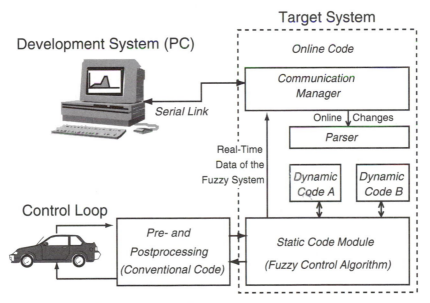

Figure 5.34   The fuzzyTECH Online Edition features both visualization of the running system and modifications "on-the-fly."

The anti-skid steering system case study shows the applicability of fuzzy logic technologies for very complex control problems. The design of the fuzzy logic system was straightforward without a mathematical model of the process. Existing engineering heuristics were implemented in fuzzy logic rules and linguistic variables rapidly delivering a working prototype. During development, the control strategy was easy to optimize because of the linguistic representation in the fuzzy logic system.

5.3.5　Heating, Ventilating, and Air Conditioning in Cars

Sections 5.2.1, 5.2.2, and 5.6.4 of this book show the benefits of fuzzy logic design technologies in heating and air conditioning of residences and offices. Hence, it is no surprise that many car manufacturers also use fuzzy logic for heating, ventilating, and air conditioning (HVAC) control in cars. While most car manufacturers work on such systems, only a very few publish their efforts. Also, the control approach in general, and hence the use of fuzzy logic in the design, differs very much for each manufacturer. In this section, I use an example developed by Ford Motor Company, in the U.S. [31].

The fundamental goal of HVAC in cars is to make vehicle occupants feel comfortable. Human comfort, however, is complex to define, involving physical, biological, and psychological responses to given conditions. Because comfort cannot be mathematically formulated, but only empirically expressed, the goal of comfort is not easy to define. Typical sensors of an HVAC include a car interior temperature sensor, ambient temperature sensor, sun heating load sensor, humidity sensor, and others. Typical actuators are variable-speed blowers, means for varying air temperature, ducting, and doors to control the direction of air flow and the ratio of fresh to recirculated air. This multiple-input, multiple-output control problem does not fall into any convenient category of traditional control theory.

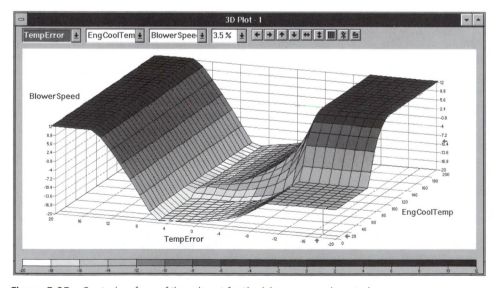

Figure 5.35　Control surface of the rule set for the blower speed control.

Figure 5.35 shows the control surface of a part of an HVAC system, the blower speed control. Blower speed depends on two input variables. One is the temperature error, that is the in-car temperature minus the set point temperature. The other one is the engine coolant temperature. Figure 5.36 shows the rule base. If the temperature error is small, low blower speed is desired. If it's hot inside, (i.e., the temperature error is positive), high blower speed is needed to cool the interior. If the error is negative (i.e., it's cool inside, and the engine is cold), little blower speed is needed for defrost. If the error is negative but the engine is warm, high blower speed is needed to heat up the interior.

Matrix	IF		THEN	
Utilities	EngCoolTemp	TempError	DoS	BlowerSpeed
1		zero	1.00	low
2	high	negative	1.00	high
3		positive	1.00	high
4	low	negative	1.00	med_low
5				

Spreadsheet Rule Editor - Blower Control

Figure 5.36   Rule base of the blower speed control.

5.3.6   Other Applications

This section contains other examples of fuzzy logic control in automotive engineering in brief. For more information, refer to the papers cited in the References.

Autonomous Intelligent Cruise Control [14]

Peugeot Citroën Corporation of France developed a fuzzy logic system for an intelligent cruise control. The system combines functions for autonomous intelligent cruise control: following another vehicle, stop and go procedures, and emergency stop. The system uses three fuzzy logic blocks with four inputs, one output, and 30 rules each. Optimization and verification of the rule base used a Citroën XM sedan with automatic transmission and ABS brakes as the test vehicle. The fuzzy logic controller runs on an 8-bit microcontroller. As sensors, the car uses a speed sensor and a single-beam telemeter for the distance to the next car. The actuators command brake pressure and the accelerator. The tests show that the fuzzy logic controller can handle the cruise control under all the tested conditions. See also [160] and [179]. A system that evaluates the behavior of other drivers by a fuzzy estimation model is described in [103].

Fuzzy Control of a Speed Limiter [169]

Future regulations by the European Community require speed control for the limitation of truck speeds on the European roads. Today's speed limiters use adaptive PIDs type controllers. However, the resulting truck behavior is not satisfactory compared to an experienced driver. For these reasons, a number of recent designs use fuzzy logic control to achieve robust performance, even under the strong load changes can occur with commercial trucks.

Fuzzy Logic Traction Control System [137]

This paper by Ford Electronics describes the design of a fuzzy logic traction control system for a radio-controlled model car. The fact that Ford publishes model car applications is symptomatic of the fear of many automotive manufacturers to admit that they use fuzzy logic as a design technique.

5.4   Industrial Automation and Process Control

In industrial automation, fuzzy logic technologies enable the efficient and transparent implementation of human control expertise. Here, the individual control loops of single process variables mostly remain controlled by conventional models such as PIDs. The fuzzy logic system then gives the set values for these controllers based on the process control expertise put in the fuzzy logic rules. The following case studies show different ways of integrating conventional control techniques and fuzzy logic.

5.4.1   Optimization of a Decanter

This case study is about a fuzzy logic solution in biochemical production [185] at the world's largest oral penicillin production facility in Austria. After extracting the penicillin from the microorganisms that generated it, a waste-water treatment plant further processes the remaining biomass. Fermentation sludge obtained in the course of this process contains microorganisms and remnants of nutrient salts. It is the basic material for a high-quality fertilizer and is sold as a by-product of the penicillin production. To obtain the fertilizer, the sludge is concentrated in a decanter and then cleared of the remaining water in a vaporizer. The vaporizing step uses high-temperature steam and, thus, is very energy consuming. In order to reduce energy costs of the vaporizing process, the separation of water and dry substance in the decanter must be optimized. Before the implementation of the fuzzy logic solution, operators controlled the process manually.

Fuzzy Logic Replaces Manual Control

Due to the complexity of this control process, operators control the proportions of precipitants in the decanter manually. The draining control in the decanter is very crucial. To save energy costs in the vaporizing process, the decanter must extract as much water as possible. However, this operating point is close to the point where the decanter becomes blocked. Because such a blockage requires stopping the process and cleaning the decanter manually, the operators run the process far away from this point. Alas, this results in high operational energy costs. In this case study, a fuzzy logic system replaced the suboptimal manual control by operators.

Fuzzy Logic Applications in the Chemical Industry

A number of conventional control techniques exist to automate continuous processes in the chemical industry. To keep single variables of a process constant, PID controllers or similar control models are most commonly used. Even though most technical processes are nonlinear and PID controllers are based on a linear model, this often works fine. This is because within most continuous processes, the behavior of the process can be well-approximated to linear near the operation point. In processes with no dead time, even simple P (proportional) controllers and bang-bang controllers often suffice.

While keeping single process variables at their command values is relatively easy, the determination of the optimal operating point is often a complex multivariable problem. In most cases, a solution based on a mathematical model of the process is far beyond acceptable complexity. In some cases, the derivation of a mathematical model of the plant consumes many years of effort. Hence, in a large number of plants, operators control the operation point of the process manually.

In these cases, fuzzy logic provides an efficient technology to put the operator control strategies into an automated solution with minimum effort [39, 51, 135, 170, 204]. Figure 5.3 shows how to combine the fuzzy logic system with underlying PID controllers. In practical implementations, the PID controllers run on the same Distributed Control Systems (DCS) as the fuzzy logic controller. Figure 3.22 shows the technical integration of fuzzy logic into a DCS.

Decanter Control

The sewage of the fermenters contains about 2% dry substance. In the first step, milk of lime neutralizes the sewage. Second, a fermenter biologically degrades the sewage. Third, bentonite is added in a large reactor. This results in precoagulation of the sludge. Now, the slurry is enriched with cationic polymer before the water is separated in the decanter. The cationic polymer discharges the surface charge of the sludge particles and hence leads to coagulation (Figure 5.37).

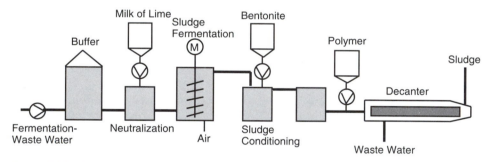

Figure 5.37   Process diagram of sludge draining.

Bentonite and polymer addition exert a fundamental influence on the drainage quality obtained in the decanter. In order to achieve high drainage quality, the gradation of the chemicals has to be optimized. A changed bentonite proportioning causes only a slow change in the precipitation process because of the dead time of the reactor, about 20 minutes (reactor capacity 30 m^3 at a volume flow of 90 m^3/h), and the dead time of the decanter of about five to seven minutes. An increase in bentonite addition principally results in an improvement in coagulation. An implementation of only a polymer-proportioning controller must only consider the dead time of the decanter. At first, an increase in polymer addition results in coagulation improvement, but with further addition it impairs coagulation.

The control strategy of the operators uses two measured variables:

■ A turbidimeter measures the purity of the water. High turbidity indicates a high remaining solids content of the water.

■ A conductimeter measures the draining degree of the slurry. A high conductibility of the slurry indicates a high water content.

Control Strategy Objectives

The prime objective of the control strategy is to minimize the operational cost of the total drying process. In particular, the objectives are:

■ Minimize amount of precipitants. The polymer that is used is very expensive.

■ Minimize remaining water content. The vaporization of remaining water consumes large amounts of energy.

■ The biological mass content of the sewage water of the decanter should be 0.7 g/l. Exceeding a value of 1.5 g/l reduces the operability of the clarification plant and can even result in a breakdown of the next sewage stage because of its limited capacity to degrade biological mass.

The third objective has absolute priority over the other ones to ensure safe operation. If the biological mass content reaches its upper limits, the control strategy will reduce it regardless of economic considerations. Below the critical biological mass content of the sewage water, only the first two objectives are relevant. A rough cost estimation shows that the most effective way to reduce the expenses of the process is to minimize the energy used in the evaporators. If the dry substance content of the thick slurry is increased by 1% (this corresponds to a change of conductibility of about 0.5 mS/cm), the costs of energy (used in the evaporator) could be reduced by $140 per day. A reduction of bentonite addition by 10% saves about $30 per day, and a decrease of polymer addition by 10% reduces costs by $40 per day. A small decrease of chemical gradation can result in a significant reduction of dry substance contents in thick slurry. Therefore, the main objective of optimization is to obtain the best possible result of draining with the least use of chemicals.

Designing the Fuzzy Logic Rule Base

An increase of polymer addition results in an increase of drainage grade. This reduces the degree of turbidity of the sewage water (degree of suspended matter) and conductibility of the thick slurry (water content). Exceeding the optimum polymer gradation, further addition of polymer leads to a decline of the separative power in the decanter. The separative power on polymer gradation $L = f(dm_{polymer}/dt)$ follows a parabolic curve (Figure 5.38). Conductibility of the slurry is used as an indicator for the separative power obtained. Hence, the control strategy is to find the minimum of conductibility by modifying the polymer addition.

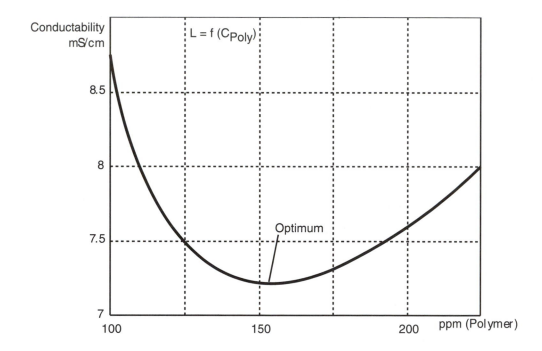

Figure 5.38   Conductibility of the thick slurry over polymer proportion.

The problem with this is that the shape of the curve, and hence the level and position of the minimum, may strongly vary over time. The only way to find out the direction to the minimum from the current operating point is to apply a change in the polymer gradation and evaluate the effects of this. If the draining of thick slurry improves, the conclusion is that this decision was correct and can be repeated. If the decision results in a decline, the fuzzy logic controller pursues the opposite strategy. The stronger the system's reaction to a change in polymer addition, the greater the current operation point's distance to the optimum.

Likewise, an increase in bentonite addition leads to an increase in the separative power of the decanter until an optimum is reached. If more bentonite is added beyond this point, neither improvement nor decline will occur.

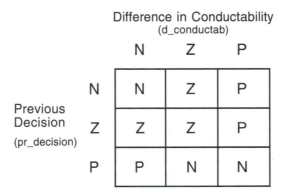

Figure 5.39   Matrix representing the control strategy of polymer proportion. N represents "negative," Z represents "zero," and P represents "positive."

Thus, an increase in bentonite addition beyond the optimal point is less critical than an increase in polymer addition. However, bentonite addition should be kept as low as possible to minimize operating costs.

Structure of the Decanter Controller

A change in bentonite addition has a far greater long-term effect than a change in polymer addition, due to the longer dead time. As a correlation between bentonite and polymer addition exists, it is important to change the polymer addition dependent on the separative quality in the short term and to let the bentonite controller run with delay.

Sewage quality is only restricted by an upper limit, whereas slurry quality is of great economic importance. For these reasons, polymer addition is controlled by a first set of rules in correlation to the slurry quality. An absolute point of reference does not exist because of the changing optimum of the polymer addition characteristics. Hence, no absolute input or output values are used. The controller determines its position in the objective function from a prior change in polymer addition and the resulting reaction of conductibility.

The first rule block of the fuzzy logic controller works on targeting. Input values for this rule block are the increment of the set point in the previous cycle (pr_decision) and the resulting change in conductibility (d_conductab). The output of the rule block is the increment (polymer1) on the set point of the polymer PID controller. Figure 5.39 shows the control strategy of this rule block as a matrix. The entries in the matrix represent the output variable polymer1 of the rule block.

A positive change in conductibility implies a decline in the plant's operating state. If the controller in the previous cycle (pr_decision) recommended "negative" (reduce polymer addition) and conductibility increased as a reaction to this, the controller must now operate in the opposite direction and increase polymer addition. If the controller recommended "positive," polymer addition must be reduced. Conductibility may increase although the controller has not given a recommendation in the previous cycle (pr_decision = 0). In this case, the optimum moved due to external influence and action must be taken.

Since the fuzzy logic controller does not know in which direction the optimum moved, it has to choose one direction. For this it increases polymer addition to test the reaction of the process. It tests with a polymer increase rather than a decrease as the curve in the figure rises more gently in the positive direction and an increased use of polymer is cheaper than the raised energy costs that stem from the evaporation process.

If the test result is favorable, this will be confirmed in the next cycle. If it is negative, the controller will simply change the signs of the output in the subsequent cycle (see matrix in Figure 5.39). This only represents the basic principle of the rule block. The final implementation of the rule block contains additional rules that more finely differentiate the input values. By that, the fuzzy logic controller can differentiate between several cases and thus adapt the size of gradation change to the reaction of the process; that is, to the proximity to the optimum.

The turbidity of the sewage water forms a restriction that in some cases forbids reduction of precipitant addition. Therefore, a second rule block evaluates the turbidity of the sewage water (turbidity) and the output of the first rule block (polymer1) to determine the final polymer addition increment (polymer2). Figure 5.40 shows the structure of the fuzzy logic system. As long as turbidity units are below 2500 TE/F, the second rule block transfers the first block's recommendation to the output. Starting at about 3000 TE/F, all recommendations of the first rule block are transferred, except recommendations to reduce polymer addition. If about 3500 TE/F is exceeded, the second rule block always recommends an increase of flocculent addition. Only the rate of increase of flocculent addition is changed, depending on the recommendation of the first rule block.

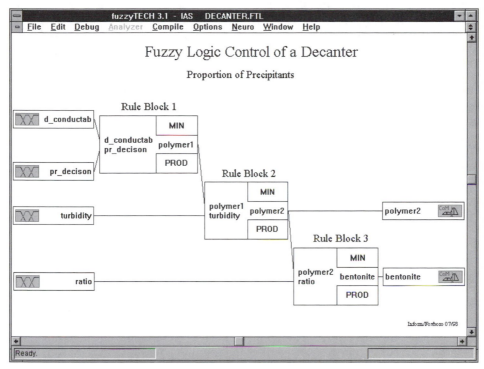

Figure 5.40 Structure of the fuzzy logic controller.

To determine the amount of betonite addition, a third rule block uses the output of the second rule block and a fourth input variable, called ratio. The ratio is calculated outside the fuzzy logic system.

Integrating the Fuzzy Logic Controller in the System

Figure 5.41 shows the total structure of the entire control system. In addition to the fuzzy logic system, function blocks (CALC, RATIO) provide preprocessing of the sensor signals, ramp generation, and ratio control. The entire control system is implemented using a standard distributed process control system (DCS).

The most important input variable of the controller is the change in the conductibility of the slurry. Unfortunately, the conductimetry signal is subject to strong noise. Hence, a low-pass filter is used that determines each minute the average change in conductibility during the last ten minutes. This forms the input variable d_conductab of the fuzzy logic system. Turbidity, the fuzzy system's second input, uses a similar filter.

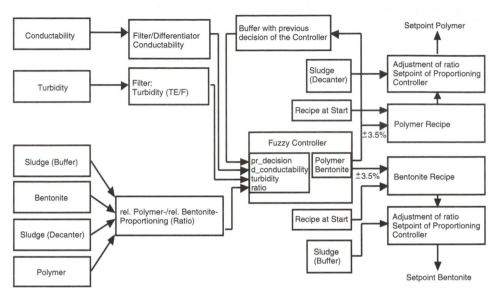

Figure 5.41   Total controller structure with preprocessing and postprocessing.

Results

About two months of engineering effort was required to develop the application. Compared to manual operation, the fuzzy logic controller saves about $70,000 in energy costs per year.

5.4.2   Optimization of a Refuse Incineration Plant

Refuse incineration is a complex process, the multivariable control problems of which cannot be solved conventionally by deriving an exact mathematical model of the process. For a refuse incineration plant in Hamburg-Stapelfeld, Germany, an adaptive fuzzy logic controller provides online process optimization [187]. The plant uses the generated heat to produce electric energy. The objective for the plant controller is to achieve stable energy production and minimize the exhaust of toxic gases.

Refuse Incineration

Because of the heterogeneous composition of home refuse, most incineration plants are manually controlled by operators observing the combustion chamber. Figure 5.42 shows the layout of the refuse incineration plant in Hamburg.

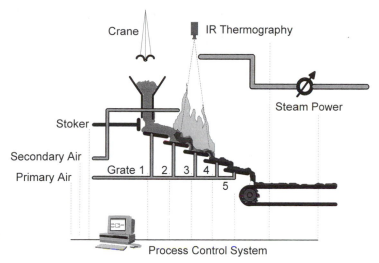

Figure 5.42   Layout of the refuse incineration plant in Hamburg-Stapelfeld.

A bunker stores all incoming refuse; from there, a grapple crane transports it into the feed hopper of the incineration plant. The refuse lands on the first grate via the downshaft and feeder. The grate consists of two parallel tracks with five undergrate air zones each. The optimum position of the fire is in the middle of the third grate, since at this point the refuse is well predried and there is still enough time to ensure complete burnout.

Operator Control Strategy

Although the crane operator attempts to homogenize the refuse by mixing, it is impossible to maintain uniform feed quality. As this disturbs the heat generation and thus the energy production, the operators have to constantly intervene. The operator observes the furnace and adjusts refuse feed and grate operating mode.

While the quantities of refuse to be incinerated steadily increase, the environmental laws for refuse incineration constantly become more restrictive. This is mostly due to recent insights on the toxicity of chlorinated organic pollutant emissions. To minimize toxic emissions, the controller must:

- Control the O_2 concentration in the flue gas to keep it constant

- Maintain a uniform thermal output

- Maintain optimal flow conditions in the furnace and first boiler pass with as little variation as possible

The most important control variable is steaming capacity. This is mainly affected by primary air admitted to the various undergrate air compartments. Disturbances here occur as a result of the inhomogeneous refuse composition at localized points. The primary air distribution must therefore match the requirements of the individual grate zones. Since O_2 content in the flue gas must be kept constant, secondary and primary air are controlled to counterbalance each other.

Between the feeder and the combustion zone, there is always a quantity of uncombusted refuse. The amount of this varies with the feed quality. As a result of this "storage" effect, there is no simple and immediate connection between feeder movement and the position of the fire on the grate. The position can only be identified visually by the plant operators or video picture evaluation.

The automated control solution of this plant with fuzzy logic uses infrared thermography to monitor the combustion. Figure 5.43 shows the observation area of the infrared camera. Because of the furnace geometry, the area that must be observed lies mainly in grate zone 3, but also to some extent in zones 2 and 4, which are not completely observed. Conventional video processing and filtering techniques determine the position and width of the combustion zone. This data preprocessing step also identifies existing secondary combustion zones.

Fuzzy Logic Controller Structure

In addition to the signals from the infrared thermography, the fuzzy logic controller uses other input signals, such as temperatures at various positions of the furnace and gas sensors in the exhaust. Also, observations by the operators are inputs to the fuzzy logic controller. Figure 5.44 shows the overall structure of the control system. In addition to the control variables for the furnace, the fuzzy logic controller also outputs diagnosis data used for malfunction analysis.

Figure 5.45 shows the internal structure of the controller, consisting of three stages. Each stage implements a short-term and a long-term strategy. The first stage controls power generation. Here, a short-term control cycle controls steaming capacity and a long-term control cycle regulates the O_2 concentration in the flue gas.

The second stage controls the fire position by throughput of refuse and grate movement. Grate movement is responsible for short-term control of the

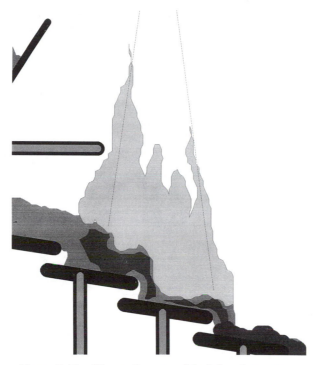

Figure 5.43   Observation area of the infrared camera.

position of the fire on the grate, and feeder speed is utilized for the long-term adjustment of the amount of refuse fed to the grate. Input to this control is the fire position measured by the infrared thermography.

The third stage, which serves to optimize combustion, uses additional information from the infrared thermography. The optimization consists of two steps:

■ Control of the primary air for the various undergrate air zones

■ Control of the length of the fire by governing the feed velocity in the individual grate zones

The use of fuzzy logic permits integration of different sources of information in this step. Besides directly measurable parameters, such as steaming capacity, various identifying parameters for the position of the fire and its length are used. Each stage of the controller uses fuzzy logic modules. For the first stage, Figure 5.46 shows the fuzzy logic module structure.

The implementation of the fuzzy logic modules was done in four steps, sketched in Figure 5.47. In the first step, process data from manual operation

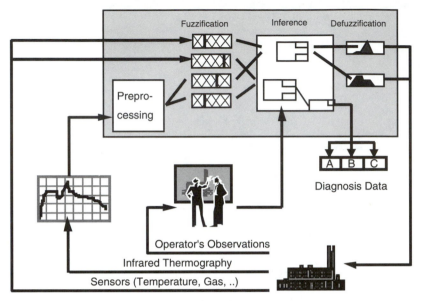

Figure 5.44   The fuzzy logic controller system of the waste incineration plant uses multiple information sources.

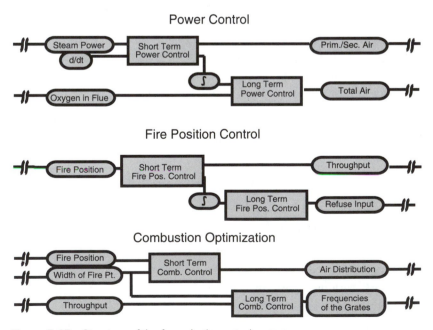

Figure 5.45   Structure of the fuzzy logic control system.

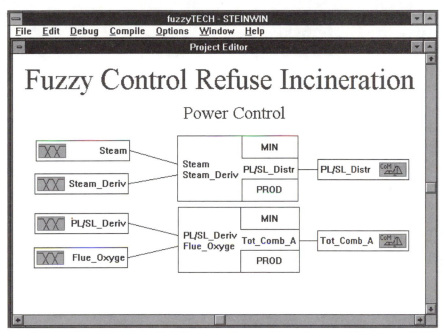

Figure 5.46   First stage "Power Control" of the controller.

was traced, for both initial analysis and for the subsequent NeuroFuzzy training. The next step involves prototypical design of the fuzzy logic modules. The first prototype of a controller uses a total of 18 linguistic variables and 70 fuzzy logic rules in nine rule blocks. The membership functions of the linguistic variables and the rules stem from discussions with the operators and observing their operation.

In the third step, the NeuroFuzzy Module [119] uses the traced process data to adapt the control strategy to the cases recorded. In the training data used, the operators gave their recommendations for the best actions to be taken in the recorded cases. The result is a fuzzy logic system that covers most of the operational situations. However, with a process as complex as this one, the sample data sets cannot be complete and unambiguous. Hence, manual fine-tuning is necessary. For this, online optimization is used in a fourth step [117]. In the case of the incineration process, however, little fine tuning was necessary. The online optimization step was mainly used for systems verification.

Note that in this application, NeuroFuzzy learning did not start from scratch but rather started from an already-working prototype. This is due to the complexity of the incineration process. If the NeuroFuzzy Module must

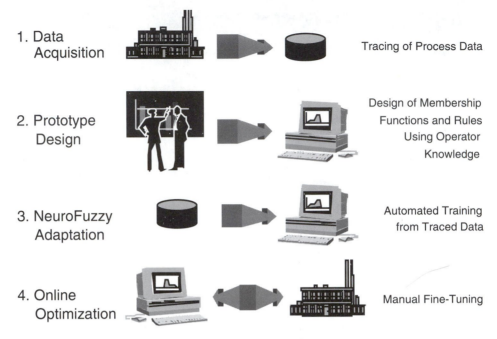

1. Data Acquisition — Tracing of Process Data

2. Prototype Design — Design of Membership Functions and Rules Using Operator Knowledge

3. NeuroFuzzy Adaptation — Automated Training from Traced Data

4. Online Optimization — Manual Fine-Tuning

Figure 5.47   Development of the fuzzy logic modules in four steps.

extract complete knowledge of how to operate the plant just from process data, much more high-quality sample data is necessary. The effort to generate this data would be prohibitive.

The entire fuzzy logic system is implemented on programmable logic controller hardware [117]. See Section 3.2.3 for details on fuzzy logic implementations on PLCs.

Other Applications in Waste Incineration

A waste incineration plant in Osaka, Japan, uses an approach similar to that described above [44]. Mitsubishi Corporation of Japan also uses fuzzy logic technologies for its waste incineration systems, but with a different approach [124, 127].

5.4.3   Fuzzy Logic in Ethylene Production

Many ethylene production plants in Japan and Europe already use fuzzy logic control techniques. This section presents three case studies that cover different components of the ethylene production process. First, a brief introduction to the ethylene production process follows (see Figure 5.48).

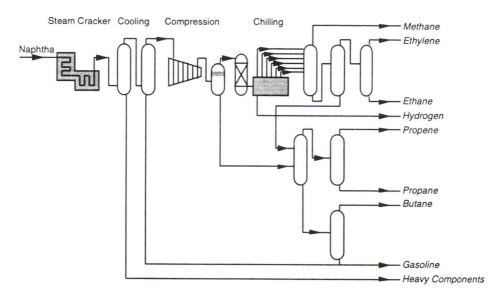

Figure 5.48 The industrial production of ethylene comprises the steps of cracking, cooling, compression, liquefying, and distillation.

The basic material for ethylene production is naphtha. First, a steam cracker cracks the naphtha into smaller molecules. The resulting gas mix leaves the steam cracker at a temperature of 800°C to 900°C and a pressure of 0.5 to 1 kg/cm^2. A first cooler cools the gas mix to about 400°C, resulting in a condensation of oil and heavier components. A second cooler cools the gas mix to environment temperature, resulting in a condensation of gasoline . The cooling process generates steam that other parts of the chemical plant use. A compressor compresses the gas mix to 30 to 35 kg/cm^2 and, after separation of the acid components (H_2S, CO_2), a cooler liquefies the gas mix. Subsequent distillation steps separate the gas mix into ethylene and its other components.

Load Distribution Control of Steam Crackers

Most ethylene plants use multiple parallel steam crackers to crack the naphtha. Figure 5.49 shows the layout of such a steam cracker. The raw naphtha is preheated to 100°C to 130°C and fed at a pressure of 2.5 to 6 kg/cm^2 into the cracker. The upper part of the cracker further heats up the naphtha to 450°C to 650°C. Then, the naphtha is mixed with steam and heated to up to 850°C in the lower part of the steam cracker. This process breaks the naphtha into lighter components.

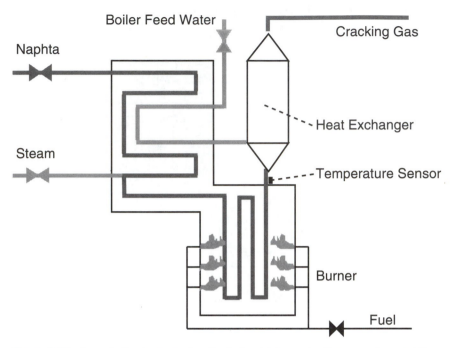

Figure 5.49   Layout of a steam cracker. Control variables are heating as well as naphtha and steam flow.

The difficulty of operating this process lies in the condensation of carbonaceous substances on the inside wall of the reaction tubes in the furnace. To clean the reaction tubes, the cracker must be shut down periodically for decoking. To ensure continuous operation, most ethylene production plants use at least 10 parallel crackers. The operators must divide the load of the shut-down cracker to the other crackers. The optimum load balance depends on the deterioration state of each cracker. A cracker with medium coke deposition is overloaded by applying the same feed rate an uncoked cracker can process. Cracker overload results in both expedited coking and dispersion of the cracking process. For these reasons, Mitsubishi Kasei Corporation of Japan uses a fuzzy logic load-balancing system in its plant in Mizushima [176].

The input variables of the fuzzy logic load balancing system are:

■ Temperature of the gas mix leaving the steam cracker

■ Current naphtha feed rate

■ Current steam feed rate

■ Temperature of the gas mix after the heat exchanger

■ Exhaust gas temperature of the steam cracker

■ Temperature at the outside of the reaction tube in the burning zone

■ Operation time of the steam cracker since its last decoking

The output variable of the fuzzy logic load-balancing system is the load distribution for all crackers. Since the fuzzy logic system only has to compute this load distribution every time a cracker is shut down or switched on, it runs off-line on a PC. The operators enter the input data manually in the PC, start the fuzzy logic inference, and implement the determined load distribution

The fuzzy logic load-balancing system operates the plant more stably. Therefore, the average production capacity can be set closer to the maximum plant capacity. Table 5.2 compares the results for the products ethylene and propane. In addition, the smoother operation reduces the coking process in the crackers, resulting in a slight decrease of required cracker-cleaning steps in a given interval.

Table 5.2   Capacity Usage of Fuzzy Logic
Versus Manual Operation

Product	Manual Control	Fuzzy Control
Ethylene	97.0 ± 2.8	99.1 ± 0.7
Propene	97.7 ± 2.2	99.2 ± 0.7

Temperature Control in the Bottom of a Distillation Column

To separate cracking gas into its components, distillation columns are used in ethylene production (Figure 5.48). Due to the temperature gradient in the column, the heavier components can be withdrawn at the bottom and the lighter components at the top. In its ethylene production plant in Chiba, Idemitsu Petrochemical of Japan uses a fuzzy logic temperature controller [51].

Figure 5.50 shows a distillation column that separates the light components (hydrogen, methane) from the heavy components (ethylene, ethane, propene, propane, butane). As the boiling point of these substances is well above the environment temperature, distillation is carried out at relatively low temperatures and very high pressure. To monitor the process, gas chromatographs measure the outgoing gas mixes. The gas chromatograph at the bottom detects methane. The one at the top measures the concentration of methane and ethylene. A heat exchanger delivers heat to the bottom of the distillation column using steam from other steps of the process.

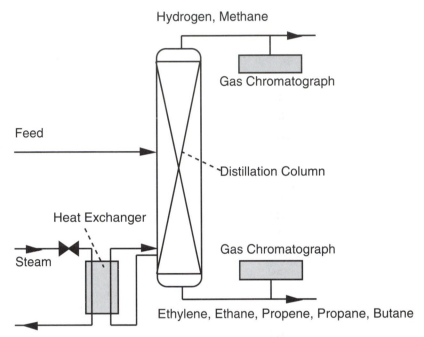

Figure 5.50   Layout of a distillation column in an ethylene production plant. The raw material fed into the column is separated into heavy and light components by the temperature gradient in the column.

Keeping the temperature gradient in the column constant is essential for ensuring a high quality of distillation. However, temperature control in the distillation column is difficult because strong disturbances are present. The temperature and feed rate of the incoming cracking gas fluctuate because of variations in the steam cracking process step. Another general property of distillation columns is the existence of long dead times that are hard to quantify and depend on the composition of the cracking gas. Idemitsu Petrochemical's previous attempts using conventional automation techniques did not deliver satisfying results, leaving the plant under manual control.

In a new automation attempt, Idemitsu Petrochemical finally succeeded by using a combination of fuzzy logic and conventional control techniques. The resulting controller uses the following input variables to determine the steam flow in the heat exchanger:

- Heat flow of the incoming cracking gas (Feed)
- Pressure in the distillation column
- CH_4 concentration in the lower fraction
- Bottom temperature in the distillation column

The combination of a fuzzy logic controller and a conventional controller has operated the plant continuously since 1989 and does not require manual intervention. After an extended online optimization phase during operation, the final solution delivered more robust operation compared to the manual control. Even strong variations in the feed rate of the cracking gas caused by shutdowns of crackers are well under control.

Quality Control in Polyethylene Production

Most of the ethylene produced is converted to polyethylene by a polymerization reaction. One product made of polyethylene is foil, some as thin as a few micrometers. Such products are made from HDPE polyethylene, which must have a very constant quality.

In the polymerization, the ingredients ethylene and a solvent react using a catalyst. The quality of the final product depends on many factors. Some of these are the purity of the ingredients, the reaction pressure and temperature, and the concentration of the substances. The measurement of these factors during the reaction is incomplete. Only analyzing the resulting polyethylene reveals the quality of the final product. However, this analysis information is only available a few hours later. In the worst case, an unusable product is made.

To control the quality of the polyethylene produced during the reaction, Hoechst Corporation of Germany uses a fuzzy logic supervising controller in its Münchsmünster plant. This controller estimates the quality of the current polyethylene production on the basis of the existing sensor signals. Every ten seconds, the fuzzy logic controller adjusts the set values of the process accordingly. Figure 5.3 shows the total structure of the control system.

In a similar application, Polysar Rubber Corporation of Canada uses a fuzzy logic process controller to ensure stable polyethylene quality [135]. The fuzzy logic system controls the catalyst feed using three input variables that stem from online process sensors. The fuzzy logic system uses 75 rules and has reduced the standard deviation by more than 40% since its first operation in 1990.

5.4.4   Control of a Coke Oven Gas Cooling Plant

Since 1989, Dai-Dan Corporation of Japan has used fuzzy logic in the control of a coke oven gas cooling plant [171]. The plant itself was set up more than 20 years ago. Since then, Dai-Dan started many efforts to automate the control of the plant using conventional automation techniques. Because all these efforts failed, operators control the plant manually.

Figure 5.51 shows the layout of the plant. The coke oven gas flows through four cooling towers sequentially. The water circulations of the towers are linked in parallel. Sensors measure the temperature of all incoming and outgoing gas and water flows continuously. Control variables of the plant are the valve settings of the cooling water flow for each tower. The cooling towers have quadratic surface of 3m by 3m and are 10m high. The capacity of the plant is 16,000 Mn^3.

Figure 5.52 shows the layout of a single cooling tower. While the coke gas cools down, impurities condense at the circular cooling water tubes. These impurities degrade the cooling power of the tower. A cleaning system periodically removes the impurities by spraying a chemical solvent over the cooling tubes. During cleaning, the respective tower must be bypassed for the gas flow. The resulting reduction to three towers changes the control characteristics substantially. If another tower is bypassed for maintenance work, the plant must be operated with only two towers for a short time.

Control Objectives

The primary objective for the control operation is to keep the temperature of the gas exiting the plant at 35°C. Manual control by the operators can only meet this objective within a range of about ±5°C. This is due to the complex interdependencies of the plants' parameters. All temperatures must be considered when balancing the loads of the water flows through the valves. Also, the cleaning procedure disturbs the process significantly. In detail, the problems are:

1.   The time constants of the plant are relatively high (the lag time between entrance and exit of the gas is about five minutes).

2.   The mass flow of the incoming coke gas varies greatly due to the inhomogeneities in the burning of the coal in the previous process step.

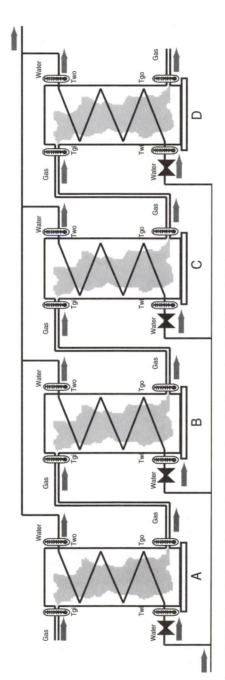

Figure 5.51   The plant uses four cooling towers in serial. The water circulations of the towers are linked in parallel.

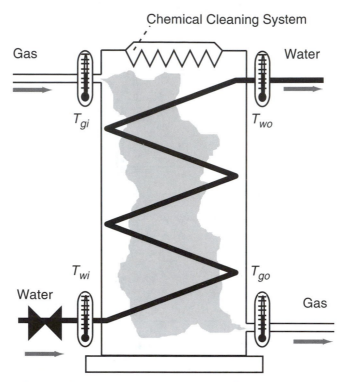

Figure 5.52   Layout of one cooling tower. The incoming gas flows in from the upper end and leaves the tower at the lower end. The cooling water flows in circular tubes in the opposite direction.

3   The cooling performance of the towers degrades continuously due to the condensation of impurities on the cooling tubes.

4   The bypassing of cooling towers during maintenance or chemical cleaning changes the control characteristics of the plant significantly.

5   Cooling performance also depends on the external temperature as the cooling towers are uninsulated.

Problem areas 2, 3, and 4 are especially difficult to tackle using conventional control techniques.

While the manual control by the operators was satisfactory in the past, new laws require much better accuracy of the gas temperature for future operation. This makes an automated control solution mandatory. Dai-Den employed fuzzy logic for the automated solution due to the following reasons:

■ Conventional automation techniques failed mainly because of the large number of parameters that have to be considered at the same time which have nonlinear relations to each other.

■ Knowledge of the correlation between the parameters and experience in plant operation exists from the years of manual control. The reason manual control does not perform better lies more in the fact that applying all these control rules simultaneously overwhelms the operators.

■ Although the dead times of the process are known, the human observation capabilities of slow trends in the process parameters are limited.

Fuzzy Logic Control

The fuzzy logic controller Dai-Dan implemented uses five input variables:

E1:   Temperature error of the gas leaving the cooling plant

E2:   First time derivative of E1

E3:   Second time derivative of E2

E4:   First time derivative of the temperature of the incoming gas

E5:   Second time derivative of the temperature of the incoming gas

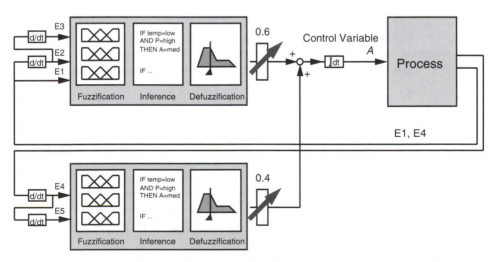

Figure 5.53   Structure of the fuzzy logic controller of the coke oven gas cooling plant. The outputs of two fuzzy logic control modules are combined to give the change of the cooling water flow.

The output of the fuzzy logic system is the total change of the cooling water flow, ΔA. Figure 5.53 shows the total structure of the control system. It is structured as two fuzzy logic control modules whose outputs are combined to result in ΔA. An integrator computes the control variable A of the process. The upper fuzzy logic control module contains 31 rules, the lower one, 7. All linguistic variables use Standard MBFs. E1 and E2 have five terms each, E3, E4, and E5 have three terms each. The output variables have five terms each and use standard membership functions of Lambda type.

The control variable A only controls the total flow of cooling water in the system. A simple heuristic controls the distribution of this water flow to the individual towers. Due to the simplicity of this heuristic, it was not implemented as a fuzzy logic system but rather as a simple mathematical formula. First, two characteristic parameters are computed for each cooling tower as a measure of how efficient each tower currently operates:

$$\eta_g = (T_{gi} - T_{go})/(T_{gi} - T_{wi})$$
$$\eta_w = (T_{wo} - T_{wi})/(T_{gi} - T_{wi})$$

where T_{gi}: Temperature of incoming gas

T_{go}: Temperature of outgoing gas

T_{wi}: Temperature of incoming water (same for all towers)

T_{wo}: Temperature of outgoing water

The heuristic for the distribution of the total cooling water flow to the individual towers is based on the fact that the efficiency of tower W, η_w, should be equal for all towers to achieve the best overall efficiency. Hence, the heuristic decreases the water flow of the tower with the highest efficiency until all towers have the same efficiency.

Results of the Field Test

After the first prototype implementation, Dai-Den conducted a field test in early 1989. During the test period the external temperature ranged from 6°C to 31°C and included operation with just two towers. Operation was tested with two set temperatures (37°C and 35°C). In spite of these strong disturbances, the fuzzy logic controller kept the outflowing gas temperature within a tolerance of just ±1°C. Compared to manual control, this was a significant improvement.

Preventive Maintenance Using Fuzzy Logic

Inspired by the good performance of the fuzzy logic controller for gas temperature, Dai-Den started to further use fuzzy logic data analysis for preventive maintenance. The system monitors the operation of each tower continuously and determines the optimal point in time for the chemical cleaning of each tower.

The plant operators determine the necessity of cleaning a cooling tower by a subjective estimation of the efficiency of each tower. To mimic this estimation with a fuzzy logic system, the first two characteristic parameters are derived from the sensor data. These parameter α_i and β_i are measures of the relative efficiency of the tower:

$$\alpha_i = (\text{water flow in tower } i) / (\text{average of water flow in all towers})$$
$$\beta_i = \eta_{gi} / \max \{ \eta_{gi} \mid \forall \, i = 1\text{--}4 \}$$

These two parameters, together with the total water flow, are the input variables of the fuzzy logic data analyzer. Figure 5.54 shows the structure of the system; Figure 5.55 shows part of the fuzzy logic rule base. The input variables "Beta" (β) and "WaterFlow" (A) as well as the output variable "MaintenRequest" have five terms each. The input variable "Alpha" (α) only has three terms. All membership functions are of standard types.

The fuzzy logic data analyzer continuously monitors operation parallel to the fuzzy logic control of the gas temperature. The output variable of the fuzzy logic data analyzer, however, is not fed back into the process as a control variable. It is instead displayed as a trend curve to the operators. They use this information to schedule the cleaning and maintenance procedures for the plant. Figure 5.56 shows the example of such a trend plot.

5.4.5   Waste Water Refinement Plant Control

In most industrialized countries, the recycling of waste water is gaining more importance. The actual recycling process is a combination of mechanical, chemical, and biological processes in multiple steps. Such a process is of a multivariable nature, and the interdependencies of the control variables are highly nonlinear. In addition to this, the laws governing waste water recycling have become increasingly strict over the past few years. Also, the combination of wastes constantly gets more complex.

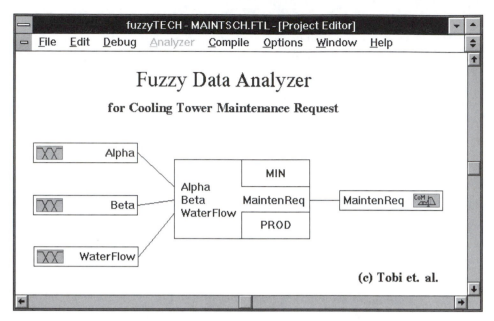

Figure 5.54   Structure of the fuzzy logic data analysis module that determines the necessity of a tower-cleaning step. This system is identical for each tower and uses three input variables.

While operation of such a plant requires well educated and experienced personnel, the reality is different. In plants operated by the government, often one operator with limited education must control multiple plants alone. This is due to the comparatively low salaries and the social prestige of such jobs. Hence, the automation of waste water treatment processes becomes a prerequisite.

Fuzzy Logic Control

As with the applications previously cited in this section, the design of an adequate mathematical model of the plant is a laborious effort. On the other hand, experienced operators do know how to operate a waste water treatment plant without a mathematical model. As this is exactly the type of application where fuzzy logic often excels, it is no surprise that many such applications exist. For example, a plant in Florida uses fuzzy logic for direct sludge flow control [213]. A waste water treatment plant in Vienna, Austria, has been using a fuzzy logic data analysis system since April 1992 to detect abnormal biological conditions [181] (see also [204]).

Matrix	IF			THEN	
#	Alpha	Beta	WaterFlow	DoS	MaintenRequest
1	low		high	1.00	very_high
2		medium		1.00	medium
3	medium		high	1.00	high
4		low	high	1.00	very_high
5	low		medium	1.00	high
6	low		low	1.00	medium
7	high		high	1.00	low
8	medium		medium	1.00	medium
9		very_low	high	1.00	very_high
10	high		medium	1.00	very_high
11		very_low	medium	1.00	very_high
12		low	medium	1.00	high
13		very_high	low	1.00	very_low
14					

fuzzyTECH - MAINTSCH.FTL - [Spreadsheet Rule Editor]
File   Edit   Debug   Analyzer   Compile   Options   Window   Help

Figure 5.55   Rule base of the fuzzy logic data analyzer shown in Figure 5.54 (13 of the total 24 rules shown).

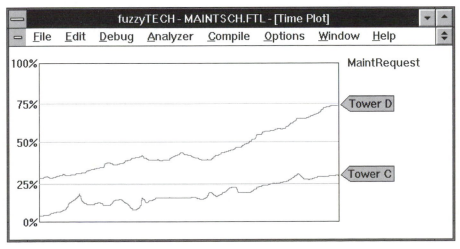

Figure 5.56   Trend plot of the output variable of the fuzzy logic data analyzer (tower A and B not in operation).

Oxygen Control of an Aerobic Processing Step

Hoechst AG of Germany uses fuzzy logic control for an aerobic processing step in a waste water recycling plant for chemical waste water. This process was previously controlled by operators manually and is now successfully automated by fuzzy logic control. The basin is 70 m long and can contain up to 6 million liters. Figure 5.57 displays the layout. A pump delivers the waste water in the basin where it is mixed with pressurized air in propulsion jets. This provides the oxygen to the microorganisms needed for the biological degradation of the waste substances. The size of the air bubbles depends on the controlled air pressure and the controlled waste water flow. A sensor continuously measures the concentration of oxygen in the basin.

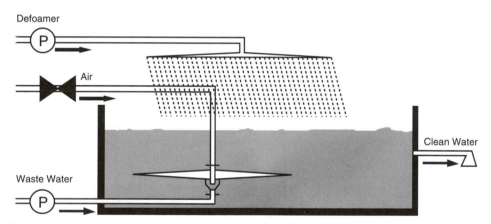

Figure 5.57   Layout of the aerobic processing step in an industrial waste water treatment plant. Sensors measure waste water flow, defoamer flow, air pressure and flow, water level, foam level, and oxygen concentration.

The oxygen concentration must be kept above a threshold to sustain the life of the microorganisms and hence keep the cleaning process active. On the other hand, excessive air inflow both results in energy cost for the compression and causes the generation of foam. To remove the foam, a mixture of tensides and silicon oil is sprayed on the foam. The typical annual use of defoamer is in the range of 50 to 70 tons. Each ton of the defoamer costs about $2,500. In addition, some defoamer remains in the water and thus pollutes the environment.

The control variables of the process are waste water flow, air pressure, and defoamer flow. The operators control the air pressure according to the oxygen pressure and the defoamer flow with respect to the foam level. This task is difficult to automate using conventional control techniques due to the following:

- A PID controller would be very difficult to tune as the characteristics of the process vary greatly depending on the combination of waste chemicals in the waste water.

- The dead time of the process can be longer than half an hour.

- The control loops are interdependent.

The first fuzzy logic control solution Hoechst built realized acceptable performance with just 15 fuzzy logic rules. All membership functions are of standard types and the linguistic variables have between two to five terms. Some examples of fuzzy logic rules are:

1	IF	OxygenConcentration = low
	AND	FoamLevel = normal
	THEN	AirPressure = increase
2	IF	FoamLevel = very_high
	THEN	WasteWaterPumpFlow = decrease

The output of the fuzzy logic controller is the increment or decrement of subsequent PI controllers. Figure 5.3 shows the structure of such a combination of a fuzzy logic controller with conventional control elements. In a field test, the new solution decreased the use of defoamer by about 50%. Another application in sewage water treatment is shown in [61].

5.4.6   Fuzzy Logic in Food Processing

Food processing reveals a high potential for fuzzy logic automation. This is due to the fact that most processes are nonlinear and involve multiple parameters. In addition, the fluctuation in the quality of the raw material makes robust control necessary. In this section I will present a case study of a fuzzy-logic-controlled baking oven for candy bar biscuits. For this control problem, no conventional solution exists. Standard PID-type control cannot be applied due to the nonlinearities and the multiple parameters involved. Model-based control cannot be applied due to the lack of an appropriate mathematical model of the baking process. However, skilled operating personnel are able to control the baking process reasonably well using heuristic knowledge. Hence, fuzzy logic technologies are used to convert this heuristic expertise into a control solution.

The Biscuit Baking Process

Figure 5.58 shows the layout of the existing oven line for the continuous baking of biscuits. The primary quality characteristics are color, moisture, and dimensions of the biscuit. The settings of the oven influence these quality characteristics. Adjustments can be made to the level and distribution of the temperature along the length of the baking oven and to the setting of baking flaps. The flaps control the channeling of hot air to specific oven areas.

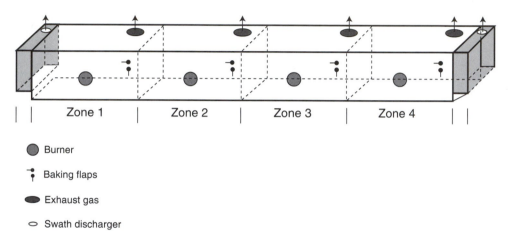

Zone 1   Zone 2   Zone 3   Zone 4

⬤ Burner

⦙ Baking flaps

⬬ Exhaust gas

⬯ Swath discharger

Figure 5.58   Basic layout of the oven line.

The baking process is subject to statistical fluctuations. These stem, on one hand, from variations in the mixing process and, on the other, from the inconsistent harvest quality of the natural raw materials. Also, physical and biochemical characteristics of dough alter during the baking process. In addition, it is subject to the prevailing temperature conditions and the condition of the dough itself. The process is further subject to uncertainties relating directly to the system itself (air distribution in the oven, contact pressure of the dough-shaping roller, external air pressure, etc.).

The system is time-variant. The oven's operating characteristics change when it has been in operation for a certain time. The product is conveyed through the oven on a meshed steel belt. The conveyance speed, and subsequently, the baking time, are variable and are adapted to production requirements. In the course of time, dough residues collect in the mesh of the belt. The oven belt becomes soiled and gradually alters the manner in which the temperature characteristics of the oven are transferred to the product to be baked.

For several years now, operating personnel have successfully regulated the process manually based on acquired experience. In the course of the manual control process, product samples are taken at regular intervals. Color and moisture of biscuits are measured. If the measured values are outside the specified tolerance limits, the operator reacts in order to move the process back in the direction of the required parameters. The appropriate actions to be taken here depend primarily on the operator's personal experience.

Design of the Oven

The oven line is a four-zone baking oven consisting of four equivalent ovens connected in series. A gas burner is installed in the middle of each zone. The temperature of each zone is adjusted individually. The temperature in each zone is kept constant by individual temperature controllers. Air heated in one oven zone is subsequently distributed through the oven via air ducts by a main circulating fan. Located in the ducts are baking flaps that enable the flow of hot air to be directed onto the product. Each zone is provided with four baking flaps—two for the front part and two for the rear part, with one of the two being for upper and lower heating, respectively, in each part.

The baking flaps enable specific adjustment of the speed of the air flow, and subsequently of the heat current that is transferred to the product. Connected to each zone is an air discharge pipe with a facility for adjusting the air flow rate. At each end of the oven there is a swath discharge fan that prevents volatile products from entering into the production room. Figure 5.59 shows a burning zone of the oven in detail.

The biscuits are conveyed through the oven via a meshed steel transport belt, the "oven belt." The oven belt speed is variable and adapted to production requirements. Since the length of the oven, l_o, is constant, the belt speed, v_B, determines the baking time, t_b. The baking time is an important factor in oven control. The oven belt runs between upper and lower baking jets in the bottom quarter of the oven (Figure 5.59). Over time, the belt becomes soiled and its specific heat capacity and thermal conductivity change.

As a first step, a conventional mathematical model for the thermal characteristics of the oven was built. The results obtained show that the conditions in the oven are nonlinear and are not suitable for meaningful mathematical modeling because of their complexity. The amount of time required, combined with the fact that significant influences such as external air pressure, the posi-

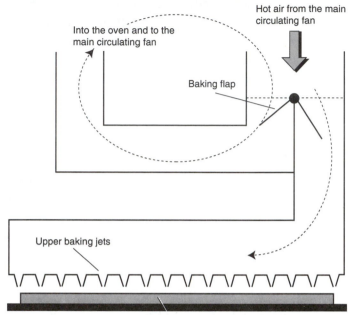

Figure 5.59   Principle of hot-air control by baking flaps.

tions of the exhaust air flaps, and soiling of the oven belt have yet to be taken into account, necessitated the abandonment of conventional mathematical modeling at this stage. The results are described in detail in [32]. However, these studies helped in understanding the baking process and provided a basis for the subsequent acquisition of operator knowledge, dimensioning of the membership functions, and development of the control strategy.

Development of a Heuristic Control Strategy

Three variables influence the baking process:

- Zone temperatures
- Baking flap settings
- Exhaust air flap settings

Interviews with the operating personnel, regarding which of the above-stated manipulated variables are employed in which situations and how, provided the results for defining a control strategy. Some examples of these results are:

- The zone temperatures are the decisive manipulated variables. The process can be influenced most specifically via temperature changes. Flap settings are employed for control purposes only when all the possibilities of controlling the process via the temperature have been exhausted.

■ Temperature changes are set rather than temperatures.

■ System deviations and changes in the system deviations for color and moisture are employed as input variables.

■ Line speed and number of lines are employed to initialize the zone temperatures.

■ Exhaust air and upper heat baking flaps are adjusted in two special cases. The dough operator is informed via a monitor.

■ Lower heat flaps of the first zone are activated only in relation to the dimensions.

■ The sum total of temperature changes must not be above or below a specified upper or lower limit.

■ All upper heat flaps are 100% open and all lower heat flaps are 100% closed when the oven is started up.

■ The first zone is always in operation.

■ Different rules apply in two-zone operation than those which apply in three-zone operation. Four-zone operation is extremely rare. The empirical values that are available for four-zone operation are not sufficient to enable a rule base to be developed. Hence, different fuzzy logic control strategies need to be set up for two- and three-zone operation.

Figure 5.60 shows the structure of the oven fuzzy logic control system. Sensors measure biscuit color and moisture as well as each zone temperature. Both error and deviation of error for moisture and color are inputs to the fuzzy logic system. The outputs of the fuzzy system are set temperature changes for the three zones of the oven. Each of these controllers hence implements an integration of the output of the fuzzy logic system. By comparing the set temperatures to the actual temperatures in the oven, the burner intensities are controlled by the individual controllers. Also, initial temperatures are set at these individual controllers. The flaps are not controlled directly by the fuzzy logic module but via a message to the operating personnel.

The entire fuzzy logic controller runs on a PC connected by a serial bus system (RS485) to the sensors and the temperature controllers. Figure 5.61 sketches the integration. The PC runs under MS-Windows and uses the *fuzzy*TECH Online Edition for the fuzzy logic control and process visualization.

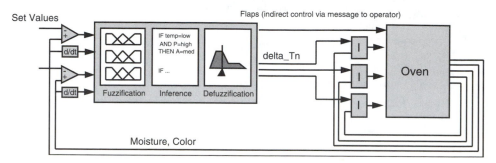

Figure 5.60 Configuration of the oven control system.

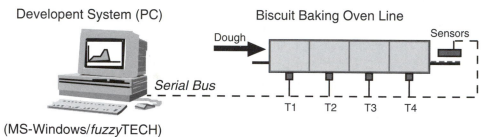

Figure 5.61 Integration of the oven control system.

Figure 5.62 shows a screen shot of *fuzzy*TECH displaying the fuzzy logic control module itself (two-zone operation). The upper left window (Project Editor) shows the structure of the fuzzy logic controller. The two lower windows show one input variable and one output variable during debugging. The left lower window shows the input variable. The input value and the fuzzification are displayed by the thin vertical line with the arrow underneath. The right lower window shows the output variable and the Center-of-Area defuzzification. The arrow under the area shows the crisp result of the defuzzification.

For all inputs and outputs, linguistic variables use standard membership functions. All input variables use three terms each, while the output variables use five terms each. Figure 5.63 shows another aspect of the debugging. The upper left window plots the partial transfer characteristic of the oven controller. The lower window exemplifies part of the rule base.

The complete rule set used for the fuzzy logic controller contains 162 rules. To illustrate the control strategy, nine example rules are shown in Table 5.3. This table shows the partial fuzzy control strategy for the case of no change in moisture and color.

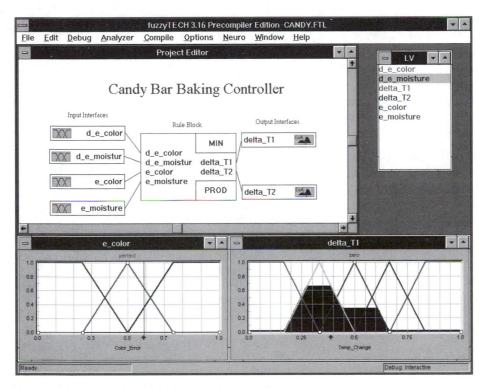

Figure 5.62   Screen shot of the fuzzy logic controller.

Optimization of the System

As a first optimization step, the controlled variables were continually recorded during the production process. The information includes the settings for the zone temperatures, the line speed, the positions of the baking flaps for upper and lower heat, and the changes in the manipulated variables relating to the zone temperatures. By connecting the fuzzy logic controller to data sets representing 10 weeks of operation and comparing the set value decisions with the experts' decisions, the control strategy was iteratively refined. Completeness of the control strategy was ensured by using *fuzzy*TECH's matrix rule representation. For the verification of the entire fuzzy controller, the *fuzzy*TECH analyzers were used (Figure 5.63).

Results

The first tests of the fuzzy logic oven control system used an open loop where the temperature changes displayed on a monitor are set by the operating personnel. The performance of the controller was supervised

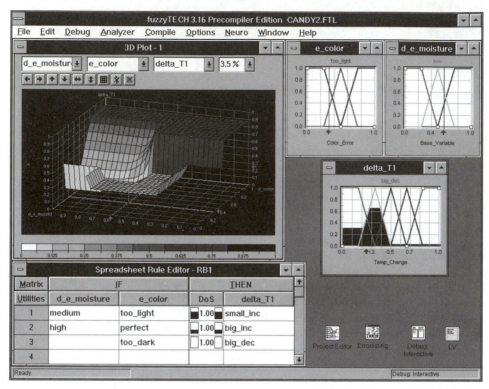

Figure 5.63 Screen shot of the fuzzy logic controller during debugging.

Table 5.3 Partial Fuzzy Logic Control Strategy
for No Change in Moisture and Color

Case No.	Deviation Color	Deviation Moisture	2-Zone Operation Action	3-Zone Operation Action
1	too dark (PO)	too moist (NE)	$\Delta T_1 = PM$ $\Delta T_2 = NM$ $\Delta T_3 = \text{—}$	$\Delta T_1 = ZR$ $\Delta T_2 = PM$ $\Delta T_3 = NM$
2	too dark (PO)	o.k. (ZR)	$\Delta T_1 = ZR$ $\Delta T_2 = NM$ $\Delta T_3 = \text{—}$	$\Delta T_1 = ZR$ $\Delta T_2 = ZR$ $\Delta T_3 = NM$
3	too dark (PO)	too dry (PS)	$\Delta T_1 = NM$ $\Delta T_2 = NM$ $\Delta T_3 = \text{—}$	$\Delta T_1 = ZR$ $\Delta T_2 = NM$ $\Delta T_3 = NM$

Table 5.3 Partial Fuzzy Logic Control Strategy
for No Change in Moisture and Color *(Continued)*

Case No.	Deviation Color	Deviation Moisture	2-Zone Operation Action	3-Zone Operation Action
4	o.k. (ZR)	too moist (NE)	$\Delta T_1 = PK$ $\Delta T_2 = PK$ $\Delta T_3 = {-}$	$\Delta T_1 = ZR$ $\Delta T_2 = PM$ $\Delta T_1 = ZR$
5	o.k. (ZR)	o.k. (ZR)	$\Delta T_1 = ZR$ $\Delta T_2 = ZR$ $\Delta T_3 = {-}$	$\Delta T_1 = ZR$ $\Delta T_2 = ZR$ $\Delta T_3 = ZR$
6	o.k. (ZR)	too dry (PS)	$\Delta T_1 = NK$ $\Delta T_2 = NK$ $\Delta T_3 = {-}$	$\Delta T_1 = ZR$ $\Delta T_2 = NM$ $\Delta T_3 = ZR$
7	too light (NE)	too moist (NE)	$\Delta T_1 = PM$ $\Delta T_2 = PM$ $\Delta T_3 = {-}$	$\Delta T_1 = ZR$ $\Delta T_2 = PK$ $\Delta T_3 = PK$
8	too light (NE)	o.k. (ZR)	$\Delta T_1 = ZR$ $\Delta T_2 = PM$ $\Delta T_3 = {-}$	$\Delta T_1 = ZR$ $\Delta T_2 = ZR$ $\Delta T_3 = PK$
9	too light (NE)	too dry (PS)	$\Delta T_1 = ZR$ $\Delta T_2 = ZR$ $\Delta T_3 = {-}$	$\Delta T_1 = ZR$ $\Delta T_2 = NM$ $\Delta T_3 = PK$

continuously by the operators for evaluation. After the first optimization step, the controller already performed as well as experienced operating personnel in standard operation. Hence, the oven operation was successfully automated.

The primary benefit of having used fuzzy logic in this application lies in the quick and easy implementation of operator experience. In addition to baking processes, this is also of great benefit to many other food processing applications. For example, a Japanese corporation uses fuzzy logic to control a sake brewing process [125].

5.4.7   Other Applications

This section contains other examples of fuzzy logic applications in the area of industrial automation and process control in brief. For more information, refer to the papers cited in the References.

Automatic Train Operation [208]

This is the often cited "classic" fuzzy logic application in Japan. The subway system of the Japanese city Sendai uses fuzzy logic for train operation. The producer, Hitachi, compared fuzzy logic in this application with conventional control techniques and manual control. In comparison with manual control, the fuzzy logic system is more energy-efficient. In comparison with the conventional control solution, the fuzzy logic controller reaches the stopping points with much higher accuracy.

Start-Up and Shut-Down Control in a Power Plant [22]

Goldstar Corporation of Korea uses a fuzzy logic controller for start-up and shut-down control in a fossil power plant in Seoul. In this application, not only is the continuous operation controlled, but the optimal point in time for certain operation sequences is also determined by a fuzzy logic system.

Load-Follow Operation of a Pressurized Water Reactor [55]

Mitsubishi Heavy Industries Corporation of Japan uses a combination of fuzzy logic and conventional controllers to control the boron concentration of a nuclear pressurized water reactor. The extension of the conventional controller with fuzzy logic was necessary because the conventional controller could not cope with the long dead times of the reactor. The long dead times stem mostly from the transportation of the boron water in the tube system of the reactor. Another application of fuzzy logic in nuclear power plants is shown in [134].

Optimizing Control of a Hydrogenation Plant [185]

The optimal control of a chemical process that uses a catalyst which ages over time is difficult. This is primarily due to the fact that all control parameters of the process also change over time. One example of such a process is the C2 hydrogenation reaction from ethine to ethene in the petrochemical industry. In this process, two chemical reactions occur. First, ethine reacts with hydrogen to ethene. This is the wanted reaction. Second, ethine reacts with more hydrogen to ethane. Ethane is the unwanted by-product that must be separated from the ethene later. The reaction is exothermic, causing a temperature rise over the length of the catalyst. The reaction velocities of the two reactions strongly depend on the temperature in the catalyst. A moderator substance mixed with the ethine and hydrogen flowing in the reaction chamber controls the reaction velocities in the catalyst. Another difficulty in the control of this process lies in the strong disturbances of the ethine mass flow. Control variables of the process are temperature of the influx and mass flow of the moderator substance. Each of these variables is kept constant by conventional PID controllers. Operators give the set values of these control loops to define the operation point of the process based on observation of the process. To automate this task, Foxboro Corporation used fuzzy logic to implement the operator's knowledge in a fuzzy logic system. Foxboro used fuzzy logic because the design of a mathematical model required an extreme effort. The design and implementation of the fuzzy logic controller only required a two-month effort. Comparing the fuzzy logic controller with the most skilled operator crew revealed that the operators only kept the optimal operation point with an accuracy of 7%, while the fuzzy logic controller kept an accuracy of 1.2%. In addition to smoother operation, this equals energy savings of at least 4%.

Fuzzy Logic Control of a High-Purity Distillation System [157]

To separate the azeotropic mixture of ehtanol and water, in this application, a fuzzy logic controller was combined with conventional control strategies.

Control of a Differential Distribution Weighting Means [167]

Carl Schenck Corporation of Germany uses a fuzzy logic system to control a differential distribution weighting means. Bulk material is discharged from a buffer by a feeder. The amount of material fed at a certain time is determined by differentiation of the buffer weight and is used as an actual value for controlling the rotational speed of the feeder. Many interferences corrupt the weight signal. Also, the control must correct fluctuations in the material flow and nonlinearities of the feeder. The resulting fuzzy-logic-based system implements higher precision and a more robust operation compared to the previous conventional solution.

Blast Furnace Control [69]

NKK Corporation of Japan has used fuzzy logic since 1989 to control blast furnaces in the steel industry. A long-term study revealed that the fuzzy logic controller delivered a more stable operation, even in the presence of disturbances and changing process characteristics.

Control of a Granulated Medium Refining Machine [24]

Granulated medium refining machines are used, for example, to skin rice. The control of such a machine involves strong nonlinearities and disturbances. The disturbances are due to strong mass flow fluctuations caused by other processing steps of the entire plant. A fuzzy logic system using four inputs and two outputs was designed for control.

Neutralizing Chemical Waste Water [199]

The cited plant neutralizes chemical waste water in two stages. Because of the use of buffered neutralizing agents, the behavior of this process is highly nonlinear. Also, the two stages strongly influence each other. In this application, a fuzzy logic solution implemented on a programmable logic controller delivered excellent results after only four weeks of engineering. A similar application of Hartman & Braun Corporation of Germany is shown in [98].

Automatic Control of Sewage Pump Stations [26]

The city of Shanghai in China uses the combination of a fuzzy logic controller and a neural net to optimize the operation of their sewage pump stations. The fuzzy logic system controls the number of active pumps and their power in a most energy-efficient way. The neural net predicts the load of the sewage system from the known parameters (day, time, season, rain amount, and other weather data).

Fuzzy Logic Control of a Cold Strip Mill [109]

Nippon Steel Corporation of Japan has used fuzzy logic control in a six-stand tandem cold strip mill since 1989. The objective is to produce steel with the most constant thickness. In such a mill, material to be rolled is set on a payoff reel to be unwound. The unwound plate is welded to the end of the already-set plate now being rolled and leaving the reel. The welded coil passes through a louver to be led to the six-stand tandem roller. After rolling to a preset thickness, the sheet is wound up at the tension reel to be shipped. The conventional method requires input of variables that are difficult to measure and that are therefore taken as assumption values only. As a result, unexpected errors occur resulting in difficulty in automating the rolling process. The implemented fuzzy logic controller showed a more constant steel thickness compared to the manually operated process.

Shorter Operation Times with Electrical Discharge Machining [112]

Sodick Corporation of Japan uses a fuzzy logic controller to reduce operation times with electrical discharge machining (EDM). Depending on material and machining depth, the fuzzy logic controller shortens operation times from 5% to 80%, compared to manual parameterization of the machine. Also, Mitsubishi Corporation of Japan and AGIE Corporation of Switzerland use fuzzy logic in their electrical discharge machines.

Weld-Line Tracking Control of an Arc Welding Robot [105]

Mitsubishi Heavy Industries of Japan uses fuzzy logic to control the weld-line tracking by a robot. Sensor signals are horizontal and vertical displacements of the welding point. As these signals contain much noise and many artifacts, the controller uses fuzzy filter techniques. Another application of picture recognition in robot technology is described in [147].

Tank-Level Control in a Refinery [45]

Elf Antar Corporation of France uses fuzzy logic to control the floating level in a tank on top of the atmospheric distillation column of a refinery. An existing controller was not performing satisfactorily. Hence, Elf first translated the algorithm of the existing controller into a fuzzy logic controller. Then this fuzzy logic controller was further optimized in the plant. The resulting fuzzy logic controller is now in continuous operation in the Donge refinery in France, where it shows entirely satisfactory performance.

Temperature Control of a Naphtha Hydro-Desulfurizing Plant [163]

To control the top temperature of a naphtha hydro-desulfurizing plant, Idemitsu Kosan Corporation of Japan uses a fuzzy logic controller in parallel with a PID controller. Figure 5.6 shows the structure of such a controller. The resulting controller performed well, not only in steady state, but also when subjected to transients such as in feed-oil switching.

Steam Turbine Prewarming Automation [16]

General Electric uses a fuzzy logic system to control the prewarming of large steam turbines after extended periods of maintenance or inactivity. Before, the prewarming procedure was controlled manually.

Fuzzy Logic Control of a Wind Tunnel Temperature Process [48]

For the control of its Mach 6 wind tunnel, NASA uses a fuzzy logic system. The PID-type controller used previously failed to provide acceptable control of the tunnel temperature. The fuzzy logic solution, running on an i486 board controlled by a master PLC, delivered very satisfactory results in tunnel preheating and temperature control in operation.

Cement Kiln Control

The application of fuzzy logic in cement kiln control started in 1972 in Denmark as a direct result of Mamdani's first fuzzy logic. Since then, a large number of cement kilns have been automated by fuzzy logic. For an overview, see [129]. A case study of an implementation is contained in [38]. The control of a chamber ball mill in the cement industry is presented in [123].

AC Motor Control Using Fuzzy Logic

Many publications in the area of AC and other types of motor control exist. Reference [29] shows how fuzzy logic control can be employed to optimize the energy efficiency in AC motor variable-speed control. Reference [59] shows a flux and torque control by fuzzy logic direct self-control.

5.5   Fuzzy Data Analysis

The analysis of complex data sets often requires human-like evaluations and decisions. Mathematical models used for this have severe limitations in representing such evaluations. Also, in many applications, the data material is noisy or contains artifacts. Here, conventional data analysis methods soon reach their limits. This section describes the use of fuzzy logic in data analysis. Section 5.5.1 shows how fuzzy logic is combined with data analysis techniques. Section 5.5.2 describes the combination of software tools for fuzzy data analysis. As case studies, Section 5.5.3 shows an application of fuzzy data analysis in an embedded application, Section 5.5.4 in industrial automation, and Section 5.5.5 contains an overview of other applications in the area.

5.5.1 Using Fuzzy Logic in Data Analysis

Most data analysis methods try to derive structural information out of given data sets. This structural information will represent the system that produced the data sets. The goal is to identify internal parameters of the system that cannot be measured directly.

Today, many different methods and algorithms for data analysis exist. Most of these algorithms have difficulties coping with noisy data and data that contains artifacts. These applications have to use very robust data analysis techniques that can cope with errors and artifacts in the data material.

But what can fuzzy logic do for this? Here is a simple example: look at Figure 5.64. With the human eye as sensor, this looks like a nonsensical collection of gray squares. The human eye is already a very precise sensor that can distinguish about 100 different shades of gray, but even with better sensors, the figure remains a collection of gray squares. Only if you squint to the point that the entire picture becomes "fuzzy," do you see that the collection of gray squares is actually a picture of Abraham Lincoln. The lesson learned is that even the most precise method will not give you the information of what is contained in the picture. Even if you were to modify the grayness of some of the squares, the "fuzzy" look would still recognize Abraham Lincoln.

To employ fuzzy logic in data analysis applications, many different combinations of fuzzy logic and conventional techniques exist. Which one is best depends strongly on the application. We will now discuss the most common combinations of fuzzy logic and conventional techniques.

Fuzzy Cluster Analysis

Cluster analysis maps objects to predefined classes. For a quality control system, the classes could be *bad* and *good*. For this mapping, a vector of parameters describes each object. Each parameter denotes a certain property of the objects. For the classification of acoustic signals, these parameters could be the result of a Fourier transformation. Most cluster analysis algorithms use training algorithms to configure themselves from given sample data sets.

Using fuzzy logic in cluster analysis allows for the definition of "fuzzy" classes. The benefit of this is that even when unique classification of some pa-

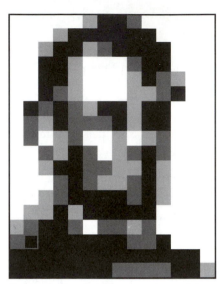

Figure 5.64   Only if you squint until the picture becomes "fuzzy," can you recognize Abraham Lincoln.

rameters is not possible, a good final solution can still be derived. For more general information on fuzzy cluster analysis, refer to [21, 72, 196, 221].

Fuzzy Rule-Based Methods

Cluster analysis methods derive all necessary structural information by training from given sample data sets. This demands a very high quality of the sample data sets used. Also, there are no explicit modifications of the resulting system. This makes optimization and verification difficult tasks.

Fuzzy rule-based methods work differently. Here, "if-then" rules represent the entire classification. This is very similar to the application of fuzzy logic in intelligent control as described above. In contrast to fuzzy logic in control applications, fuzzy logic classification uses different inference and defuzzification methods.

The benefit of fuzzy rule-based methods over fuzzy cluster analysis is that the information flow in the system is completely transparent. As fuzzy logic systems are self-explanatory, explicit optimization and verification are easy. The disadvantage of fuzzy rule-based methods is that the entire system has to be built up manually. In contrast to fuzzy cluster analysis, no automated training exists.

However, fuzzy rule-based methods are the basis of many successful applications in data analysis and signal classifications. Section 5.5.7 presents some of these applications.

Adaptive Fuzzy Rule-Based Methods

In summary, the advantage of fuzzy cluster analysis lies in its trainability while the advantage of fuzzy rule-based methods lies in the inherent transparency of the system. However, some applications need both trainability and transparency at the same time. Here, the combination of a training algorithm with a fuzzy rule-based method can provide a successful solution. Because the training algorithm adapts the fuzzy rules and membership functions so that the behavior represents the sample data sets, this combination is called the "adaptive fuzzy rule-based method."

Although there are many ways to adapt a fuzzy logic system, the only approach that has been used widely in industrial applications is the Neuro-Fuzzy technique. Here, learning algorithms developed for neural nets are modified so that they can also train a fuzzy logic system. Section 4.2 of this book treats this technique in detail.

The benefit of such a technology is that it can learn from given sample data sets, and the learned result can be further enhanced by hand. Especially for applications where only partial information for the solution stems from sample data, adaptive fuzzy rule-based systems are the best choice. Another advantage is that the system developed is a "pure" fuzzy logic system which can be implemented even on very inexpensive hardware platforms. Section 5.5.3 shows a good example of this.

5.5.2   Software Tools for Fuzzy Data Analysis

In most fuzzy data analysis systems, the input data needs extensive preprocessing before it goes into the fuzzy logic system. This preprocessing can include filtering, linearizations, or Fourier transformations. These functions are not part of most fuzzy logic applications in industrial control, and hence are not part of most fuzzy logic software development tools.

For the *fuzzy*TECH development system described in Section 4.1.1, complete data analysis functionality is provided by an add-on tool, the so-called DataAnalyzer Module [120]. Figure 5.65 shows how *fuzzy*TECH, the DataAnalyzer Module, and the NeuroFuzzy Module can be linked to form an integrated design environment. Linking all three components allows for the design of an adaptive fuzzy rule-based solution. If the NeuroFuzzy Module is left out, only fuzzy rule-based solutions are possible.

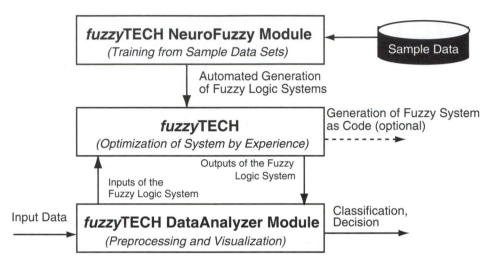

Figure 5.65   Linking the DataAnalyzer Module, the NeuroFuzzy Module, and *fuzzy*TECH creates an integrated development environment for fuzzy data analysis systems.

Figure 5.66 shows the visual design of a fuzzy data analyzer solution that supervises the wear of a machinery tool during operation. The two upper left function blocks drive the A/D channels of a standard PC plug-in board. The upper channel links to a tension stripe sensor that acts as a microphone; the lower channel links to a temperature sensor mounted on the tool. The acoustic signal is preprocessed by a Spectrum block (fast Fourier transformation) and input to the fuzzy logic function block. The second input to the fuzzy logic function is the temperature signal filtered by a low-pass filter. The third input to the fuzzy logic function block is the direct temperature signal after a Threshold function block. A fourth input comes from a visual inspection of the machine operator and is input by a slide in a separate window.

Both a a meter and a spectrum scope visualize the outputs of the fuzzy logic function block. In case of an overload, a D/A channel outputs a speed overwrite signal to the machine to avoid destruction of the machinery tool. For documentation, a File function block writes the evaluation result on disk. The NeuroFuzzy Module resides on top of *fuzzy*TECH (Figure 5.65), hence, it is not displayed in Figure 5.66.

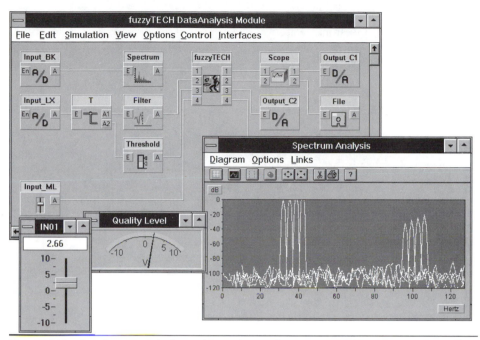

Figure 5.66   Development of a fuzzy data analyzer solution is completely graphical. By configuring predefined function blocks, conventional signal analysis techniques and fuzzy logic are integrated. Fuzzy logic is also represented as a function block.

5.5.3   Fuzzy Data Analysis in a Medical Shoe

After knee surgery, patients are required to limit the strain on the knee during a long convalescent period. The problem is that humans have no strain sensor to control this. When pain occurs, the knee has already suffered damage. To solve this problem, a tension sensor and a fuzzy logic data analysis system was used to design a bio-feedback shoe inlay [189]. Figure 5.67 shows how this setup works. A silicon inlay contains a tension sensor made of conducting polymer. The sensor is wired to an electronic unit that sits in a belt attached over the ankle by velcro. The electronic unit hosts a microcontroller, battery, alarm, and a keypad. The alarm warns the user when the strain limit is reached. A/D conversion, signal preprocessing, and the fuzzy data analysis system all run on the 8-bit microcontroller.

The objective for the fuzzy data analysis system is to estimate the internal strain on the knee from the tension signal. If 80% of the maximum acceptable load is reached, a beep warns the user to take it easy. If 90% of the maximum acceptable load is reached, a repeating beep tells the user to not use

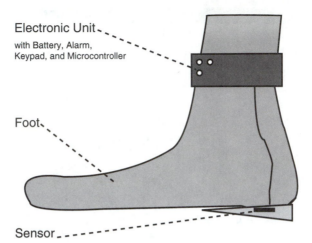

Figure 5.67   The orthopedic shoe consists of an electronic unit attached by velcro over the ankle and a sensor in a silicon inlay.

the leg for a while, and if the strain is over the maximum threshold set by the doctor, the beep sounds continuously.

The difficulty of this is to estimate the internal strain on the knee from the tension signal. Figure 5.68 displays the tension sensor signal for a typical sequence of steps. To get more information from the tension sensor signal, preprocessing derives additional inputs to the fuzzy data analysis system. In total, this yields four inputs to the fuzzy logic function block:

- *Act_Peak:*
  Peak tension of the current step.
- *Act_Slope:*
  Slope of the tension signal of the current step.
- *Hist_Short:*
  Feedback of the average output signal of the fuzzy logic function block over the last five minutes. This input is an indicator for the current strain situation in the knee.
- *Hist_Long:*
  Feedback of the average output signal of the fuzzy logic function block over the last 48 hours. This input is an indicator for the long-term strain situation in the knee.

Figure 5.69 shows a screen shot of the fuzzy logic system in the data analyzer. The upper window draws the structure of the system. The output vari-

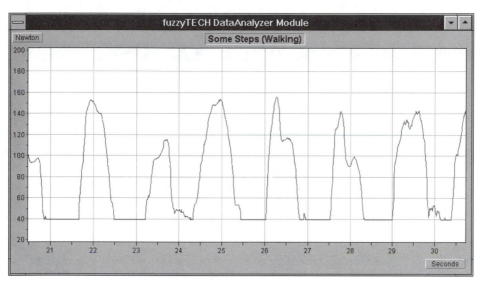

Figure 5.68 Typical tension sensor signal for a sequence of steps.

able "Alarm" stems from a rule block with the input variables "ActualLoad" and "TimeLoad." Both of these variables are outputs of other rule blocks. ActualLoad computes from the two input variables Act_Slope and Act_Peak, which are input variables of the fuzzy logic function block. The DataAnalyzer Module computes these variables from the tension sensor signal.

TimeLoad computes from the two input variables, Hist_Short and Hist_Long, which the DataAnalyzer Module computes out of the output signal from the fuzzy logic function block by averaging. The left lower window shows a typical membership function definition. Most linguistic variables use two or three membership functions of standard MBF type. The lower right window shows four rules of the upper rule block. The total number of rules in the system is 39.

The rules were derived in close cooperation with orthopedic doctors. Under the nomenclature of Section 5.5.1, this application uses "fuzzy rule-based methods." Another advantage of using fuzzy logic in this example is that the rule set is easy to modify. For example, by designing a rule set that evaluates the steps and their fit to an optimal curve, runners could improve their running style with this intelligent bio-feedback technique.

Figure 5.70 shows the total implementation on the microcontroller. First, the analog-to-digital conversion transforms the resistance of the tension sensor into a digital 10-bit value. Preprocessing and filtering gets the four in-

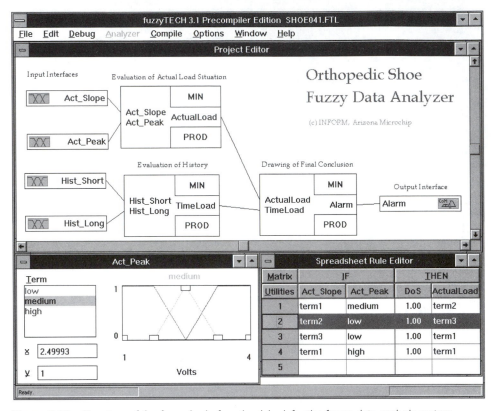

Figure 5.69   Structure of the fuzzy logic function block for the fuzzy data analysis system.

put variables for the fuzzy logic computation shown in Figure 5.69. Last, depending on the strain rating, the speaker outputs the alarm and the keypad is scanned. The fuzzy logic system requires about 20 bytes RAM and 500 byte/words of ROM on the microcontroller. This enables even very small microcontrollers to run this complex system efficiently.

5.5.4   Fuzzy Data Analysis for Cardio-Anesthesia

This section uses a more complex case study of fuzzy data analysis in medical systems. In open heart surgery, achieving a stable anesthetic condition is a prerequisite. However, the large amount of data available makes it hard for the anesthetist to comprehend the patient's overall situation. To support the anesthetist during open heart surgery, the medical school of Aachen University developed an intelligent alarm system [17].

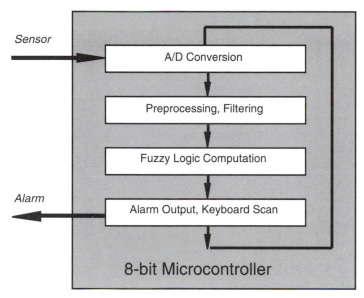

Figure 5.70   Implementation of the fuzzy data analyzer system on a microcontroller.

The fuzzy data analyzer uses input data such as the systolic arterial pressure (SysArtPress), left heart chamber arterial pressure (LAP), the heart rate (HeartRate), and the current medication (Fentanyl, Benzo). As outputs, the fuzzy data analyzer determines the five vital parameters afterload (Afterload), myocardial contractility (Contractility), blood volume (IvVolume), depth of anesthesia (DepthAnest), and heart rate (_HeartRate). Note that the output variable heart rate is only computed by fuzzifying and defuzzifying the actual measured heart rate. By this process, the heart rate in beats per minute is translated into a nondimensional measure. Figure 5.71 shows the structure of the fuzzy data analyzer. The total system contains about 200 fuzzy logic rules and uses the γ operator for aggregation in the rule inference [116, 217].

The knowledge of the data analysis system, that is the membership functions and the rules, was determined by using structured questionnaires with a group of 13 experienced anesthetists.

The intelligent alarm system uses a dedicated user interface to ensure that the anesthetist gets all important information and only that data. Figure 5.72 shows a screen shot of the user interface. The five outputs of the fuzzy data analysis system are presented as bars next to icons representing the variables. Bars to

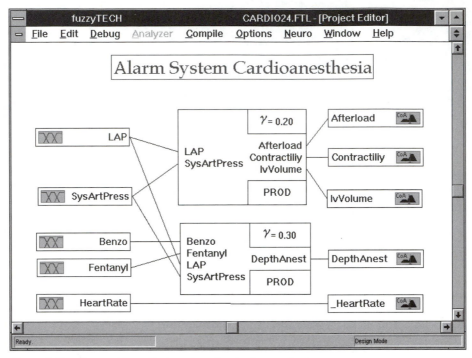

Figure 5.71   Fuzzy data analysis system for cardio-anesthesia.

the left side of the center line indicate a state variable becoming too low. Bars to the right side of the center line indicate a state variable becoming too high. When the length of the bar increases, the color turns from green to red. In the right section of the user interface, the trends of the most important hemodynamic vital parameters, LAP and SysArtPress, are plotted over time. This plot enables the anesthetist to recognize pathologic trends in the patient's circulatory functions and thus prevent deterioration of the patient's state.

The system was first optimized by testing it with recorded data from real operations. By comparing the results with the actions of the anesthetist who did the operation and discussing the strategies, the system was gradually improved and verified. Figure 5.73 shows the partial transfer characteristic of the system. Now, the system is in permanent use at the heart center of the university hospital in Aachen and delivers very satisfactory results. A similar application is shown in [34].

While this fuzzy data analysis system only supervises the patient's state, other applications use fuzzy logic to actually control anesthesia depth in a closed loop. See Section 5.6.7 for a detailed description.

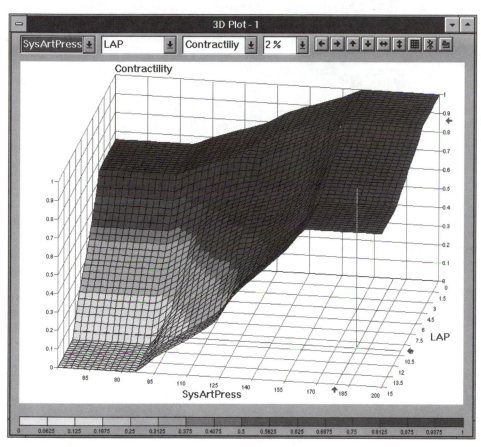

Figure 5.72 Transfer characteristic of the fuzzy data analyzer determining the contractibility out of the input variables LAP and SysArtPress. The arrows and lines denote the current values.

5.5.5   Ultrasound Sensors with Fuzzy Data Analysis

The ultrasound measurement principle allows a continuous, noncontacting level measurement in bulk solid silos and liquid storage and reaction tanks. Figure 5.74 shows the principle. A variety of products are measured: liquids, coarse-grained bulk solids such as gravel or plastic granules, and fine-grained materials such as cement or flour. Often the contents of a tank or silo change from week to week.

The level of "good" is determined by the ultrasound reflection echo using the speed of sound. However, this determination can be difficult in some cases:

■ Foaming liquids generate multiple echoes.

■ Some shapes of liquid tanks generate focusing effects.

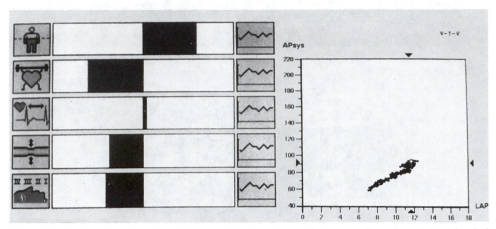

Figure 5.73   User interface of the intelligent alarm system. Left side: profilogramm, right side: vital trend visualization.

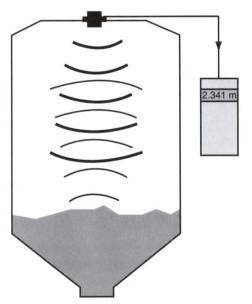

Figure 5.74   Level measurement by the ultrasonic principle. The level of goods is derived from the echo signal.

■ Internal fittings cause artifact echoes.

■ Coarse-grained bulk solids form filling mounds and outflow funnels.

These factors are very hard to cover using analytical models and conventional filter algorithms. For these reasons, Endress-Hauser Corporation of

Germany uses fuzzy data analysis to separate the level echo from the artifacts [20]. Fuzzy logic allowed the designers to use the knowledge of the experienced specialists at Endress-Hauser directly in the solution. Some examples of this knowledge are:

- Fragmented echoes are typical for outflow funnels.
- If multiple echoes have a constant distance from each other, the first "big" echo is the level echo.
- Artifact echoes from internal fittings are stationary.

The implemented expert's knowledge simplifies and expedites the setup of the sensor. Just one parameter is set to indicate one of five standard operation cases: "liquids," "fine-grained bulk solids," "coarse-grained bulk solids," "liquids with rapid level changes," and "conveyor belt."

5.5.6   Voice Recognition Using Fuzzy Logic

The recognition of spoken language is still a challenge to computerized systems. Some solutions provide limited dictation capabilities if trained for a single speaker in non-noisy environments. Speaker-independent voice recognition in noisy environments still remains limited to a few words and commands. Because there are no good mathematical models of human speech, designers have to rely heavily on experience and experiments to develop solutions. Since fuzzy logic is a technology that facilitates integration of knowledge in systems, it is commonly used in voice recognition systems.

The first application of fuzzy logic in speaker-independent voice recognition was done by the Japanese corporation Ricoh [42]. Experiments proved that with a restricted set of 120 words, the recognition averages 93% in noisy environments. The recognition rate did not depend on the language. The test languages were Japanese, English, and German.

Most voice recognition systems—with or without fuzzy logic—use fast Fourier transformation algorithms to transform the voice input data into a frequency pattern as the first step. Then, after normalization and filtering steps, pattern recognition algorithms determine the closeness of the voice input pattern to prerecorded patterns. Using fuzzy logic pattern recognition techniques rather than conventional ones has been shown to be of great benefit. For an example of such a fuzzy logic voice recognition system, refer to [50].

In some applications, fuzzy logic facilitates an even simpler solution without a Fourier transformation step. I will illustrate this with a voice command input system demonstrated in [41]. Voice command systems, in contrast to voice recognition systems, use a much more restricted vocabulary and are thus easier to design. However, for applications such as voice mail systems, remote controllers, industrial process control, or appliances only limited vocabulary is required.

Amplitude

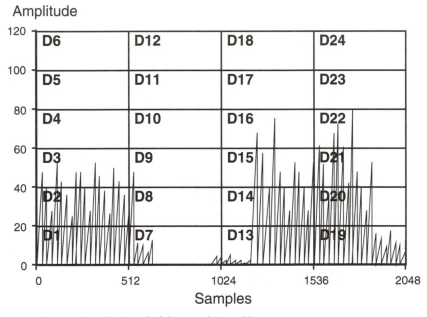

Figure 5.75   Intensity signal of the word "equal."

The cited application presents the technology using a voice input calculator recognizing 16 words (ten digits, four arithmetic operators, and the words "equal" and "clear"). The design goal was to develop a solution that does not require the computation and code-intensive Fourier transformation. Instead, the system samples an utterance at an 8-kHz sample rate, obtaining up to 2048 samples. Within the sampling, the utterance would show up as a simple graph of amplitude with higher density in regions of higher frequency. Figure 5.75 shows this graph for the word "equal," Figure 5.76 for the word "four."

After the microcontroller samples the utterance, the graph is divided into 24 squares. Then each square is characterized in terms of the sample density that falls into it. By inspecting the graph and deciding which regions carried the identifying characteristics for each word, the designers determined

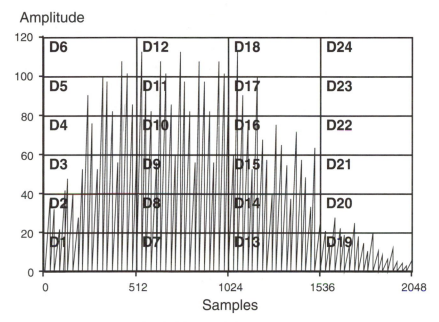

Figure 5.76   Intensity signal of the word "four."

Matrix	IF				THEN	
Utilities	D20	D21	D9	D10	DoS	Word
1	some_high	some_high	very_low	very_low	1.00	equal
2	very_low	very_low	average	average	1.00	four

Figure 5.77   Typical rules for "equal" and "four."

the fuzzy logic rules that interpret the graph. Figure 5.77 shows typical rules for the words "equal" and "four."

Such an approach has its limits. For example, the word "equal" cannot be distinguished from the word "sequel." However, for many voice command applications, this simple approach may well suffice. A first prototype, after two months of development, was capable of 90% recognition for the same speaker. The system is currently under optimization to achieve the same recognition rate for speaker-independent recognition.

The benefit of the fuzzy logic solution is the short development time and few resources required for the implementation of the system. The resulting fuzzy logic system contains 19 rules, one output variable, and 13 input variables (not all densities were used). This requires only 2.3 KB of ROM memory on a 16-bit microcontroller or 1.8 KB of memory on a 8-bit microcontroller. The computation time for the fuzzy logic system is 0.5 milliseconds on an average 16-bit microcontroller and 5 milliseconds on an average 8-bit microcontroller. The incremental cost added by such a voice command module to a design that already uses a microcontroller is, hence, very low.

5.5.7   Other Applications

This section contains other examples of fuzzy data analysis systems in brief. For more information, refer to the paper cited in the References.

Active Noise Cancellation in Airplanes [78]

One approach to reducing noise in airplanes is active noise cancellation. Here, microphones record the noise and a filter algorithm transforms the signal so that, using an amplifier and speakers, this signal cancels part of the original noise. The problem is to parameterize the filters for the best result. Optimal parameter values change with the operational conditions. This application by Boeing Corporation uses fuzzy logic to evaluate the quality of the current cancellation process and adapts the filter characteristic to always obtain the best results. An extension to the case of multiple primary sources with low correlation between them is presented in [79].

Quality Control of Quartz Light Tube Production [56]

In the production of quartz light tubes, the parameters of the plant have to be retuned for every new shift. Some of the parameters are flow of cooling gas, position of the burner flame, and press duration of the tube end. In this application, a fuzzy logic system monitors the process by a video camera, interprets and evaluates the melting process, and determines corrections for retuning the parameters.

Traffic Control Using Fuzzy Logic [142]

The traffic control system of the Osaka-Sakai Highway in Japan uses fuzzy logic to ensure continuous traffic flow. Traffic control systems are common in Japan, where congestion is the rule rather than the exception. Traffic lights at the entrances to the highway limit the number of cars that enter. Another way to limit the number of cars entering a certain part of a highway is to close lanes at the toll booths. Fuzzy logic is used to estimate the likelihood of a traffic jam on certain parts of the highway. Based on this estimation, the number of cars is limited to prevent the traffic jam. Compared to the mathematical models that were used before, the fuzzy logic solution resulted in higher accuracy and faster adaptability, and required only a fraction of the development time.

Passive Sonar Signal Classification [86]

To identify water vessels, most submarines use passive sonar. Here, sensitive microphones record the sound emitted from ships, other submarines, and torpedoes. In a conventional solution, a monitor plots the signal transformed into the frequency domain over time. These plots are called "waterfall diagrams," and either a human or a conventional classification system interprets them. Atlas Electronic Corporation employs a fuzzy logic system to interpret the transformed signal. The fuzzy logic system first estimates revolution speed of the screw and the number of blades per screw. Then the vessel type is estimated. Comparisons between the fuzzy-logic-based solution and the previous conventional solution show that the fuzzy logic solution performs with much higher accuracy while taking less development time. A similar application is shown in [91].

Optimization of Picture Quality for Video Printers [43]

The Japanese company Sanyo uses fuzzy logic to optimize the picture quality in video printers. By evaluating the color signals of the video signals, the fuzzy logic system compensates for color shifts that are common with other video printers.

False-Alarm Reduction with Fire Detectors [168]

One common approach to detecting fires is to use an ion detector that spots smoke in the air. Alas, false alarms can be triggered by air flow caused by air conditioners and other circumstances. Another cause of false alarms is high humidity that condenses inside the ionization chamber. The Swiss company Cerberus uses fuzzy data analysis to circumvent this problem. Kendel-Tau functions estimate the noise contents and the gradient of the signal. Three parameters derived from these functions describe the ionization signal. These parameters are inputs of the fuzzy logic system that make the decision on whether to trigger the alarm. The company states that fuzzy logic helped them to put the expertise that the engineers had gained over years of experiments right into a successful product.

Mask Alignment Using Fuzzy Logic [66]

The Japanese company Canon uses fuzzy logic for a picture recognition system in a mask alignment system in its 16-Mbit DRAM process. Canon states that the desired alignment accuracy had not been achieved with conventional methods. The fuzzy logic system was implemented as an extension of an existing mask alignment unit.

Automated Classification of Defects in Semiconductor Wafers [131]

IBM Corp. developed a fuzzy logic classification system for defects in 16-Mb DRAM semiconductor wafers. The classification result is used for yield prediction, rework/scrap decisions, and process evaluation. While many vision systems already exist on the market that can locate defects on semiconductor wafers, they give little information about the defects themselves. Thus, it is common practice for automatically detected defects to be reviewed manually and classified by human operators. The classification process is much more time-consuming than the initial inspection, so only a sample of the identified defects are classified by the operators. Manual defect review and classification is very monotonous and subjective. There is a great deal of inconsistency among operators and studies have shown that classification accuracy is seldom better than 60%. The fuzzy logic system was qualified by the end-user on eight of the 14 defect types associated with the first 16-Mb DRAM process step. The system then classified about 75% of all the defects found after this process step. Approximately 85% of these defects were classified correctly. Similar results were obtained with other process levels. IBM used a training method to generate the rules for the classifier from sample data.

Handwritten Letter Recognition [15]

Intel Corp. designed a handwritten letter recognition system prototype using fuzzy logic. The prototype was developed in 1.5 months and showed fair recognition quality for single handwritten letters. It is still inferior to conventional letter recognition systems but has been developed in a very short time. There should be enormous potential in enhancing existing handwritten letter recognition systems with fuzzy logic. Sony Corp. of Japan already uses fuzzy-logic-enhanced handwritten letter recognition in a palmtop product. This recognition system, however, is dedicated to Kanji characters.

Identification of Signatures [164]

To identify human signatures, many different approaches already exist. The problem is that signatures are relatively easy to fake since even the same person can sign in very different styles. The identification of a signature off-line (i.e, after it was written) is especially hard. The cited solution by the Japanese company Omron uses fuzzy logic to identify signatures while signing. With the additional timing and draw speed information, the accuracy is much higher. Signature identification can replace passwords at pen computers and enable fraud detection with credit cards.

Credit Card Fraud Detection [30]

Much credit card fraud is committed by copying the contents of the magnetic stripe to a blank card and using it at many ATMs at the same time. A new system by XTEC Corporation of Florida uses fuzzy logic data analysis to analyze the magnetic "fingerprint" of information recorded on the card. This fingerprint is unique due to the different alignment of each card, the different wear on each card, and the different machines that recorded the information. The fuzzy data analysis system can tell the original from the copy, even if the information on the cards is identical.

Processing of Ultrasound Pictures in Cancer Diagnosis [10]

At Kawasaki Medical School in Japan, a fuzzy logic system processes ultrasound pictures to diagnose prostate tumors. First, conventional signal processing derives a total of eight parameters from the ultrasound picture. Such parameters are the shape of the tumor, the echo signal strength within the tumor, and the hypoecho. These eight parameters are the inputs of the fuzzy logic system. The fuzzy logic system evaluates whether the tumor is considered malignant or benign. In a field study, the fuzzy logic system reached a 90% match rate with the pathological result for the diagnosis of a malignant tumor. This match rate equals that of a good medical doctor.

Multisensor Array for Gas Mix [68]

Matsushita Corp. of Japan uses fuzzy logic for a multisensor array that analyzes gas mixes. Each sensor detects a group of gases; hence, most gases are detected by more than one sensor. Using the different nonlinear characteristics of the sensors, the fuzzy logic data analysis system differentiates and quantifies the ingredients of a gas mix.

Ultrasound Quality Control for SMD Production [192]

Today, the production process of SMDs (surface mounted device) is highly automated. To ensure that every part of the board is placed correctly, this application uses an ultrasound sensor. This sensor scans a height profile of the board, moved by step motors. Signal processing compares the measured height profile with the height profile of a reference board by cross-correlation. Conventional filter techniques derive parameters such as "shape difference," "asymmetry," "energy difference," and "time delay" of the cross-correlation function. These parameters are the inputs of a fuzzy logic system that interprets the differences between the two height profiles. The output of the fuzzy logic system tells whether the board is considered good or it should be further inspected manually. The fuzzy system has a total of 65 rules.

Control of a Wind Energy Converter [46]

The utilization of wind energy for the environmentally friendly generation of electricity has become very attractive during the past decade. To optimize energy generation, the controller has to take multiple factors into account, such as mechanical stress resulting from gusty winds and stability of the generated power. As the operation point of the wind generator is determined by the wind, no steady state is achievable. Due to these reasons Aerodyn Corporation, Husumer Schiffswerft, and Klockner-Moeller Corporation of Germany cooperatively use a fuzzy logic system on a PLC for control.

5.6   Other Applicational Areas

Fuzzy Logic is a very general technology for engineering applications. Hence, fuzzy logic is used in a wide variety of applications. Some of the most interesting applications that do not fit under the previous sections of this chapter are contained in this section. Section 5.6.1 shows how an intelligent battery charger can drastically prolong the life expectancy of NiCd batteries. Section 5.6.2 shows the application of fuzzy logic in hard disk and optical disc drive control. Section 5.6.3 explains the digital image stabilizer technique commonly found in today's camcorders. Section 5.6.4 presents the application of fuzzy logic in climate control systems for large buildings. Section 5.6.5 explains fuzzy logic elevator group control. Section 5.6.6 deals with fuzzy logic control of cameras. Section 5.6.7 covers the closed-loop control of anesthesia during operations, and Section 5.6.9 presents more applications in brief abstracts.

5.6.1   Rapid Charger for Batteries

Portable appliances, ranging from Walkmans, portable and cellular phones, camcorders, and notebook PCs to electric tools and shavers, are becoming increasingly popular. Most of these devices use rechargeable NiCd batteries. The advantages of this battery type are high peak current, low cost, and the availability of a complete spectrum of sizes and shapes. Unfortunately, NiCd batteries also have disadvantages:

- Charging batteries that are not completely empty will decrease battery capacity (memory effect)

- Overcharging of the battery also decreases capacity and life cycles

- Overdischarge damages the battery

Alas, the charge level of a NiCd battery cannot be measured easily. Many indirect parameters have to be considered for a charge-level estimation. Hence, many applications use an intelligent, microprocessor-controlled system for power management. The charge level estimation is a complex, multiparameter signal interpretation for which no good mathematical model exists. On the other hand, a lot of engineering expertise is available that can be used to design a fuzzy logic solution. Another reason to use fuzzy logic is that fuzzy logic can implement quite complex systems using very little RAM and ROM resources. Hence, low-cost microcontrollers can be used for this complex signal interpretation task.

Rapid Battery Chargers for Portable Tools

BOSCH Corporation of Germany used fuzzy logic for the design of their new NiCd rapid charger, AL12FC. The name means: "AL" for "akkulader" (battery charger), "12" for 12-minute charging time, and "FC" for "fuzzy controlled." BOSCH designed this charger for electric tools, such as a portable drill. The users of these tools cannot wait for the standard 14-hour charge time of a NiCd battery. Hence, many companies designed rapid charg-

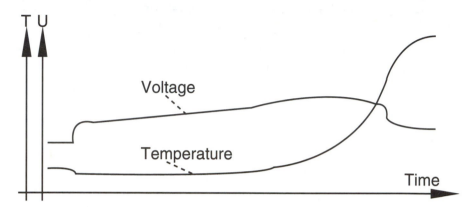

Figure 5.78   Temperature and voltage of a NiCd battery during rapid charging process using a constant-current charge.

ers that charge the NiCd battery in just 12 minutes. The problem of these chargers in general is that due to the high charge current, even an overcharge of one minute can permanently damage the NiCd battery. Due to this, the average life expectancy of about 1000 charging cycles drops down to 300. Also, due to the higher likelihood of undercharging, the capacity of the battery degrades.

Figure 5.78 shows the temperature and voltage of a NiCd battery during charging. The batteries used have an integrated temperature sensor. The objective for the charger controller is to determine the ideal shut-off point. The problem is that many parameters influence the ideal shut-off point:

- The used NiCd batteries can be from different manufacturers, hence showing slightly different characteristics.

- The temperature sensor is mounted differently with different batteries.

- The charge level at the beginning of charging is unknown. Many users do not completely discharge the battery prior to charging.

- The age and the history of the battery are unknown to the charger since one charger is used for many NiCd batteries in most cases.

- The number of cells in the battery is unknown.

- The environment temperature is unknown (only the battery temperature is known).

Conventional Rapid Charge Algorithms

To determine the ideal shut-off point for the charging process, a number of conventional methods exist. The most popular ones are:

1   *Negative Delta U*

This algorithm is the most commonly used for rapid charge. During charge, the voltage maximum is determined, and, after it has been detected, the current is shut off (Figure 5.78). However, the ideal shut-off point lies before the voltage maximum. Also, in some cases, no voltage maximum occurs. This is the case for batteries not used for a longer period, as the individual cells self-discharge differently over time. With hot batteries (>40°C), the maximum is very flat, if not nonexistent. With cold batteries (<10°C), the voltage may reach the maximum long before the battery is completely charged.

2   *Voltage Threshold*

This approach uses a fixed threshold for the voltage to determine the shut-off point. The disadvantages are similar to those in 1.

3   *Delta T*

The charge is shut off when the actual temperature rises to more than 15°C over the precharging temperature. This approach heats up the batteries unnecessarily, and batteries that are already hot cannot be charged as the temperature rise would destroy the battery.

4   *Time Limit*

This, the simplest approach, shuts off the charging process after a certain period of time. Rapid chargers cannot use this, since the initial condition of the battery is unknown.

The previous generation of BOSCH rapid battery chargers used a negative delta U algorithm. In addition to the low life cycles of the batteries, the large number of possible disturbances caused frequent error shut-offs during operation. The only solution is to not restrict the charge control to just a single parameter, but to combine them. However, due to the complex interdependencies of the parameters, a simple way to combine the parameters does not exist.

For these reasons, BOSCH used fuzzy logic to evaluate the charge condition and to determine the ideal shut-off point. The fuzzy logic system monitors the temperature and voltage signal over time. By that, it estimates inter-

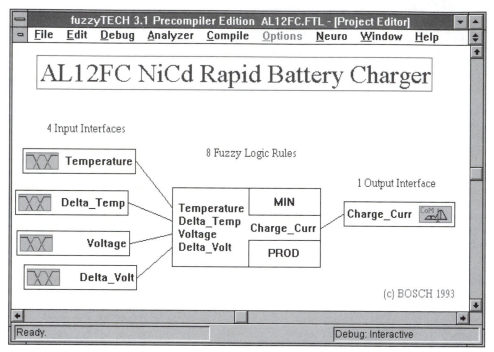

Figure 5.79   Structure of the fuzzy logic system. In total, the fuzzy logic system consists of four inputs, eight rules, and one output.

nal conditions of the chemical charging process. BOSCH implemented the fuzzy logic system on a low-cost 8-bit microcontroller that only provided 2 KB of ROM and 32 Bytes of RAM. The fuzzy logic system uses four input variables, one output, and eight fuzzy logic rules. The computing time is about 10 milliseconds, much faster than required for this application. In addition to the fuzzy logic system, the microcontroller hosts other code that controls LED indicators and self-checks of the charger.

Figure 5.79 shows the structure of the fuzzy logic system while Figure 5.80 plots the linguistic input variable "Temperature" and Figure 5.81 the linguistic variable "Charge_Current." All membership functions use standard-MBFs that can be efficiently computed on a microcontroller. Figure 5.82 lists some of the fuzzy logic rules used in the system, and Figure 5.83 shows the final product.

Using fuzzy logic, the new charger revealed many advantages over the previous one that used a conventional (negative delta U) algorithm:

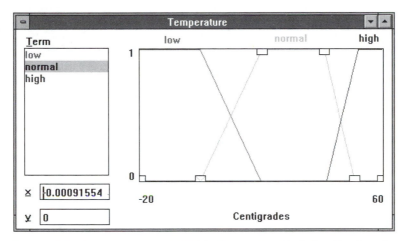

Figure 5.80   The linguistic input variable "Temperature" is defined by three linguistic terms.

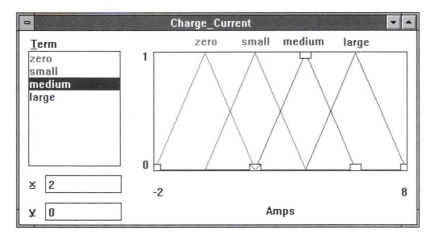

Figure 5.81   The linguistic output variable "Charge_Current" is defined by four linguistic terms.

■ Smaller temperature increase of the NiCd battery during charging. This results from increased charge efficiency.

■ Shorter charge time for the same charge level.

■ No more error shut-offs during charging.

■ The specified temperature range of the charger was extended from 10–45°C to 0–60°C.

Matrix	IF				THEN	
Utilities	Delta_Temp	Delta_Volt	Temperature	Voltage	DoS	Current
1				high	1.00	zero
2			low		1.00	small
3	positiv		normal		1.00	small
4		positiv	normal		1.00	large
5	negativ		high		1.00	small

Spreadsheet Rule Editor

Figure 5.82　Rule base of the fuzzy logic system.

Figure 5.83　The BOSCH fuzzy logic battery charger.

■ The life expectancy of the NiCd batteries used was extended to 3000 cycles.

The methods used in this case study can, in principle, also be used for other types of rechargeable batteries. Also, the discharging process can be monitored and optimized in a similar way. Other applications of fuzzy logic power management include charge gauges that determine the remaining charge of rechargeable batteries. The applications of these power management functions are in electric cars, portable digital assistants, and cellular phones. Applications similar to the one discussed here are shown in [139] and [133].

5.6.2   Controlling Optical Disk Drives

While positioning with servo motors is a typical control task, some applications have very specific demands. The head-positioning control of hard disk drives and optical disk drives is such an application area. This section presents a case study in optical disk drive control (CD) [209]. Applications of fuzzy logic in hard disk drive control are presented in [1] and [212] . The first factor that makes head positioning difficult is the high demand for control precision. The data density of a CD is up to 325,000 bits per square millimeter. The track-to-track distance on a CD is 2 μm. Hence, the head positioning must cover the stroke of 5 cm (2") with a precision of 0.1 μm. This is equivalent to a relative precision of 0.0002%.

A single servo drive cannot implement such precision. Hence, most CD players use a combination of two servo systems. A coarse actuator covers the entire stroke width, while a fine actuator implements a fast response and high resolution. Figure 5.84 shows the layout of such a compound actuator. The control of the compound actuator represents certain difficulties. To reach a certain position, the coarse actuator moves the head until the target position is in reach for the fine actuator. Then the fine actuator positions the head precisely.

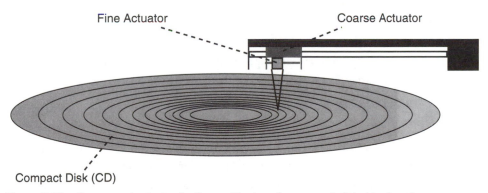

Figure 5.84   Compound actuator for the positioning of a compact disk drive head.

A standard control approach is to make the fine actuator follow the tracking error and make the coarse actuator follow displacement of the two actuators. Because the coarse actuator is slower, it will follow the slower motion and leave the fast movement to the fine one. Most manufacturers that use this control approach tune the PID-like controllers for this entirely by experience [209]. This is partially due to the fact that mathematical models cannot cope with the limited resolution of the low-cost sensors used.

One disadvantage of this approach is that the coarse actuator "blindly" follows the fine actuator. This results in high power consumption for the coarse actuator. To reduce the power consumption for battery-powered CD drives, the cited application uses fuzzy logic for the implementation of heuristic knowledge. In this application, an estimation model determines the position of the coarse actuator and a capacitance sensor measures the position of the fine actuator. Some examples of the engineering heuristics are:

1 If the fine actuator can do the positioning alone, only use the fine actuator.

2 If the target position is out of reach for the fine actuator, only move the coarse actuator.

3 If the distance to the target position is very large, use the estimated position of the coarse actuator for feedback.

4 If the distance to the target position is not very large, use the displacement between the two actuators for coarse feedback.

5 If the fine actuator has reached the end of its stroke, reduce the fine control effort just enough to keep it in position.

To develop the fuzzy logic controller, the optical disk drive was equipped with a laser displacement sensor. This enables verification of control performance in the practical experiments. A comparison of the achieved fuzzy logic solution with the conventional approach proved that the fuzzy logic controller reaches the target position faster and uses less energy on average.

5.6.3 Digital Image Stabilizer for a Camcorder

Many appliances undergo a continuous trend for miniaturization. This is especially true of camcorders (video cameras with integrated VCR) that now fit in the palm of a hand. The small size and weight of these camcorders, however, creates the problem of blurring. One reason for this is the lightness of these camcorders in comparison with earlier generations that rested on the shoulder. To compensate for shaking produced by unstable camera holding, different methods exist:

■ Mechanical systems (inertia)

■ Electromechanical systems (motor-controlled lens)

■ Electronic systems (digital image processing)

The electronic system only records a subarea of the picture frame of the CCD sensor. Moving this subarea against the movement of the camera compensates for the shaking. Figure 5.85 shows an example. The important task here is to determine the motion vector of the camera out of the picture frame of the CCD sensor. This task is difficult since one typically uses camcorders to film scenes with moving objects. Consider a children's playground, where everybody moves around in different directions. How can the camcorder detect which objects to use for orientation?

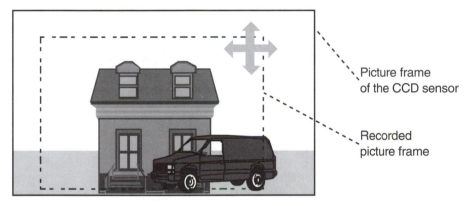

Picture frame
of the CCD sensor

Recorded
picture frame

Figure 5.85   Principle of the electronic image stabilizer using fuzzy logic.

In the following, I will present the solution; Matsushita Corporation of Japan ("Panasonic") uses in its "Palmcorder" products [37]. This approach divides the picture frame area of the CCD sensor into four areas. Each area itself consists of 30 subregions. In each subregion, the algorithm identifies a significant feature. The displacement of this significant feature in the sub-region between two subsequent pictures is computed by signal correlation. The minimum of the displacements in each area results in the area motion vector V_1–V_4 (Figure 5.86). In addition, the algorithm computes two "confidence factors" for each area that express whether the determined motion vector is caused by a moving object or by the motion of the camcorder. One confidence factor describes the consistency of the displacement vectors of the subregions. The other confidence factor describes the change of the area motion vector over time.

The eight confidence factors are inputs to a fuzzy logic system that determines the motion vector of the camcorder, V. Other inputs of the fuzzy logic system are the area motion vectors V_1–V_4 and their differences [178].

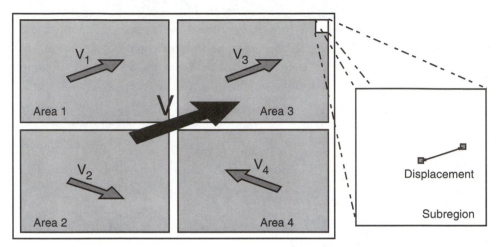

Figure 5.86 Determination of the camcorder motion vector by computing motion vectors of four areas. Each area consists of 30 subregions, where the displacement vectors of the most characteristic feature of the subregion is computed.

Since the computation of the camcorder motion vector must be made 25 times per second, the computing effort for the fuzzy logic system is rather large. The use of standard high-performance processors would involve prohibitive costs. Hence, the entire fuzzy logic system, along with pre- and post-processing, is implemented as an ASIC. The ASIC uses an ad hoc implementation of the fuzzy logic algorithm; that is, it does not contain a general-purpose fuzzy logic computation unit.

The product proved to be a big market success for Matsushita in all countries of the world. However, the product literature for the U.S. and Europe does not mention the fact that fuzzy logic is used. Matsushita feared confusing customers ignorant of fuzzy logic as a technology by using the term "fuzzy" when describing the features of a camera. In Japan, Matsushita touts the fact that fuzzy logic technologies were used and calls the system "fuzzy gyro." I have used the camera myself. It does not compensate for big shakes, but it takes a fair share out of the trembling that occurs as a result of free-hand filming. Recently, most other camcorder manufacturers have introduced similar systems for their top-of-the-line products.

Other camcorder manufacturers also use fuzzy logic in their products. For example, Sanyo Corporation of Japan uses fuzzy logic for its auto-focus and auto-iris systems [110]. Since this application does not require the same fuzzy logic processing power as the image stabilizer, Sanyo uses a software implementation of the fuzzy logic algorithm on an 8-bit microcontroller.

5.6.4   Fuzzy Logic in Climate Control

Especially in Japan, many applications of fuzzy logic exist in building control and climate control. This section demonstrates a case study of a fuzzy logic central climate control system for large buildings [170].

The objective of a climate control system is to keep temperature and humidity at a constant level under varying environmental conditions. A climate control system achieves that by combining three stages (Figure 5.87):

1   Cooling

2   Heating

3   Humidification

To maintain temperature and humidity at constant levels with minimum energy, the controller must set the three stages in accordance with the load of the building and the external weather conditions. This continuous control problem is multiparametric and nonlinear. In addition to this, a large number of constraints and many alternative control strategies exist. Thus, a control solution based on a mathematical process model is too complex.

On the other hand, there is a lot of engineering knowledge on how to control a climate control system under varying conditions. This control strategy also depends on the specific requirements of the building. Some industrial manufacturing buildings require that the humidity be kept within a very small tolerance. In office buildings, the combination of temperature and humidity plays an important role. For these reasons, the cited application uses fuzzy logic to implement the control strategy.

In the first stage, the mix of outside air and return air from the building passes the cooling stage. When the temperature of the air leaving the cooling coil is higher than the dew point of the air entering the coil, it will work almost entirely for cooling. When it is lower, it will work for both cooling and dehumidifying. The second stage can heat up the air. If the cooling coil works in dehumidifying mode, the heating coil works for reheating. If the incoming air is too dry, a steam jet humidifier is used. Since the humidifier cools the air, the heating coils must preheat the air if necessary.

Conventional Control Strategies for Climate Control

Many conventional control strategies for climate control exist. One approach, the so-called dew-point control, uses three unlinked control loops. The first control loop uses a dew-point sensor to control the cooling. The sec-

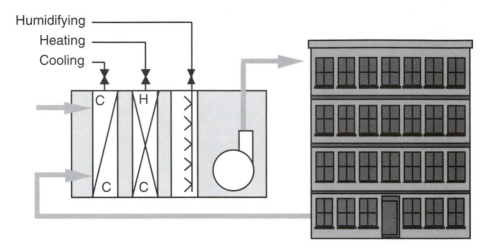

Figure 5.87   Outline of a centralized climate control system. Outside air and return air from the building are mixed and pass the cooling, heating, and humidifying stages.

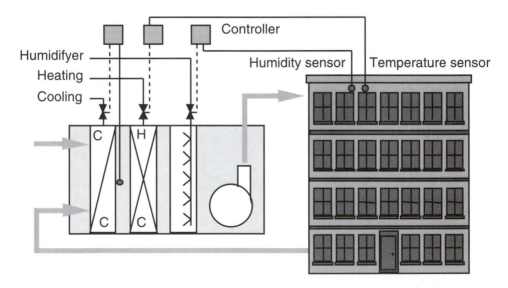

Figure 5.88   The conventional dew-point control strategy uses three independent control loops that each have a sensor.

ond control loop controls the heating coil using room temperature sensors in the building, and the third control loop controls the humidification using humidity sensors in the building. Figure 5.88 outlines the principle of the dew-point controller. This control system is efficient, but not economical in some cases, because all three control loops operate independently. Hence, in some · situations, all three stages can work at the same time.

A possible improvement of the dew-point control is to couple the humidity control loop with the temperature control loop for cooling-valve control. This ensures that the cooling valve opens if both dehumidification and cooling are necessary. Figure 5.89 outlines this. With this improvement, operation is economical, but may be suboptimal in certain situations.

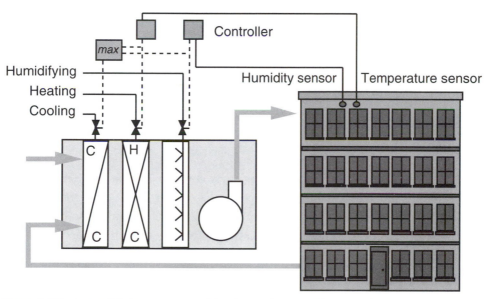

Figure 5.89 A possible improvement of the dew-point control is to couple the humidity control loop with the temperature control loop.

Fuzzy Logic Climate Control

To ensure both high-performance and economical operation, this application uses a fuzzy logic control strategy. The rules of the fuzzy logic system identify the different operational situations and set the valves of the three stages. Figure 5.90 shows the structure of the fuzzy logic system. Inputs are temperature and humidity errors and the actual valve positions. The fuzzy logic system uses a total of 60 rules; most linguistic input variables have three or five terms, most linguistic output variables five terms.

The fuzzy logic rule base contains three types of rules. The first group contains rules that identify the control strategy for simple operating conditions such as pure heating, pure cooling, and pure humidification. The

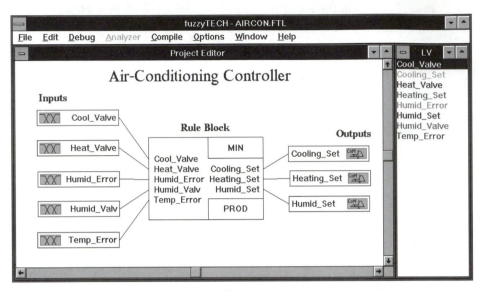

Figure 5.90   Structure of the fuzzy logic climate controller.

second group contains rules that cover complex situations, such as dehumidification. With a third group of rules, the fuzzy logic system identifies operational conditions under which the same performance can be reached with less energy. These rules overwrite the outputs of the second group.

An existing climate control system with a controller as shown in Figure 5.89 served as a testbed for optimization of the fuzzy logic control strategy. One result was that adapting the control strategies to various operational conditions was much easier compared to the conventional controller. Also, the fuzzy logic controller reached a better performance in both energy efficiency and keeping temperature and humidity at a constant level. This is due to the fact that with the tuning of the conventional controller, many compromises had to be made. With the definition of the fuzzy logic control strategy, for each operational condition, the optimal control strategy was definable as an individual fuzzy logic rule. For the exact results, refer to [170]. A similar application for clean rooms is described in [207].

5.6.5   Elevator Group Control

Large high-rise buildings use groups of elevators for interfloor transportation. With these groups of elevators, an intelligent control strategy can minimize the average waiting time for passengers. There are cases in which it is better for an elevator to not stop on a floor, although passengers are waiting there. For the total situation, it may be better to let another elevator service the passengers even though it gets to the floor later.

Figure 5.91 illustrates such a situation. A passenger waits on the fourth floor to go down for four seconds, while other passengers are waiting on the first floor to go up for 28 seconds. Elevator 2 is at the fourth floor going upwards with a passenger inside requesting to stop at the fifth floor. Elevator 3 is at the fifth floor going downwards with a passenger inside requesting to stop at the second and first floors.

Now, even if elevator 3 could get to the passengers on the fourth floor first, the better decision is to let elevator 2 serve the fourth floor passengers, first, because elevator 2 would probably deliver the passengers to their destination faster, which most likely is the first floor. Second, the passengers on the first floor have already been waiting a pretty long time. If elevator 3 were to stop at the fourth floor, they would wait even longer.

To determine the best operating strategy for the elevator group control, a number of information sources exist:

- External calls (passengers request transportation from a certain floor)
- Internal calls (passengers request a stop at a certain floor from the elevator)
- Time of day ("… in the morning from 8 to 10 a.m., most passengers go from the first floor to upper levels …")
- Statistical analyses ("…from the fourth floor, people go to lunch in the sixth-floor cafeteria pretty early …")
- Detection of peak loads ("… it seems that a large meeting just ended on the second floor …")
- Cabin load (also allows detecting how many people enter at each floor)
- Number of pushed call buttons on each floor ("… risky parameter, some people habitually press all buttons …")

With more effort, even more information can be gained. For example, the number of waiting passengers can be approximately determined by a passive infrared sensor.

To come up with a decision model for the optimized control of such elevator groups, mathematical modeling is a prohibitive effort due to the com-

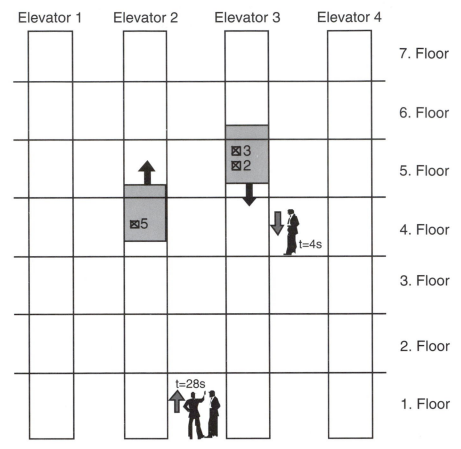

Figure 5.91   Optimizing group elevator control: elevator 3 does not stop at the fourth floor, even though passengers are waiting there.

plexity of the model and the nonlinear relations between the parameters. Also, using a mathematical optimization model, the decision would be too slow. Decisions on whether an elevator should stop at a certain floor or not must be made in fractions of a second.

Also, many parameters and goals can only be defined subjectively rather than by mathematical functions. For example, the primary optimization goal is to not annoy passengers too much. But how do you model "annoyance" mathematically? Figure 5.92 shows the definition of "annoyance" from a Japanese fuzzy logic elevator controller.

In addition to the static control strategy, the elevator control must adapt itself to different buildings and changing situations. An elevator group con-

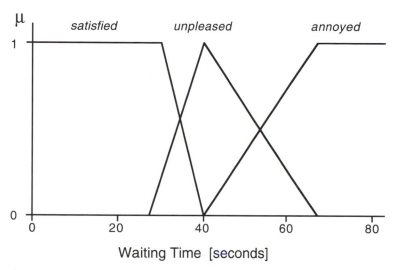

Figure 5.92 Linguistic variable "passenger satisfaction" defined for the waiting time for the elevator.

troller of Toshiba [67] uses NeuroFuzzy techniques. Here, the fuzzy logic rules are predefined in the controller delivered with all elevator group controllers. In a test phase, the NeuroFuzzy system tunes the rule weights of the predefined rules to adapt the controller for the building. To ensure that the NeuroFuzzy system does not train implausible control strategies, meta fuzzy logic rules guide the training process.

5.6.6 Fuzzy Logic in Cameras

The application of fuzzy logic in cameras started with the first application from Canon Corporation of Japan in 1986 [148]. Most manufacturers use fuzzy logic to improve their auto focus and automatic exposure systems. In 1991, Minolta Corporation introduced their first camera in which all control and decision functions use fuzzy logic (Minolta 7xi). Figure 5.93 shows an overview of the various fuzzy-logic-controlled functions.

The fuzzy logic system uses four types of input information:

- ■ Four auto focus sensors (Figure 5.94a)
- ■ 14 metering cells for exposure value calculation (Figure 5.94b); 13 sensors in a honeycomb pattern, one sensor for the background area
- ■ Focal length
- ■ Orientation of the camera (horizontal/vertical)

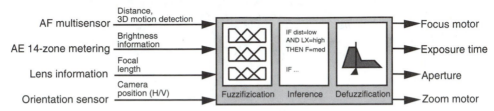

Figure 5.93 Integrated fuzzy logic system for auto focus, automatic exposure, and auto zoom.

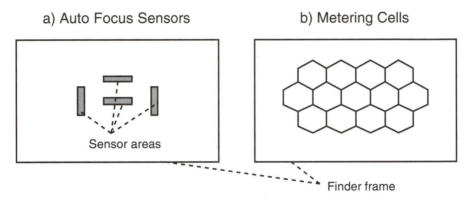

Figure 5.94 Positioning of the sensors in the finder frame.

Auto Focus, Auto Exposure, and Auto Zoom

To determine the best focus and exposure for a photo, the camera must first identify the position, distance, and brightness of the important objects of a picture. First, the "backlighting grade" is computed from the 14 metering segments' outputs and the main subject position from the auto focus sensor. From this backlighting grade and the focal length, the fuzzy logic system determines how the brightness signals of the metering cells are weighted. Other inputs of this fuzzy logic system are how close the objects contained in the segments are. Objects in the foreground and background are weighted differently.

Once the fuzzy logic system has determined focus and exposure, a degree of freedom exists in how the shutter speed and aperture shall be set. Different factors play a role in this decision:

- If the fuzzy logic system finds that interesting objects are both close and far away, the aperture should be closed as much as possible. This increases the depth of field and focuses objects both near and far.

■ The higher the focal length, the higher the risk of blurring. Hence, the larger the focal length, the shorter the shutter speed.

■ If the orientation sensor senses a trembling photographer, the shutter speed should also be short to avoid blurring. Also, shutter time should be reduced when the focus sensors detect fast-moving objects in the picture.

Aside from these major factors, the fuzzy logic system also uses the film characteristics as input. Figure 5.95 shows the exposure area in a two-dimensional plot. The vertical axis shows the aperture, the horizontal axis the shutter speed. All straight lines with a slope of −1 indicate the same exposure value. The first fuzzy logic inference step determines the exposure value. The second fuzzy logic inference step determines the combination of aperture and shutter speed.

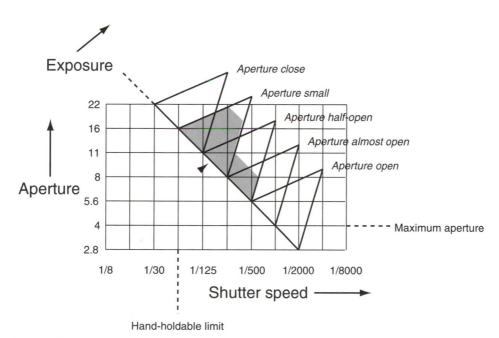

Figure 5.95   The first step of the fuzzy logic inference determines the exposure value, the second step the aperture/shutter speed combination.

The third function of the fuzzy logic system is the auto zoom. In "image size lock" mode, the fuzzy logic system adjusts the focal length automatically and continuously to keep the same image size as at invocation. This function enables taking pictures of moving subjects with constant image size. For this function, the fuzzy logic system analyzes distances and distance changes from the focus sensors to drive the zoom motor.

Minolta claims that the fuzzy-logic-controlled camera realizes significant performance improvements. The experience that the fuzzy logic controller contains delivers a proper camera setting even in nontypical cases. In earlier-generation cameras, many parameters had to be set to compromise values to make sure that picture quality would be reasonable in any possible situation. As the fuzzy logic system can dynamically set the parameters depending on the interpretation of the situation, it delivers improved performance. The nontypical cases are, for example, backlight situations, objects on a water surface, and photos with off-center subjects.

The entire fuzzy logic system runs on a standard microcontroller in the camera. The complete fuzzy logic system uses about 1.3 KB of ROM and requires a computing time of about 4 milliseconds. For the implementation of fuzzy logic systems on standard microcontrollers, refer to Section 3.2.2.

5.6.7   Anesthesia Control Using Fuzzy Logic

Section 5.5.4 already described the application of fuzzy data analysis for cardioanesthesia. For simpler operations, even closed-loop fuzzy logic control of anesthesia exists. Although it looks strange at first glance to consider a human body as a process under control, when you do this, you find some similarities to other processes where fuzzy logic has been successfully applied. The human body is multiparametral, has highly nonlinear behavior and long dead times, and shows time-variant behavior. Hence, useful mathematical models for the human body as a process under control do not exist. However, medical doctors accumulated a lot of experience and knowledge in the past on how to control anesthesia of the human body. Fuzzy logic is an excellent technology for the conversion of this knowledge into a systems solution. The remainder of this section deals with the case study of a closed-loop anesthesia controller using fuzzy logic developed in Bern, Switzerland [101].

The main task for the anesthetist during an operation is to control the depth of the anesthesia. However, the depth of anesthesia cannot be measured directly. Hence, the anesthetist uses indirect information, such as heart rate, blood pressure, pupil size, and motor activity. The anesthesia depth is controlled by medication, such as intravenous drug application and mixture of narcotic gases. A common narcotic gas is isoflurane, mixed in a concentration of 0 to 2% to the oxygen/nitrogen inspiring gas. Figure 5.96 shows the flow and signal diagram of the configuration.

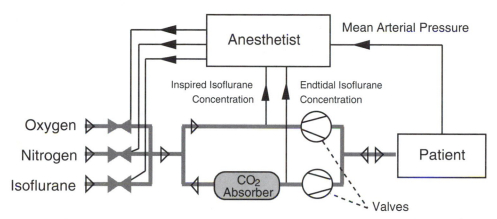

Figure 5.96 Flow and signal diagram of the configuration used during anesthesia. The anesthetist controls narcotic gases and drug application.

The exhaled air is freed of carbon dioxyde, mixed with oxygen, nitrogen, and isoflurane, and recirculated to the patient. Measuring the isoflurane concentration both in the exhaled and inhaled air, the isoflurane concentration in the patient's blood is estimated. From a control engineering view, the task for the anesthetist is to keep the depth of anesthesia between the upper bound W (awakening threshold) and the lower bound E (exitus threshold). These thresholds cannot be defined in a fixed way, and also depend on the patient's condition. Because of the operation itself and changes in the patient's condition, the actual anesthesia depth fluctuates around its set point. If a robust controller can keep these fluctuations small, the set point of anesthesia depth can be set higher, resulting in less strain on the patient. Figure 5.97 shows examples of the anesthesia depth for strong and small fluctuations.

Another reason for the automation of anesthesia is that the anesthetist is freed from the routine control task. This leaves him more time for other tasks, such as drug application, a demanding task with complex operations.

The first automation attempts using PID-type controllers were made around 1960. They were not too successful due to the strong nonlinearities involved in anesthesia control. Later attempts used adaptive controller structures but showed problems with robustness during blood circulation fluctua-

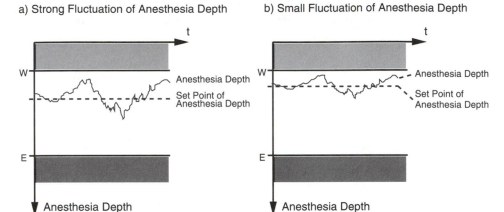

Figure 5.97   Anesthesia depth over time. The upper bound of the anesthesia depth is the awakening threshold, the lower bound the exitus threshold. A robust anesthesia control renders a smaller fluctuation of the anesthesia depth. With that, the set point of anesthesia depth can be chosen to be higher, thus limiting the impact on the patient.

tions. For example, the blood pressure can step up 10 mmHg when cutting the skin with a scalpel.

For these reasons, the cited application uses fuzzy logic control. An additional advantage is that the fuzzy logic controller can use the medical vocabulary directly. This eases development and optimization of the controller, as anesthetists can interpret and understand the system.

A set value for the anesthesia controller is the mean arterial blood pressure as a measure of anesthesia depth. The difference between the set value and the actual measured mean arterial blood pressure is one input of the fuzzy logic system. The other input is the integral of this error signal. The output of the fuzzy logic system is the set value for the isoflurane concentration. A subsequent controller keeps the isoflurane concentration of the inhaled air constant. Figure 5.98 outlines the structure of this control loop. In an experiment, the time derivative of the error signal was used as an input variable, too. However, no improved performance resulted from this.

The first rule set was derived from computer simulation results. To verify and optimize this first prototype during operations, a PC equipped with I/O boards was connected to the instruments in the operating room. During the operation, the anesthesiologist can overwrite the output signal of the fuzzy logic system at any time. Table 5.4 shows the rule set after optimization.

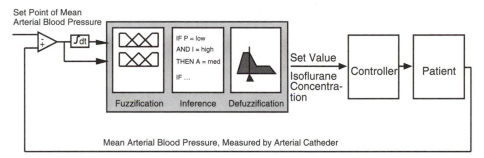

Figure 5.98 Structure of the fuzzy logic anesthesia controller. The anesthetist gives the set point for mean arterial blood pressure. The output of the fuzzy logic system gives the set value for a subsequent controller that controls the isoflurane concentration.

Table 5.4   Rule Set of the Fuzzy Logic Anesthesia Controller

	INPUTS		OUTPUTS
Rule #1	**Difference**	**Intergral of Difference**	**Set Value Isoflurane**
1	NS	–	PS
2	PS	–	NS
3	NB	–	PB
4	PB	–	NB
5	Z	Z	Z
6	Z	PS	NS
7	Z	NS	PS
8	–	NB	PB
9	–	PB	NB

All linguistic variables have five terms each: NB = negative big, NS = negative small, Z = zero, PS = positive small, PB = positive big.

In practical use, automatic control was not begun before an acceptably deep anesthesia was achieved. The field study showed that "normal" operations are handled quite well by the fuzzy logic controller. No adaptive components were necessary for these results. This is a particular advantage of the approach because the performance of adaptive systems is hard to understand. The adaptive component was not necessary because the fuzzy logic controller can cover the entire control space in a nonlinear fashion using fuzzy logic rules. Also, the fuzzy logic solution is easy to extend. Other inputs that give information on the patient's state can be added incrementally to the solution. Similar applications are described in [9, 159, 211].

5.6.8 F/A-18 Automatic Carrier Landing System

A good example of how fuzzy logic can be used to implement a nonlinear control system where the control strategy primarily depends on one input variable is the F/A-18 automatic carrier landing system discussed in [150].

This automatic carrier landing system uses a combination of conventional control modules and six fuzzy logic rule blocks. Each rule base covers a certain aspect of flight control such as roll, sink rate, throttle, lineup, glide slope, and air disturbances. Control variables are the three dimensions of the flight path, the angle of descent, and the approach speed.

Figure 5.99 shows the linguistic variable "Distance" that describes the range from aircraft to carrier. The linguistic variable Distance is contained in the "if-part" of all rules to change the control strategy as the aircraft approaches the deck. The terms of Distance are *far_away*, *in_middle*, *in_close*, and *at_ramp*. The primary control strategies that correspond to the terms of Distance are:

far_away: correct alignment errors

in_middle: correct velocity errors

in_close: compensate ship wake

at_ramp: compensate deck motion

Since all the terms of Distance are defined by overlapping membership functions, the control strategy performs a gradient transition between the rule blocks as the F/A-18 approaches the carrier for landing. For example, roll, sink rate, and throttle rule blocks grade to zero as Distance decreases. The lineup and glide slope rule blocks are concerned with correcting large errors quickly when Distance is *far_away*. When the F/A-18 is halfway through the approach, trends in drift rate are more important than small errors. Thus, when Distance is *at_middle*, the lineup and glide slope rule blocks act to cancel drift in the aircraft lineup. When Distance is *in_close*, static errors become important, and the lineup and glide slope rule blocks apply corrective action, acting to level the aircraft and avoid striking the carrier deck. The sixth rule

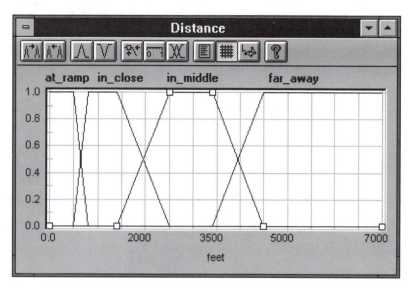

Figure 5.99   Linguistic variable Distance of the F/A-18 automatic carrier landing system from [150].

block deals with the air disturbances over the carrier deck and with carrier deck motion.

A comparison of the fuzzy logic system with the previous conventional solution proved a much better performance of the fuzzy logic controller, especially in keeping an accurate approach path when strong disturbances were present (wind gusts, ship movements, and so forth). A complete fuzzy logic autopilot is described in [27], and the application of fuzzy logic in autonomous underwater vehicles in [149]. Reference [89] describes fuzzy logic steering support for cargo ships. Another application in the area of active flight stability control is discussed in [28].

5.6.9   Other Applications

This section contains other examples of fuzzy logic systems in brief. For more information, refer to the papers cited in the References.

Dust-Adaptive Power Control of a Vacuum Cleaner [165]

You may consider this an example of "high-tech overkill" at first glance. Matsushita Corporation of Japan uses a fuzzy logic system to control the power of the motor in its new generation of vacuum cleaners. In other countries, vacuum cleaners do not even have any electronics. The reason, however, is simple. The vacuum cleaner uses an infrared sensor to measure the dust amount and type, and a pressure sensor to determine the floor type. The fuzzy logic system analyzes the signals and determines the required motor power for this floor. Thus, the vacuum cleaner can save about $22 in energy cost per year for an average home.

Ventilation Control in a Car Tunnel [197]

Toshiba Corporation of Japan uses fuzzy logic to control ventilation and filters in the four-mile-long Higo tunnel near Kyushu. The tunnel is equipped with multiple ventilators and electric dust filters. The inputs of the fuzzy logic system stem from six visibility sensors, two carbon monoxide sensors, five air flow sensors, and two traffic counters. The fuzzy logic system achieves substantial energy savings in operation.

Fuzzy Control of Traffic Lights [62]

To control traffic lights at urban intersections, the cited application uses a fuzzy logic controller with 72 fuzzy logic rules. By evaluating the running traffic, the controller tries establish maximum throughput on the intersection in any condition.

Extra-Corporal Pacemaker [4]

To better adapt the heart-beat rate of a cardiac pacemaker to the condition of the circulation, this application uses a fuzzy logic system. Inputs to the fuzzy logic system are muscle contraction activity, body temperature, and blood oxygen pressure. The build of a mathematical model for such a control problem is impossible, since the reaction of the human body cannot be adequately modeled. On the other hand, there is a lot of experience in how the human body reacts to certain stimuli. This experience was used to design the rule base of the fuzzy logic system. Another similar application is described in [156].

Artificial Heart Control [81]

The replacement of a human heart by an artificial blood pump has been tried over the last 30 years. Up to now, no solution has been found that integrates motor and power supply inside the body. Hence, today artificial blood pumps are mostly used as interim solutions until a donor heart for transplantation is found. The cited application uses an air-driven blood pump inside the body that is powered from the outside. Hence, the fuzzy logic control system is also located outside the human body. Set values of the controller are pump frequency, pump volume in the left and right parts of the heart, and medication. Input variables to the controller are pH-value of the blood, body temperature, arterial pressure, heart chamber pressure, and $O_2/CO_2/N_2$/protein/electrolyte contents of the blood. A similar fuzzy logic application involving a new type of blood pump is under development at the University of Aachen.

Field-Oriented Control of an Induction Machine [90]

This application uses fuzzy logic and neural net techniques to reduce the peak currents that are generated with the direct current pulse width modulations of the three phases. As a result, the motor is driven with a sine wave containing little harmonic waves under varying load situations. Further work done in Taiwan, targeted to control even very quick momentum changes, is described in [93].

Control of a Superconducting Actuator [82]

The position control of a superconducting piston by a magnetic field is strongly nonlinear and influenced by a hysteresis. The application uses a fuzzy-PD controller for which a stability proof is given.

Grasping Force Control of Manipulator Hand [33]

This application uses a fuzzy logic system to control the grasping force of the manipulator hand of a robot. The objective is to grasp different items, hard and soft, with constant force. An important issue is to avoid overshoot, since this can destroy the item.

Fuzzy Logic Control of an Extra-Corporal Circulation System [172]

Dai-Dan Corporation of Japan uses a fuzzy logic system for the blood volume control in an extra-corporal circulation (ECC) system. The fuzzy logic controller is quite complex and uses the input variables: systemic arterial pressure, diastolic pulmonary arterial pressure, venous reservoir height, and its time derivative. A total of 206 fuzzy logic rules use these input variables to control the parameters: volume of the blood flow pump, change in venous reservoir height, and phase change of the occluder opening. The defuzzification of the output variable "venous reservoir height" uses the Mean-of-Maximum method; all other output variables use Center-of-Maximum defuzzification.

Fuzzy Logic Control of a Yeast-Fed Batch Culture [145]

To control the batch production of yeast cultures, this application uses a fuzzy logic controller combined with a PI controller. Control variable is the flow of the feed substrate. A too-low feed rate limits the growth of the yeast bacteria. A too-high feed rate causes the bacteria to produce ethanol (alcohol) as a by-product. This by-product is wanted in the production of beer and wine, but unwanted in the yeast culture. The measured quantity of ethanol in the fermenter is one input variable of the fuzzy logic system.

Fuzzy Logic Heater Control [140]

Omron Corporation of Japan uses a combination of a conventional PI controller and a fuzzy logic controller in a waterboiler. Both controllers work in parallel, and the output is gained as a linear combination of the two controllers' outputs. The idea of this is that the rules of the fuzzy logic controller only intervene if the temperature error signal is very high. For small error signals, only the PI controller has an effect. The combined controller shows significantly improved performance with strong disturbances of the water flow and strong temperature errors.

Fuzzy PID Controller for Active Magnetic Bearings [83]

Active magnetic bearings are used in applications where high rotating speeds or minimum friction are necessary. These applications include turbo-molecular pumps, flywheels for energy storage, reaction wheels for attitude control of satellites, main shafts of electric motors of tool machines, and turbo compressors. Due to the nonlinear characteristics of the active magnetic bearing, conventional control solutions do not perform completely satisfactorily. In the cited application, direct fuzzy logic control (Figure 5.1), fuzzy logic adaptation of PID parameters (Figure 5.5), and fuzzy logic intervention (Figure 5.6) are compared.

Phase-Change Material Cooling System [49]

To utilize inexpensive electrical energy during the night for air conditioning systems, Mitsubishi Atomic Power Industries of Japan in this application uses a phase change material (PCM) which stores heat. Overnight, or when excessive capacity of the cooling unit is available, the PCM is chilled down in a storage tank. During the day, or when the air conditioning exceeds the capacity of the cooling unit, the stored heat is used. To control the different operation modes with maximum energy efficiency, Mitsubishi uses a fuzzy logic control approach.

Image Processing for a Driverless Transport System [71]

Fujitsu Corporation of Japan uses a combination of conventional image processing algorithms and fuzzy logic for the control of a driverless transport system. The image processing system delivers the information on the track to follow and obstacles; the fuzzy logic system implements the strategy to command the vehicle. A survey on autonomous operating vehicles and robots is contained in [136]. Another vision-guided autonomous mobile vehicle is described in [23].

Mixing Faucet Using Fuzzy Logic [177]

Matsushita Corporation of Japan showed a prototype of a mixing faucet controlled by fuzzy logic. In contrast to a mechanical system, the fuzzy-logic-controlled system delivers the set temperature much faster. The resulting savings on hot water justify the higher cost of the electronic unit versus the mechanical one. In comparison to a PID-controlled mixing faucet, the fuzzy logic controller in addition eliminates any overshoot, even in cases where the water pressure fluctuates. This avoids any scalding in difficult operation states.

Stabilization of Multimachine Power Systems [57]

To stabilize load fluctuations, this application uses a fuzzy logic system to control the excitation voltage of power generators. Excitation control is a very fast way of influencing a generator's output power. The fuzzy logic system analyzes the load fluctuations in the main's supply and adjusts the excitation voltages of the generators to compensate for the fluctuations.

Fuzzy-Logic-Based Banknote Transfer Control [143]

Oki Corporation of Japan uses a fuzzy logic system for banknote transfer control. These devices are used in automatic teller machines and cash dispensers. The fuzzy logic system drives a step motor that controls the gap between a feed roller and a gate roller. In comparison to the previous conventional solution, the fuzzy-logic-controlled system lowers the chance of the banknotes getting jammed.

Minimizing Vibrations in Step Motor Control [130]

Step motors are often used for positioning since the current position can be determined by counting the number of pulses applied to the motor, avoiding the cost of a position sensor. However, in continuous operation with changing momentum, the movement becomes jerky. To avoid this, Mycom Corporation of Japan uses a fuzzy logic controller that modifies the phase control of the motor driver. Mycom uses this controller for pen plotters.

Glass Melting Furnace Temperature Control [8]

Temperature control of glass-melting furnaces is a difficult task. One reason for this is the long dead times in the control loop. In addition, the temperature of the glass cannot be measured directly. In the cited application, Nippon Electric Glass Corporation of Japan uses a fuzzy logic system to estimate the glass temperature on the basis of the existing sensors. On the basis of this temperature estimation, a second fuzzy logic system controls the furnace. This structure is similar to the one of the anti-skid steering systems shown in Figure 5.33. The fuzzy logic controller has been in continuous use in two glass-melting furnaces in Japan since 1989.

Blood Glucose Control for Diabetics [73]

A conventional approach to controlling continuous insulin dosing uses conventional PD controllers. In field tests it was shown that this controller type is not capable of keeping the command value for the blood glucose level within the tolerance for some patients. This is mostly due to the long dead time of the control loop. The cited application uses other input variables such as information on food intake in a fuzzy logic system to process this information.

Control of Shield Tunneling Machines

Okumura Corporation of Japan uses a fuzzy logic system for the control of shield tunneling machines. Shield tunneling machines are used to construct water pipe systems, sewage pipe systems, electric main supplies, and subway systems. In comparison to human operator control, the fuzzy-logic-controlled system had smaller deviations from the desired position of the tunnel.

Fuzzy Control of Jet Engines [63]

The cited paper treats the application of fuzzy logic to jet engine control. The total rule set contains 35 rules and controls burner fuel flow and nozzle area. Inputs to the fuzzy logic system are engine operation mode, surge margin, blowout margin, fan speed, burner pressure, and turbine exit gas temperature. Simulation studies show that the fuzzy logic controller performs extremely well in both steady state and transient conditions.

6

Fuzzy Design Cookbook

In Chapter 2, I described the basic technology of fuzzy logic systems. In this chapter, I treat in detail how you can develop a fuzzy logic system for your application. I will present the development methodology that has been used with the majority of recent successful applications. Standard software development tools such as the *fuzzy*TECH design tool, which I described in Section 3.1, also support this methodology. Figure 6.1 provides an overview of the development steps.

Step 1: System Design

In the first development step you design the system by:

- Creating the linguistic variables of the system. The linguistic variables are the "vocabulary" of the system in which the rules work.

- Designing the structure of the system. The structure represents the information flow within the system; that is, what input variables are combined with which other variables via rule blocks and so on.

- Formulating the control strategy as fuzzy logic rules. These are the "guts" of the system containing the engineering knowledge.

- Selecting the appropriate defuzzification method for your application.

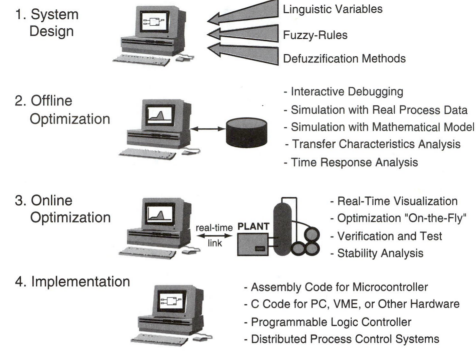

1. System Design

Linguistic Variables

Fuzzy-Rules

Defuzzification Methods

2. Offline Optimization

- Interactive Debugging
- Simulation with Real Process Data
- Simulation with Mathematical Model
- Transfer Characteristics Analysis
- Time Response Analysis

3. Online Optimization

real-time link   **PLANT**

- Real-Time Visualization
- Optimization "On-the-Fly"
- Verification and Test
- Stability Analysis

4. Implementation

- Assembly Code for Microcontroller
- C Code for PC, VME, or Other Hardware
- Programmable Logic Controller
- Distributed Process Control Systems

Figure 6.1   Development methodology for fuzzy logic systems in four steps.

Step 2: Offline Optimization

In the second development step, you simulate and test the prototype designed in the first step. The technologies that you use here depend very much on the application type. The offline optimization step is completely supported with state-of-the-art software development tools. You can either use prerecorded data from the process or a process simulation written in a programming language. Refer to Section 3.1.2 for more details on offline optimization methods. In this step, you can also use NeuroFuzzy techniques to optimize a system. All techniques used in the second development step are offline; that is, you work on the PC with no connection to a running process in real-time.

Step 3: Online Optimization

For certain closed loop control systems you cannot use simulation techniques because no good mathematical model for the process exists. With some of these, the use of prerecorded process data is of limited use since the reaction of the system in realtime to the fuzzy logic controller output is not fed back into the process. In this case, you can use online optimization techniques that support "on-the-fly" modifications on a running system. Refer to Section 3.1.2 for more details online optimization methods.

Step 4: Implementation

After completion, you can implement the fuzzy logic system on your target hardware platform. Depending on the target hardware, different implementation techniques exist. Refer to Section 3.2 for more details on implementation alternatives.

In the remainder of this chapter, I will concentrate on the first development step. Section 6.1 treats the definition of linguistic variables and membership functions, Section 6.2 deals with the creation of a rule base, and Section 6.3 helps you to identify the appropriate defuzzification method for your application. Section 6.4 contains a few remarks on verification and stability analysis of fuzzy logic systems.

6.1   Definition of Linguistic Variables

Section 2.3 already explained the concept of linguistic variables. In this Section, I will show you how to set up linguistic variables for a given application.

Basic Terminology

The possible values of a linguistic variable are "linguistic terms," mostly just referred to as "terms." These terms are linguistic interpretations of technical figures. For example, the technical figure "Distance," which is measured in yards, can have the linguistic interpretations {far, medium, close, zero, too_far}. The technical figure described by a linguistic variable is called the "base variable" in fuzzy logic design.

How Many Terms for a Linguistic Variable?

The first design decision to make when creating a linguistic variable is to choose the number of terms to be defined. Most applications use between three and seven terms for each linguistic variable. Rarely does one use fewer than three terms, since most concepts in human language consider at least the two extremes and the middle between them. On the other hand, one rarely uses more than seven terms because humans interpret technical figures using their short-term memory. The human short-term memory can only compute up to seven symbols at a time.

Another observation is that linguistic variables often have an odd number of terms. This is due to the fact that most linguistic variables are defined symmetrically, where one term describes the middle between the extremes. Hence, most fuzzy logic systems use either three, five, or seven terms.

To determine whether to use three, five, or seven terms, different approaches exist:

- ■ Formulate a few typical fuzzy logic rules. With that you get a good idea of which terms, and how many, you need to define the complete rule base.

- ■ If advance formulation of rules is difficult, you can start your design by defining three terms for each linguistic input variable and five terms for each linguistic output variable. Experience shows that this is the minimum number of terms for most applications. You can add new terms as you need them in later design steps.

Membership Functions

The degree to which the value of a technical figure satisfies the linguistic concept of the term of a linguistic variable is called degree of membership. For a continuous variable, this degree is expressed by a mathematical function called membership function (MBF). The membership functions map each value of the technical figure to the membership degree in the linguistic terms. Usually, one draws the membership functions for all terms in the same diagram as shown in Figure 6.2.

Standard Membership Functions

Many different shapes of membership functions are proposed in scientific literature. However, most practical implementations only use so-called "Standard Membership Functions" (Standard-MBFs). Four different types of Standard-MBFs exist: Z-type, Λ-type (lambda), Π-Type (pi), and S-type. Figure 6.3 sketches these four types. Standard-MBFs are also normalized; that is, their maximum is always $\mu = 1$, their minimum $\mu = 0$.

The linguistic variable plotted in Figure 6.2 uses three types of Standard-MBFs (Z-, Λ-, Λ-, Λ-, and S-type). Standard-MBFs have a number of advantages. First, they are the simplest functions that are sufficient to design most

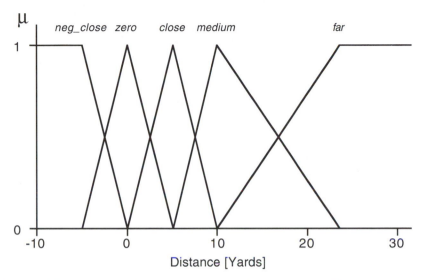

Figure 6.2   Membership functions of all terms of a linguistic variable.

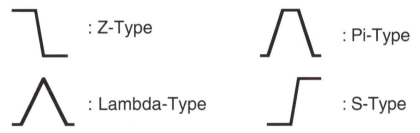

Figure 6.3   Standard membership functions.

fuzzy logic systems. Second, they always remain easy to interpret. Third, the implementation of Standard-MBFs is computationally very efficient on most target hardware platforms. To define Standard-MBFs, follow these four easy steps:

Definition of Standard Membership Functions

Step 1

For each term, define the value that best fits the linguistic meaning of the term. This most typical value for each term gets the membership degree $\mu = 1$.

Step 2

For each term set the membership degree $\mu = 0$ where the terms next to it have their most typical value.

Step 3

Connect the point $\mu = 1$ with the points $\mu=0$ by straight lines. This results in membership functions of Λ-type for the inner terms.

Step 4

No terms lie beyond the rightmost term nor below the leftmost term; thus, points in these regions belong to the respective membership functions with $\mu = 1$.

Figure 6.4 illustrates the four steps for the term "zero." Three values define the Λ-type membership function: the typical value for "zero" defines the point $\mu = 1$, the typical values for "neg_close" and "close" define the points $\mu = 0$.

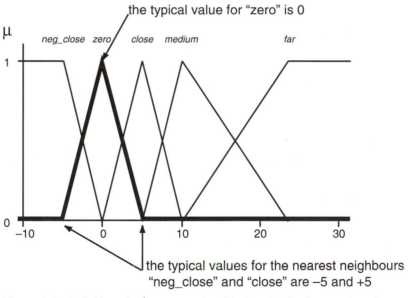

Figure 6.4   Definition of a Λ-type membership function for the term "zero."

In some applications, the typical value of a term is an interval rather than a value. If, for example, you consider any position ±2 yards from 0 to be completely "zero," define a Π-type membership function as shown in Figure 6.5.

Note that the edges of the Standard-MBFs do not correspond to edges in the transfer characteristic. Standard-MBFs are sufficient for most control applications and many other applications. However, for more complex data

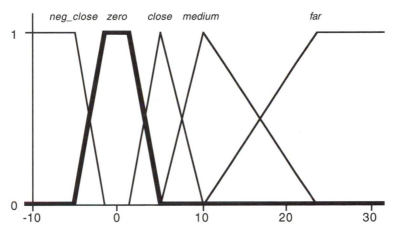

Figure 6.5   Definition of a Π-type membership function for the term "zero."

analysis and decision support applications, spline membership functions proved better performance.

Spline Membership Functions

Standard MBFs are only an approximation of the way humans linguistically interpret real values. Psycholinguistic studies have shown that membership functions should follow a set of axioms:

- ■ *μ(x) is continuous over X.*
  A small change of the base variable value cannot result in a step in its evaluation.

- ■ *d(μ(x))/dx is continuous over X.*
  A small change of the base variable value cannot result in a step in its evaluation rate.

- ■ *d²(μ(x))/dx² is continuous over X.*
  Necessary for the following axiom.

- ■ *μ(x): min$_\mu$ (max$_X$ (d² (μ(x))/dx²)).*
  The change of slope is minimal.

where μ is the membership degree, μ(x) is the membership function, and *X* is the universe of the base variable.

These axioms are satisfied by the interpolative cubic spline function. To use them for membership function definitions, you follow the same steps as with Standard MBFs. The only difference is that you use the cubic spline function (S-shape) to connect the $\mu = 0$ and $\mu = 1$ points rather than straight lines. Figure 6.6 shows such a definition for the variable Distance of Figure 6.4.

Other Membership Function Definitions

Quite a few other types of membership functions are proposed in scientific literature. Some examples are:

- Analytical functions, such as $1/(x_0-x)^2$. These functions have been proposed because of certain mathematical properties. However, membership functions shall represent human intuition, not mathematics.

- Stochastic functions, such as the Gaussian distribution. Proposed primarily by those who want to link statistics and fuzzy logic. However, membership functions shall represent linguistic fuzziness, not stochastic uncertainty.

- Empirical functions. These are membership functions that have been defined using an empirical approach to derive a membership function for a certain term out of a simulated decision process [220]. This approach is of prohibitive effort for most applications.

- Piecewise linear functions. During optimization it is sometimes useful to approximate an empirical function with a piecewise linear function.

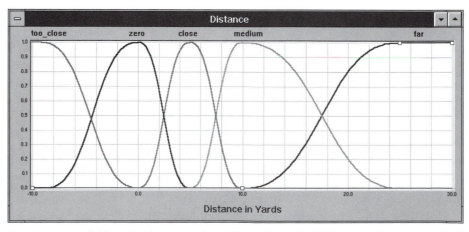

Figure 6.6   Definition of S-shape membership function for Distance.

In current practical applications, none of these types of membership functions play any significant role. Whenever they have been used, they could have been replaced with L-shape or S-Shape functions. For more details on membership functions refer to [221, p. 344].

Membership Functions for Output Variables

Everything presented so far deals only with membership function definitions for input variables of a fuzzy logic system. For output variables, most applications only use Λ-type membership functions. Here, the $\mu = 1$ and $\mu = 0$ points are defined the same way as described before. For the rightmost and leftmost membership functions, a symmetrical membership function is defined.

6.2   Creation of a Fuzzy Logic Rule Base

The rules of a fuzzy logic system represent the knowledge of the system. They use linguistic variables as the vocabulary to express the control strategy of a fuzzy logic controller. This section explains how you define the rules for your application.

Normalized Rule Representation

Normalized fuzzy logic rules only allow for the AND operator in their precondition. The rule:

IF A = a OR B = b THEN C = c

converts to the two rules:

(1) IF A = a THEN C = c
(2) IF B = b THEN C = c

As this example shows, you may need more normalized rules to represent a certain context than rules that use any logical operator. In spite of this, most fuzzy logic applications use only normalized rule bases. The advantage of using normalized rules is that the rule base is much easier to comprehend. Consider a fuzzy logic system with 10 of the following rules:

IF ((Temp = very_high) AND NOT ((Press = above_norm) OR (Antech_Press = low)) AND (O2_Frac = NOT normal)) THEN (CH4_Val = throttled AND Carb = low)

Such a rule base is very difficult to comprehend, especially during optimization. Using normalized rules instead, even systems with some 100 fuzzy logic rules remain lucid (see Section 5.2.2). Also, state-of-the-art fuzzy logic software tools optimize the rule base automatically, so the computational efficiency of a normalized rule base is even better.

Definition of a Rule Block

In a fuzzy logic system, rules are structured in blocks. For small systems with few input variables, follow these four easy steps to define the rules of each rule block:

Definition of Rules

Step 1

For each combination of terms of the variables in the if-part of the rule, define one rule. Select a DoS (degree of support) of 1 for these rules. Select the most plausible term for the then-part of the rule. If you have three input variables and one output variable with five terms each, this totals 125 rules.

Step 2

If a certain output variable term does not depend on one input variable, define a rule where this input variable is not included (don't care rule).

Step 3

During optimization you may find that the effect of certain rules is too high or too low. Modify the DoS to express the relative importance of the rules.

Step 4

Once the system works fine, you have to remove unnecessary rules. There are two kinds of unnecessary rules:

1 Redundant rules
2 Rules that never fire

Redundant rules are those that have no impact in the system. Consider rule #1, "IF In1 = low AND In2 = medium THEN Out = high," and rule #2, "IF In1 =l ow THEN Out = high." Here, rule #1 is redundant and can be removed. Rules that never fire are rules where the if-part describes a situation as a combination of input variable values which never occurs. These rules are hard to identify as the occurrence of certain situations also depends on the system under control. However, software development tools that support statistical analyzers can support the identification of such rules [116].

Although this approach works fine with small systems, with large systems, Step 1 can be of prohibitive effort because of too large a number of rules. Here, you first implement rules that use only one or two of the input variables. These rules cover much larger subspaces in the control space. Later, you refine this coarse strategy by adding the other rules.

6.3   Comparison of Defuzzification Methods

The result of the fuzzy logic inference is the value of a linguistic variable. Consider the output variable "Steering" of the anti-skid steering system presented in Section 5.3.4. The terms of Steering are: {strong_left, left, straight, right, strong_right}. A possible inference result could be {0, 0, 0.3, 0.8, 0}, linguistically expressed as "pretty much right, just slightly straight." The conversion of such a linguistic result to a real value, representing the steering angle that the steering servo shall carry out, is called defuzzification. I introduced the basic principle in Section 2.3. Here, I will compare different methods and identify the requirements of different application areas.

Requirements for Defuzzification Methods

The objective of a defuzzification method is to derive the non-fuzzy (crisp) value that best represents the fuzzy value of the linguistic output variable. Similar to the different membership function types, different methods for defuzzification exist. To select the proper defuzzification method, you need to understand the linguistic meaning that underlies the defuzzification process.

Best Compromise vs. Most Plausible Result

Experience shows that two different linguistic meanings of defuzzification are of practical importance:

- Determine the "best compromise."

- Determine the "most plausible result."

One defuzzification method is the Center-of-Maximum (CoM) method already described in Section 2.3. CoM first determines the most typical value for each term and then computes the best compromise of the fuzzy logic inference result. Example 9 and Figure 6.7 illustrate this for the linguistic variable Steering.

Example 9

Let the most typical values for the terms of the linguistic variable Steering be:

strong_right	−30°
right	−15°
straight	0°
left	15°
strong_left	30°

Let the fuzzy logic inference result be:

$$\{0, 0, 0.3, 0.8, 0\}$$

To obtain the best compromise value for the result of the fuzzy logic inference (right with 0.8, straight with 0.3) as a real number, the inference results are considered "weights" at the positions of the most typical values of the terms. The best compromise is where the defuzzified (crisp) value balances the weights. In Figure 6.7 the value (result of defuzzification) is −12°.

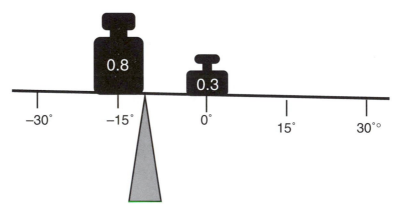

Figure 6.7   The Center-of-Maximum defuzzification method balances out the fuzzy logic inference result.

In some cases, this defuzzification approach does not work. Consider the example shown in Figure 6.8. The straight direction is blocked, while the paths to the right and left are open.

In such a situation, the result of the fuzzy logic inference is that no evidence exists suggesting that the car should go straight, while equal amounts of non-zero evidence call for both a right and left turn. Figure 6.9 shows this

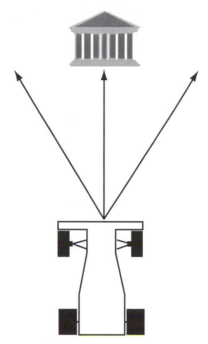

Figure 6.8   Driving situation in which the pathway is blocked straight ahead, but open to the left and right.

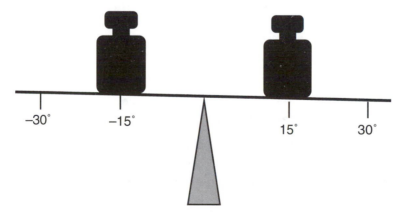

Figure 6.9   Possible inference result for the situation in Figure 6.8.

result. If you use the Center-of-Maximum method for defuzzification, the "best compromise" is to go straight. Why does the defuzzification fail so drastically here? To find out why, consider Example 10 which demonstrates how humans handle such decisions.

Example 10

Consider yourself driving a car with your spouse and your mother-in-law. You do not know the neighborhood, and both your spouse and your mother-in-law give you directions. Now, the road on which you are driving ends in another road with no pathway straight ahead.

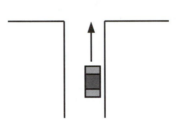

What if your spouse says you should turn right while your mother-in-law wants you to turn left? The compromise, to go straight, is no good as a solution here.

Here, the best compromise as illustrated in Figure 6.9 is clearly not the method of choice. In Example 10, you want the "most plausible result." One defuzzification method that delivers the "most plausible result" is the "Mean-of-Maximum" method (MoM). Rather than balancing out the different inference results, MoM selects the typical value of the term that is most valid. For the situation shown in Figures 6.8 and 6.9, the defuzzification result would only be either −15° or +15°, whatever term is more valid.

Center-of-Area Defuzzification Method

The first closed-loop control application of fuzzy logic [39] used a different defuzzification, the so-called Center-of-Area (CoA) method, sometimes called Center-of-Gravity. This method first cuts the membership function at the degree of validity of the respective term. The areas under the resulting functions of all terms are then superimposed. Balancing the resulting area gives the compromise value. For the example of Figure 2.11, Figure 6.10 shows the defuzzification of the same result using Center-of-Area defuzzification. Note that the results are different.

There are some implausibilities in the Center-of-Area method. Consider the linguistic variable defined in Figure 6.11a. If an inference result of

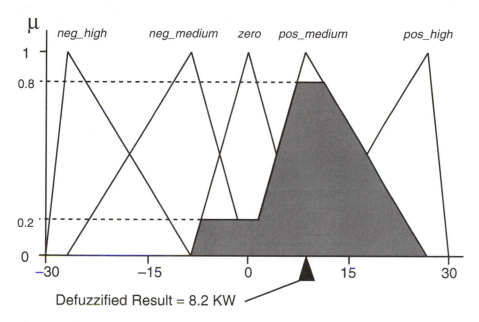

Figure 6.10   "Center-of-Area" defuzzification method.

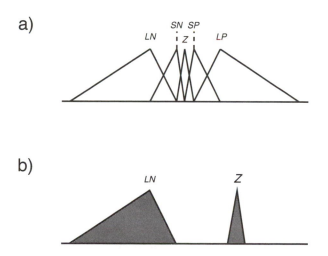

Figure 6.11   Implausibilities in Center-of-Area defuzzification. With a linguistic variable defined as in part **a**, the term LN would have a much greater impact in a defuzzification than term Z.

$\mu_{LN} = \mu_Z = 1$ should be defuzzified as shown in Figure 6.11b, the term LN has a much greater impact than the term Z due to the larger area under the membership function of the term LN. However, the only reason the area under LN is larger is that the best-fit values of the neighboring terms are further apart than for Z.

Another disadvantage of the Center-of-Area defuzzification method is its high computational effort. The center of the area is computed by numerical integration that can take up to 1000 times longer than the computation of the center of the maximum, depending on the resolution and type of processor. For these reasons, most software development tools and fuzzy logic processors use an approximation of CoA, the so-called fast-CoA. Fast-CoA computes the individual areas under the membership functions during compilation to avoid numerical integration during runtime. This approach neglects the overlapping of the areas; hence, it is only an approximation of the "real" CoA.

There are also variants of the Mean-of-Maximum defuzzification method. They differ from MoM by the computation of the most typical value of a membership function. For Λ-type membership functions, the most typical value is uniquely defined. For Π-type membership functions, variants are possible (Figure 6.12). They have gained very little practical relevance, as one can achieve the same result by shifting the membership function.

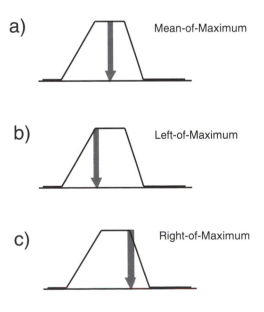

Figure 6.12   Variants of MoM: LoM and RoM.

Comparison of the Defuzzification Methods

Table 6.1compares the three presented defuzzification methods CoA/CoG, CoM, and MoM. Depending on the application, either CoM or MoM shall be used.

Table 6.1   Comparison of Different Defuzzification Methods

	Center-of-Area (CoA, CoG)	Center-of-Maximum (CoM)	Mean-of-Maximum (MoM)
Linguistic Characteristic	"Best compromise"	"Best compromise"	"Most plausible solution"
Fit with Intuition	Implausible with varying MBF shapes and strong overlap of MBFs	Good	Good
Continuity	Yes	Yes	No
Computational Efficiency	Very low	High	Very high
Applications	Control, decision support, data analysis	Control, decision support, data analysis	Pattern recognition, decision support, data analysis

An important property of defuzzification methods is continuity. The definition of continuity is as follows.

Consider a fuzzy logic system with a complete set of rules (for each combination of input variables, at least one rule fires) and overlapping membership functions. A defuzzification method is continuous if an infinitesimally small change of an input variable can never cause an abrupt change in any output variable.

CoM and CoA/CoG methods are continuous, while MoM/LoM/RoM are discontinuous. This is due to the fact that the "best compromise" can never jump to a different value for a small change of the inputs. On the other hand, there is always a point where the "most plausible solution" jumps to a different value. In the example shown in Figures 6.8 and 6.9 this means there will be a point at which an arbitrary small change in the inputs will cause the decision to turn to the other side.

Which Defuzzification for What Application?

The continuity property is important for most closed-loop control applications. If the output of a fuzzy logic system directly controls a variable of the process, jumps in the output variable of a fuzzy logic controller can cause instabilities and oscillations. Hence, most closed-loop control applications use CoM defuzzification. Only when the output of the fuzzy logic system proceeds to an integrator first is MoM a possible alternative (Figure 5.2). In this case, the integrator keeps the control variable continuous.

Pattern recognition applications mostly use MoM defuzzification. If you want to identify objects by classification of a sensor signal, you are interested in the most plausible result. Some applications do not even use any defuzzification at all. The vector of membership degrees for the output linguistic variable is the result of the classification because it gives the similarity of the signal to the objects. Section 5.5 presents the techniques used for fuzzy logic data analysis in more detail.

In decision support systems, the choice of defuzzification method depends on the context of the decision. Use CoM for quantitative decisions, such as budget allocation or project prioritization. Use MoM for qualitative decisions, such as credit card fraud detection or credit worthiness evaluation.

Information Reduction by Defuzzification

Mathematically, defuzzification is the mapping of a vector (value of the linguistic variable) to a real number (crisp value). This mapping is not unique, that is, different values of a linguistic variable can map to the same defuzzified crisp value (Example 11). In cases #1– #3, the result of the defuzzification is the same even though they come from different linguistic values.

Example 11

Let OUT be a linguistic variable with the terms {LN; SN; Z; SP; LP}. Consider the following three values of OUT:

#1: {0; 0; 0.7; 0; 0}

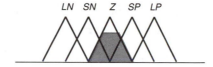

#2: {0; 0.3; 0; 0.3; 0}

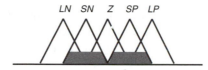

#3: {0.8; 0; 0; 0; 0.8}

All three values of the linguistic variable would be defuzzified to the same crisp value by CoA/CoM defuzzification methods.

This example shows that the defuzzification step involves a reduction of information. Although the "best compromise" is the same for all three linguistic variable values, the three cases are not the same. In case #1 the best compromise was very clear, while in #3 much more in conflict.

For most technical fuzzy logic applications this is no problem, and information about the unequivocalness of the defuzzified result is not useful. In decision support applications, this is different. Here, advanced defuzzification methods exist, especially to rank membership functions [175, 220].

Practical Experience with Defuzzification Methods

■ In practical applications, the only difference between defuzzification methods is whether they deliver the best compromise (CoM, CoA, CoG) or the most plausible result (MoM, LoM, RoM).

■ Within these groups, no relevant differences exist that cannot be equalized by modifying membership functions or rules.

■ Complex membership function shapes do not deliver better results for output variables. Use only Λ-type membership functions. CoM and MoM defuzzification methods only use the maximum of the membership functions anyway.

■ In closed-loop control, use only CoM defuzzification. Exceptions are situations in which the output of the fuzzy logic system proceeds to an integrator or in cases such as described in Figures 6.8 and 6.9.

■ The widespread use of CoA/CoG defuzzification has historical reasons. Depending on the overlap and different areas of the membership functions, CoA/CoG can deliver implausible results. Use CoM instead.

■ Some applications use CoA defuzzification with singleton membership functions. This is completely the same as CoM defuzzification with any membership function type.

■ Fast-CoA, which is used in most software tools and fuzzy logic processors, is equal to a weighted CoM defuzzification.

6.4 Stability and Verification of Fuzzy Logic Systems

Many critics of fuzzy logic claim wrongly that there is no such thing as a stability proof for fuzzy logic systems in closed-loop control. Some of these criticisms stem even from a sound scientific background. In some countries, the discussion about fuzzy logic and stability analysis has almost turned into a "religious war." Let me give you some of the more practical facts on the topic here. For an excellent general treatment of this story, refer to [97, p. 341].

Stability Proof for Fuzzy Logic Controller: The Good News

There is good news and bad news for those who ask whether a stability proof for fuzzy logic controllers exists. First the good news: of course, such a stability proof exists. Now the even better news: stability theory of conventional control completely suffices for fuzzy logic systems.

If you try to define mathematically what a fuzzy logic system is, you could state that it is a mapping of an input space $\Re^n$ into an output space $\Re^m$ with the following properties:

- *Deterministic*

  (the same input condition always results in the same output condition)

- *Time Invariant*

  (the transfer function describing the mapping does not change over time)

- *Nonlinear*

  (the output variables are no linear combination of the input variables)

Control theory classifies such a system as a "nonlinear multivariable controller" or "multiband controller." Hence, all stability analysis methods applicable to these controller types are applicable to fuzzy logic controllers as well.

However, due to the complex nonlinearities of a fuzzy logic system, an analytical solution is often impossible in most cases. This is no limitation, since fuzzy logic development tools offer links to process simulation software such as Mathlab/Simulink, VisSim and Matrixx which support numerical stability analysis (refer to Section 3.1 for more details). On the other hand, analytical stability analysis is also impossible for conventional controllers with a similar degree of complexity.

Also, there is a fair amount of research on a stability theory dedicated to fuzzy logic systems. In this scientific discipline, researchers try to establish general stability proofs for fuzzy logic systems. The methods developed so far are only applicable to very simple fuzzy logic controller architectures. Hence, this fuzzy stability theory has no practical relevance yet. On the other hand, it is a hot topic in the control theory research community. If you are interested in this work, start with[92, 95, 161, 162] and the literature cited herein.

Now the Bad News

In most engineering applications, stability analysis plays a minor role—regardless of whether these applications use fuzzy logic or conventional control techniques. Some theoreticians claim that this is due to the fact that most practitioners do not have enough background in control theory to properly conduct stability analysis. Even though this may be true sometimes, in most cases the explanation is much simpler. To do stability analysis, you need a mathematical model of the process under control. For a reliable stability analysis, the model must be very accurate. The problem is that for only a small fraction of complex applications is building such a model possible with reasonable effort.

To illustrate the role of stability analysis in industry, let me quote a friend of mine who develops closed-loop control systems for fighter airplanes:

"Every engineer who went from the campus directly into management requires us to prove stability for all control systems we design. Also, Government and the FAA require these analyses. However, the mathematical models we developed for our systems under control do not suffice to implement model-based controllers just from them. Hence, we develop most of our controllers from experience and optimize them in test flights. Likewise, the quality of our mathematical models is also not sufficient to do a sound stability proof, even though we are required to do a stability proof. So we do them and use our limited mathematical models and reference all premises and restrictions of the model. We have never had to discuss with our management or the FAA whether these premises are reasonable or not. On the other hand, the control systems we design are very stable. Our experience allows us to also evaluate the stability by experiments and test flights."

Here is another potential benefit of fuzzy logic design. In a fuzzy logic system, the individual rules represent local behavior. That is, each fuzzy logic rule describes the reaction to a certain situation. Such a situation could be one in which "high temperature AND low conversion AND medium pressure" occurs. If you encounter stability problems in this situation, you modify the respective rule. The advantage of this is that all the other rules remain unchanged. This enables a goal-oriented stability optimization approach. With conventional control techniques, in contrast, most of the parameters and fudge factors used to tweak the system have global effects on the system's performance. Hence, a modification that optimizes one situation can have bad effects on other situations. Optimization can then become a trial-and-error task.

Practical Experience with Stability Analysis

■ A stability theory dedicated to fuzzy logic systems exists. However, it has no practical relevance because it is only applicable to very small systems or special cases.

■ Conventional stability analysis techniques for multiband controllers are completely applicable to fuzzy logic controllers.

■ Stability analysis in fuzzy logic systems and conventional systems suffers from the same deficiency: mathematical models of the process under control often either require an impractical effort to derive or are not sufficiently accurate.

Using the Software

The first section of this chapter contains a brief introduction to the attached software. Further documentation
is contained with the software itself. For installation hints,
read the READ.ME file on the attached disk. Section 7.2
contains a language reference for FTL.

7.1 Getting Started with the Simulation Software

This chapter gives a quick introduction to the attached software simulations of fuzzy logic controlled systems. These simulations and their fuzzy
logic controller designs stem from various application areas and let you get
"hands-on" experience with practical fuzzy logic implementations. To run the
fuzzy logic controller that controls the simulated systems, the attached disks
also contain a simulation-only version of the professional *fuzzy*TECH® development software from Inform Software Corporation. This simulation-
only version is further referred to as the "*fuzzy*TECH Demo Edition" or
shortened to "*fuzzy*TECH."

7.1.1 Software Installation

This section guides you through the installation of the software on your
PC, for which you must have the following:

- A PC with a 386SX processor or better (a 486-class PC
  is recommended for fast simulation results)

- Minimum 4 MB main memory (RAM)

■ Minimum 10 MB free space on your hard disk

■ VGA color graphics or better (800 × 600 resolution or higher with 256 colors is recommended for complex analyses)

■ A mouse or an equivalent pointer device

■ MS-Windows 3.1 or higher running in Enhanced Mode (consult your MS-Windows manual for details)

In addition, you must have working knowledge of using MS-Windows. Please note:

■ Since the attached software may be updated faster than the revisions of this book, you should read the READ.ME file contained on the first installation disk prior to the installation of this software. You can use the MS-DOS Editor or MS-Windows Notepad to read the READ.ME file.

■ To install both *fuzzy*TECH and the software simulations, execute the file SETUP.EXE contained on the first installation diskette. You may call SETUP.EXE from either DOS or MS-Windows. However, you may not call SETUP.EXE from a DOS-Box. Follow the instructions on the screen to complete the installation.

■ The installation routine automatically installs all paths. You do not need to reboot your PC or modify any *.INI or AUTOEXEC.BAT/ CONFIG.SYS files.

■ Do not change the subdirectories the installation procedure has set up. If you want to move *fuzzy*TECH and the simulations into another directory, you have to manually change the path names in the FTWIN.INI file or reinstall from the installation disks.

■ The installation procedure generates a new program group in the MS-Windows Program Manager. This group contains the *fuzzy*TECH Demo Edition, the software simulations, and text files explaining the details of the applications.

■ To deinstall, simply erase the total contents of the directory in which you installed *fuzzy*TECH as well as all its subdirectories. The installation of this software has not modified any system files such as AUTOEXEC.BAT or CONFIG.SYS. The installation routine only adds the path of *fuzzy*TECH in the WIN.INI file. This has no side-effects and can remain in the WIN.INI file after deinstallation. Note that if you already have a version of *fuzzy*TECH installed on your PC, the installation of this software will overwrite the path in the WIN.INI file.

■ Make sure that MS-Windows runs in "386 Enhanced Mode." In the "Standard Mode" of MS-Windows you will not be able to run the process simulations interactively. To find out in which mode your installation of MS-Windows runs, you may open the "About" box in the program manager. In the lower part of this window the current Windows Mode is displayed. To find out how you can enable the "Enhanced Mode," please refer to your MS-Windows manual. Note that the installation procedure of MS-Windows automatically enables the 386 Enhanced Mode when sufficient system resources are present.

■ The software simulations have been written by *fuzzy*TECH users. The software simulations are provided as is; that is, no support can be provided by Inform Software Corporation and the author. To obtain more information about full-featured versions of *fuzzy*TECH, contact the manufacturer at the following addresses:

U.S.A./CANADA

Inform Software Corporation

2001 Midwest Road

Oak Brook, IL 60521, U.S.A.

Phone: 708–268–7550

Sales: 1–800–929–2815

Fax: 708–268–7554

JAPAN

TOYO/Inform

26-9, Yushima 3-chome, Bukyo-ku

Tokyo 113, Japan

Phone: 03–5688–6800

Fax: 03–5688–6900

EUROPE AND ELSEWHERE

INFORM GmbH
Pascalstrasse 23
D-52076 Aachen, Germany
Phone: +49–240–894–5628
Fax: +49–240–860–90

We welcome your comments about the software provided with this book. Please write or fax them to the above addresses.

If you have problems with the disks provided in this book, refer directly to the publisher.

fuzzyTECH Demo Edition Functionality

The functionality of the *fuzzy*TECH Demo Edition is almost identical to the functionality of the *fuzzy*TECH Precompiler Edition. However, the *fuzzy*TECH Demo Edition is for "simulation only" to be used with the attached process simulations. Saving and compilation of projects is disabled with the *fuzzy*TECH Demo Edition.

In this book, only components necessary to operate the process simulations are explained in brief. For more details, refer to the User's and Reference Manual of *fuzzy*TECH or the online help system of the *fuzzy*TECH Demo Edition.

The *fuzzy*TECH Demo Edition also provides a limited version of the NeuroFuzzy Module. This NeuroFuzzy Module only contains one learn method and is limited in the size of the systems to be trained. The NeuroFuzzy Module is operated as an integral part of the *fuzzy*TECH Demo Edition and is controlled by its own pull-down menu within the main window of *fuzzy*TECH.

All process simulations included with this book use the simulation interface "fT-Link" and can be used with all other editions of *fuzzy*TECH.

Conventions

- All filenames are spelled in caps, such as: "CRANE.FTL" and "SETUP.EXE."
- All user input in *fuzzy*TECH or the process simulations is also spelled in caps.

■ *fuzzy*TECH uses both the left and right mouse buttons. "Clicking" or "double-clicking" always refers to the left mouse button. Activities with the right mouse button are referred to as "click right" or "double-click right."

■ In general, clicking with the left mouse button activates pointed elements, double-clicking with the left mouse button invokes actions with the element. In *fuzzy*TECH, the right mouse button is only used for invoking "pop-up" menus in some windows. To invoke a pop-up menu, click right in one of *fuzzy*TECH's windows and select the option with the left mouse button. The pop-up menus contain functions and options that are available only for this specific window. In most windows, these functions and options are also accessible through toolbars. You can enable or disable toolbars in the Preferences dialog that is invoked by "Options\Preferences." This way of using mouse buttons and clicks is similar to most other MS-Windows software such as MS-Word or MS-Excel.

■ The "main menu" is the upper menu bar in the main window of *fuzzy*TECH. Activation (clicking) of main menu entries invokes a pull down menu for the entry. This pull down menu lists the available functions for the entry. These options in the main menu are referred to by path names. For example, "File\Open" refers to the option "Open" of the main menu entry "File."

7.1.2   Using *fuzzy*TECH: The Container Crane Simulation

This section shows the basic usage of the *fuzzy*TECH software with the crane control example from Section 2.3. If you have not read this section yet, please do so before proceeding. Each step of the following usage description has been structured so that you can follow it on your PC.

The description of the *fuzzy*TECH functionality in this book is very brief and only covers the most important features to use with the process simulations. You may obtain more detailed information by using the online help system integrated with *fuzzy*TECH. You can invoke the index of the help system by pressing the [F1] key, or to get context specific the [Ctrl]–[F1] key combination. Alternatively, you can access help by utilizing the "Help" entry in the main menu. A complete reference is contained in the *fuzzy*TECH Reference Manual.

Depending on the options enabled in *fuzzy*TECH, window elements such as status bars, toolbars, list boxes, and others may be visible or not. Hence, the windows depicted as screen shots in the following pages may look slightly different from those you see working with *fuzzy*TECH.

fuzzyTECH Program Group

The installation procedure of the *fuzzy*TECH Demo Edition creates a new program group, "*fuzzy*TECH," in the Program Manager of MS-Windows. Figure 7.1 shows this program group. The icon "*fuzzy*TECH Demo Edition" accesses the actual fuzzy logic design software. The other icons access the individual process simulations and text files that explain the process simulations. Double-click on the notepad icon named "READ ME FIRST" to view the most up-to-date information about the software.

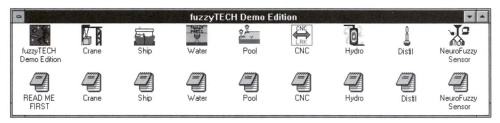

Figure 7.1   The setup routine SETUP.EXE automatically creates the program group fuzzyTECH in the MS-Windows Program Manager. This program group contains the fuzzyTECH Demo Edition and all software simulations.

All simulations may be started directly by double-clicking on their respective icons. Some of the simulations also allow for manual control of the process. To control a process simulation with *fuzzy*TECH, you have to also start *fuzzy*TECH by double-clicking on the *fuzzy*TECH icon. The *.FTL file containing the fuzzy logic controller for the respective process simulation must be opened from within *fuzzy*TECH. Files with the "FTL" suffix denote a complete fuzzy logic project.

To avoid conflicts, only one process simulation may be started at the same time. Invoking the "fT-Link" debug mode in *fuzzy*TECH lets you control the process simulation by fuzzy logic. Note that the installation procedure has created a separate subdirectory for each process simulation in the "\SAMPLES\" subdirectory. Each of these subdirectories contains a SIMULATE.EXE file as the process simulation, the *.FTL file with the description

of the fuzzy logic controller to be loaded by *fuzzy*TECH, and a *.TXT file
with a short description of the process.

Start the Container Crane Simulation

First start the container crane simulation, for example, by double-clicking
the crane symbol "Crane" in the *fuzzy*TECH program group. Figure 7.2 shows
the window of the crane simulation. The container (yellow) has already been
picked up from the ship (red). It must be positioned over the truck (green).

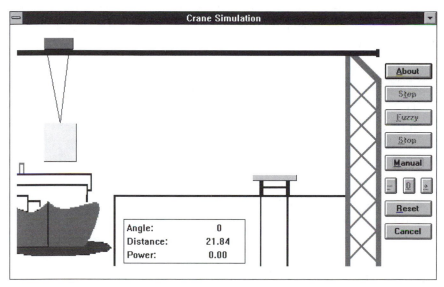

Figure 7.2   The crane simulation window animates the crane operation. The buttons let
you either operate the crane by hand or establish a link to *fuzzy*TECH for automatic operation.

The box visible in the lower part of the crane simulation window always
shows the current values for Angle, Distance, and Power. The values of Angle
and Distance are computed by the process simulation, while Power is the control variable, either set manually or by the fuzzy logic controller. Enable the
manual control mode by clicking the [Manual] button. The Distance is more
than 20 yards, and Angle and Power are zero.

To control the Power, use the [–], [0], and [+] buttons. First, click once
or twice on the [+] button. This sets the motor power to 0.75 or 1.5 kW, respectively. The jerk caused by this lets the Angle oscillate lightly, but is not
sufficient power to put the crane in motion due to the friction in the mechan-

ical system. A motor power of at least 3 kW is required to set the crane head in motion. Now further increase the motor power by clicking on the [+] button again. The [0] button resets the motor power setting to zero and the [–] button lets you apply negative motor power for braking. Alternatively, you can also use the [–], [0], and [+] keys on your keyboard. The [Reset] key sets the crane to its start position.

When you start the crane with very high motor power, you see that due to the high weight of the container, the "container drives the crane" rather than vice versa. This strong feedback of the load to the drive is typical for container cranes and causes one of the difficulties in the control of such processes.

A Crane Operator's Strategy

The crane operator must position the container over the truck so the container can be released. For that the container must not sway as releasing a swaying container could damage its contents. Two simple strategies exist to position the container without sway over the truck. One is to move the crane head so slowly that the container never starts to sway. Since you are saved from wind gusts with the software simulation of the crane, this certainly works, but may take a long time. The other simple strategy is to start with full power and position the crane head over the target position. You must then wait until the container stops swaying. This works due to the absence of wind gusts and because the sway does no harm during transportation. However, it also takes far too much time.

Both these simple strategies are not applicable for container cranes. The opportunity costs of a container ship docked in a harbor are thousands of dollars each hour. Hence, loading and unloading must be completed within minimum time. Only an anti-sway control strategy of the container crane operator can achieve this.

Try this yourself: start with medium power. If you apply full power right from the start, the container starts to sway very strongly and takes a long time to stabilize later. If the container sways a little behind the crane, you can further increase the power since this situation is stable. The increased power gets the container to the target faster. Watch the container moving. If it sways ahead of the crane head, increase the power. This reduces the sway and gets the container back in the stable position and to the target position faster at the same time. If it sways back too much, decrease power to reduce the sway because it is harder to reduce a large sway later. Section 2.3 contains more details on crane controller engineering.

Start fuzzyTECH

To use the predefined fuzzy logic controller for the container crane simulation, you have to start the *fuzzy*TECH Demo Edition first. Double-click the icon "*fuzzy*TECH Demo Edition" in the Program Manager. After a few seconds, a window as depicted in Figure 7.3 appears. This window just reminds you that you can neither save changes to a fuzzy logic system on disk nor generate any real-time code with the *fuzzy*TECH Demo Edition. Click the button [OK] to close this window. Now the main window of *fuzzy*TECH appears as shown in Figure 7.4.

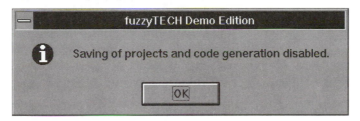

Figure 7.3   The fuzzyTECH Demo Edition does not support saving of projects and code generation.

Upon startup, the *fuzzy*TECH main window contains two subwindows: the "Project Editor" and the "LV" window (Figure 7.4). These two windows can never be closed in *fuzzy*TECH; nor can a new instance of these windows be created. However, the ▼ button iconizes these windows. Underneath the main menu a gray toolbar provides quick access to the most often used *fuzzy*TECH functions.

At the lower border, a gray status bar provides quick information on the current settings, modes, and operations of *fuzzy*TECH. The status bar consists of three fields. The left field indicates basic operations of *fuzzy*TECH, such as loading, saving, or code generation. When *fuzzy*TECH is idle, this field displays "Ready…" The left field has a second function: when the mouse pointer moves over a tool button of the toolbar, the left field displays a quick description of the tool's function.

The right field of the status bar always displays the current debug mode. Upon startup of *fuzzy*TECH, no debug mode is active; hence, the right field displays "Design Mode." The middle field displays the progress of complex

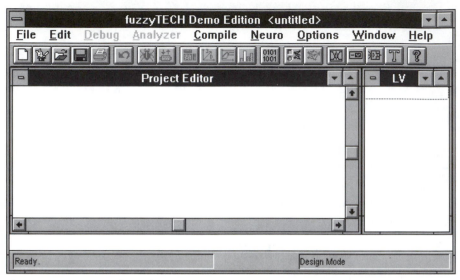

Figure 7.4   Main window of the *fuzzy*TECH Demo Edition after startup

*fuzzy*TECH operations, such as loading, saving, or the current state of a data transmission.

Load the Container Crane Controller

Open the File menu by clicking on "File" in the main menu. This menu contains all functions for opening and saving files as well as related functions. Select the option "File\Open" and open the file "CRANE.FTL" located in the subdirectory "..\SAMPLES\CRANE\." You may also click on the file name in the lower part of the File menu, if it is displayed there. Here, the last four saved files are automatically listed for quick reload. The installation routine presets this list.

While *fuzzy*TECH is opening a project, the middle field of the status bar displays which component of the fuzzy logic controller is currently loaded. Depending on the speed of your PC, this may be too fast to follow. At the end of the loading procedure, *fuzzy*TECH's Project Editor window shows the structure of the crane controller (Figure 7.5). The LV window lists all linguistic variables of the crane controller. "Angle" and "Distance" are the output variables (measured variables) of the crane simulation, and hence the input variables of the fuzzy logic controller. Power is the input variable (command variable) of the crane simulation and, hence, the output variable of the fuzzy logic controller. Linking the respective inputs and outputs of crane simulation and fuzzy logic controller closes the control loop.

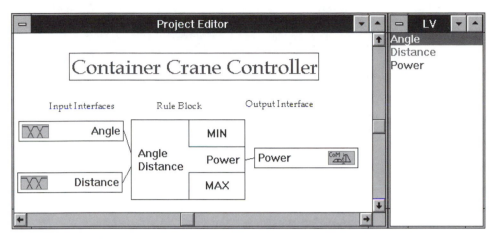

Figure 7.5   After CRANE.FTL has been opened, the Project Editor shows the system structure, and the LV window lists all defined linguistic variables.

Linking the Fuzzy Logic Controller to the Simulation

The Design Mode of *fuzzy*TECH is where you develop the fuzzy logic controller. Since you have opened the already-developed controller from the file CRANE.FTL, you can directly start debugging and test by linking the controller to the simulation. Select the option "Debug\fT-Link" (click on "fT-Link" in the "Debug" menu). For a short time, the left field of the status bar displays "Loading Knowledge Base...." During this period, *fuzzy*TECH builds an internal representation of the current fuzzy logic controller. The middle field of the status bar shows the progress. After successful completion, the left field of the status bar shows "Ready" again. The right field of the status bar now shows the active debug mode: "Debug: fT-Link." In addition, a new window titled "Debug: fT-Link" (Figure 7.6) opens. This window always shows the current values of all input and output values of the fuzzy logic controller. You should iconize this window by clicking the ▼ button when you get started with *fuzzy*TECH because you are not interested in the exact values of the variables. This also expedites the simulation on slow PCs. Closing the Debug window ends the current debug mode.

fT-Link Operation

Whenever you activate "fT-Link," *fuzzy*TECH looks for a running simulation that supports fT-Link and links to it. If you start "fT-Link" without such a simulation already running, *fuzzy*TECH tries to find a simulation named SIMULATE.EXE in the current simulation directory (set in the Di-

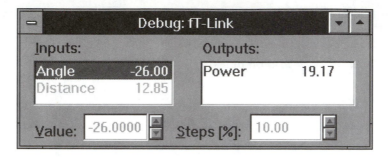

Figure 7.6   The Debug window is active in any debug mode and always shows the values of the input and output variables. In Interactive debug mode, the edit fields at the lower part of the Debug window allow you to set values for the input variables.

rectories dialog box invoked by "Options\Directories") and starts it. If *fuzzy*TECH does not find this file, an error message appears indicating "Simulation not found." Note, that all software simulations provided in this book are named SIMULATE.EXE. *fuzzy*TECH can only identify the correct simulation by the directory in which it is located.

When linking to a simulation, *fuzzy*TECH always checks that simulation and fuzzy logic controller match. The check verifies that all variable names used are the same in the controller and the simulation. You may program simulations in every program language under MS-Windows or you may use a professional simulation software package [116]. For MathLab/Simulink, Matrixx, and VisSim, special interface modules exist and M code generation is supported. Other simulation software packages can be linked by Dynamic Data Exchange with *fuzzy*TECH's DDE-Link. Note that fT-Link does require MS-Windows to run in 386 Enhanced Mode because the simulation and *fuzzy*TECH run in multitasking mode. Refer to your MS-Windows manual for details on 386 Enhanced Mode.

Start the Fuzzy Logic Control of the Crane

After you have successfully established the link to the simulation from *fuzzy*TECH, change to the crane simulation window. In the crane simulation window the button [Fuzzy] is now enabled. Click the [Fuzzy] button to start the simulation using the fuzzy logic controller in *fuzzy*TECH. In an infinite loop, the crane simulation computes the current values for Angle and Distance and sends them to *fuzzy*TECH, where they are the inputs of the fuzzy logic controller. *fuzzy*TECH then computes the value of the output variable Power and sends it back to the crane simulation. The crane simulation uses the value of Power to compute the reaction of the crane a time unit later and displays the new situation in its window. This sequence repeats itself until either the [Stop] or [Reset] button of the simulation is pressed. Depending on the computation and video performance of your PC, you see this control loop as a smooth movement of the container crane.

First, the fuzzy logic controller starts with medium power, then speeds up as the container sways a little behind the crane head. As the container is a very heavy one, it sways back stronger as a result of this. As a reaction, the fuzzy logic controller reduces the motor power to reduce the sway. Upon reaching target position, the fuzzy logic controller positions the container right over the target with one overshoot. The [Reset] button puts the container back in the start position. The [Stop] button lets you halt the simulation at any time. Pressing [Fuzzy] continues the simulation, and the [Step] button lets you single-step through the operation.

Analyzing Time Response

The graphical simulation gives you an overview of how the fuzzy logic controller controls the crane. For more in-depth analyses, *fuzzy*TECH provides numerous tools and analyzers. To evaluate the time response, *fuzzy*TECH provides Time Plots. Create a new Time Plot by selecting "Analyzer\Time Plot..." which invokes the configuration dialog as shown in Figure 7.7. The three left list boxes display elements that you can select for display. The right list box titled "Plot Items:" shows the currently selected elements for this Time Plot. To move elements from the three left list boxes to the right one and vice versa just double-click on the respective element. Alternatively, you can first highlight the elements you want to move and then use the [<<] and [>>] buttons to move the highlighted elements.

For the crane controller the leftmost list box "LVs:" shows the three input and output variables "Angle," "Distance," and "Power" in alphanumeric sequence. Double-click on all three of these variables to move them into the "Plot Items:" list box. The list box, "Terms:," is empty since the crane controller does not contain any linguistic variables without membership functions. The list box "Rule Block:" and the two fields "Rule:" and "Out:" let you select individual rules for display. Do not select any rules now. After you have selected the three linguistic variables for display, click on the [OK] button to

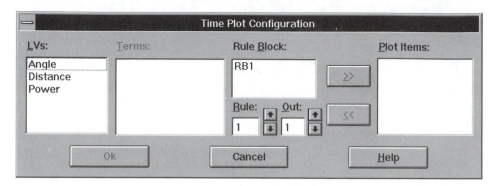

Figure 7.7   The Time Plot Configuration dialog box lets you specify linguistic variables, terms, and rules for display.

close this window. Figure 7.8 shows the resulting Time Plot. You may define up to ten Time Plots in each *fuzzy*TECH session. The title bar of each Time Plot shows its number.

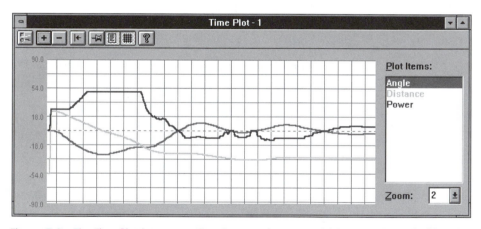

Figure 7.8   The Time Plot lets you analyze input and output variables as well as rule firing degrees over time.

At the right side of the Time Plot window, a list box shows all Plot Items selected. The left part of the window displays the plot area. Change to the crane simulation window and start the simulation with the [Fuzzy] button. If the [Fuzzy] button is not enabled, make sure that *fuzzy*TECH is running the CRANE.FTL project and the fT-Link mode is enabled. You can now see that the Time Plot window plots the value of all three control variables over time. A scale for the element highlighted in the Plot Item list box is displayed at the left border of the plot area. A dotted horizontal line in the plot area shows the zero line. Each Time Plot also has its own toolbar that can be disabled to save screen space.

Now, reset the simulation and press [Fuzzy] while watching the Time Plot window. The blue line (Power) starts with medium positive Power. After the container sways back slightly (red line declines), the fuzzy logic controller increases the motor power (blue line increases). When the sway becomes too large (red line deep down), the fuzzy logic controller reduces motor power (blue line declines). After reducing the sway (red line comes back up), the fuzzy logic controller increases the motor power again. The constantly declining green line (Distance) shows the progress toward the target.

Customizing Time Plots

To customize the Time Plot, you may set the resolution of the time axis in the "Zoom:" drop list. Also, the buttons [+] and [–] in the toolbar let you change the zoom. To freeze the display, you may use the Freeze button in the toolbar. To save screen space, you may also hide the Plot Item list box by switching off the Show Listbox button in the toolbar. Similarly, the raster in the plot area may be turned on and off by the Show Raster button. The Reset Time Plot button clears the plot area. To add or delete elements from the Time Plot, click the Time Plot Configuration button in the toolbar. Move the mouse pointer over the buttons without pressing a mouse button to see the quick description in the left field of the status bar.

You can also access the toolbar functions by the pop-up menu that you invoke by clicking right somewhere in the Time Plot window. You can turn the Time Plot toolbars on and off in the Preferences dialog box invoked by "Options\Preferences...." To close a Time Plot, double-click on the system icon ▬ . If you leave the debug mode, all Time Plots are closed automatically. If you have enabled "Save Window Position" in the Preferences dialog, all Time Plots closed when leaving the debug mode are automatically reopened.

Time Plot of Rule Firing Degrees

You may also plot the firing degrees of individual rules. Open a new Time Plot by selecting "Analyzer\Time Plot...." Then double-click on the "RB1" entry in the "Rule Block:" list box. RB1 is the name of the one and only rule block of the container crane controller. The list box "Plot Item:"

now displays the entry "RB1.1.1." The first number after the point identifies the number of the rule in the respective rule block, the second number the output variable of the rule to be plotted. Hence, "RB1.1.1" identifies the first rule in rule block RB1 and the first output variable of the rule.

Now select the second rule for display. Enter "2" in the field "Rule:" and double-click on the entry "RB1" in the "Rule Block:" list box. After pressing [OK], a second Time Plot opens that plots the firing degrees of the first two rules. Start the crane simulation again and you observe that initially the first rule fires, then the second one. When a rule is highlighted in the "Plot Item:" list box of the Time Plot, the respective rule is shown abbreviated under the plot area. You may mix any combination of linguistic variables, terms, and rules in a Time Plot.

Analyzing Control Surfaces

In addition to analyzing time response, you may also analyze the control surfaces of the fuzzy logic controller. Close the two open Time Plot windows if you have a low-performance PC to save video and computing resources. Select the option "Analyzer\3D Plot..." from the main menu. The 3D Plot, as shown in Figure 7.9, displays the control surface of the crane controller. The 3D Plot always shows two input variables on the horizontal axes and one output variable on the vertical axis. Since the crane controller has two input variables and one output variable, the configuration dialog box of the 3D Plot was omitted in the case of the crane controller. You may open up to ten 3D Plots in one *fuzzy*TECH session.

Customizing the 3D Plot

The 3D Plot also has its own toolbar. To change the resolution of the 3D Plot, click on the rightmost drop list. This displays a list of the possible resolutions. A high resolution can result in slow response of the time plot, depending on the video and computing performance of your PC. You can select the output variable using the second rightmost drop list and the two input variables using the two drop lists to the left of it. The four arrow buttons on the left side of the toolbar rotate the plot in all directions. Single-clicking on an arrow button just moves the plot one step; double-clicking starts a rotation. The hand button stops this rotation. The double-arrow buttons flip the 3D Plot for better visibility. The Change Color Palette button toggles between different color shadings of the plot surface.

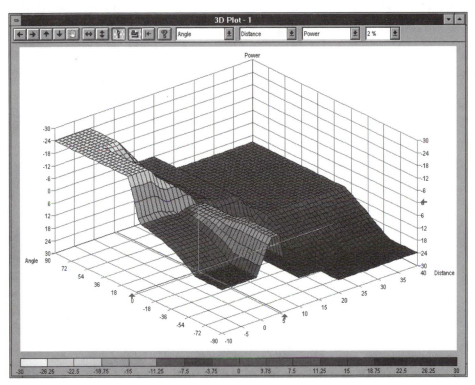

Figure 7.9   The 3D Plot draws the transfer surface for two input variables and one output variable.

If the output variable selected for the 3D Plot depends on more than the two inputs displayed, the control surface dynamically depends on these variables. If the Repaint 3D Plot button is pressed, the 3D Plot is repainted every time one of these other input variables changes to reflect the change in the control surface shape. Note that this only results in a smooth display if you have a PC with very high video and computing performance. To close a 3D Plot, double-click on the system icon ▣ . If you leave the debug mode, all 3D Plots are closed automatically. If you have enabled "Save Window Position" in the Preferences dialog, all 3D Plots closed when leaving the debug mode are automatically reopened.

Any time *fuzzy*TECH repaints the control surface, you can see that the surface is painted from back to front. This lets you also see parts of the surface hidden after the painting is completed. You can change this by turning the Background-Paint button on. Then, *fuzzy*TECH computes the new surface shape in the background and displays it instantly. This lets you see better how the surface changes, either because an undisplayed linguistic variable (and thus the control surface) has changed, or because you rotated the plot.

The red arrows at the three axes and the cyan plot lines always show the current value of the input and output variables. The Trace 3D Plot button in the toolbar lets you plot the operation point over time (green trace). Enable Trace 3D Plot and reset the crane simulation. Then start the simulation. The "green trace" starts at the start position of the crane, that is, Angle = 0 and Distance = 22, and moves to the target position, Angle = 0 and Distance = 0. The Reset Trace button clears the trace. The height of the control surface and its color indicate the reaction of the fuzzy logic controller to the combination of the input variables.

With the Time Plot and 3D Plot, you analyze the "outside" performance of the fuzzy logic controller by using input and output variables. In the next steps, you will analyze the internal structure. End the debug mode by closing the "Debug: fT-Link" window or selecting "Debug\fT-Link" again.

Linguistic Variable Editors

The LV window contains a list of all linguistic variables in the system. To invoke an editor for one of the variables, simply double-click on the respective variable name in the LV window. You may open an independent editor window for each linguistic variable. Figure 7.10 shows the editor window for the linguistic variable "Distance." To create a new linguistic variable, click on the "New Linguistic Variable" button in the main toolbar or select "Edit/Create Variable from the main menu, or use the pop-up menu in the LV window. You may also duplicate linguistic variables by selecting "Edit/Duplicate Variable…" from the main menu.

On the right side of the variable editor, a plot area shows all membership functions defined for the linguistic variable. Membership functions are always defined pointwise using definition points that can be freely positioned and dragged with the mouse. On the left side of the variable editor, the Term list box shows all terms for the linguistic variable. The definition points of the membership function of the term highlighted in the Term list box appear as small squares in the plot area. You may highlight individual definition points by clicking on the mouse and dragging them. A highlighted definition point is indicated by a filled square.

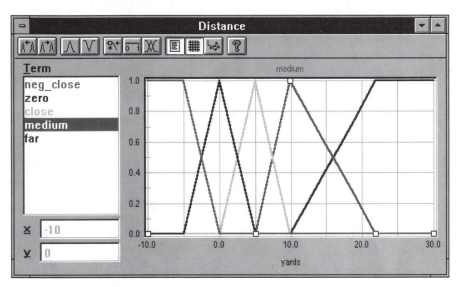

Figure 7.10   Variable Editor window for "Distance."

Pointwise Definition of Membership Functions

To erase a definition point, first highlight the point by mouse click. Then press the [Del] key. The confirm dialogs that pop up any time you erase a system component can be omitted by disabling the "Confirm Messages" option in the Preferences dialog box. The Preferences dialog box is invoked by "Options\Preferences...." Many experienced users prefer to disable confirm messages since *fuzzy*TECH provides a multistage UNDO function. You can undo most actions by pressing [Alt]-[←] (Alt-Backspace) or selecting "Edit\Undo" from the main menu.

You may also highlight more than one point at the same time. If you want to highlight individual, non-connecting points, select the first point and then hold down the [Ctrl] key while you click on the other points you want to select. The highlighted points can then be dragged or deleted at the same time. Note that you still have to keep the [Ctrl] key pressed when dragging multiple selected points. If you want to highlight connecting points, first highlight the leftmost point you want to select. Then keep the [Shift] key ([⇑]) pressed while you select the rightmost point you want to select. To create a new definition point, double-click on an empty space in the plot area.

Using the Grid Function

To ease the placement of definition points, the variable editor provides a grid function. To change the grid, click on the Grid button in the toolbar. Figure 7.11 shows the Grid dialog box. The grid resolution for base variable (horizontal axis) and membership degree (vertical axis) can be chosen independently. Enter the value "5" for "Base Variable." This sets the grid resolution in intervals of five yards, resulting in eight possible values for Distance (40 yards total distance/five yards resolution = 8 intervals).

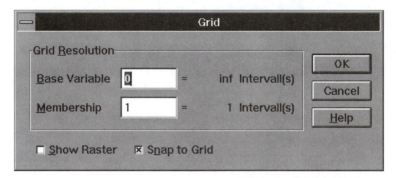

Figure 7.11   The Grid dialog lets you specify different resolutions for base variable values and membership degrees.

Enter the value "0.1" for "Membership." This allows the membership degree of definition points to be of values 0, 0.1, 0.2, ... Enable both check boxes for "Show Raster" and "Snap to Grid" and close the Grid dialog box by clicking [OK]. If you now drag definition points, only grid positions are considered.

The fields "x" and "y" show the coordinates of the nearest grid position to the current mouse cursor position while no definition point is highlighted. If one definition point is highlighted, the "x" and "y" fields show its position. You can now also enter new coordinates for this point in these fields. If more than one definition point is highlighted, these fields show the coordinates of the definition point the mouse cursor is over. If you do not want to use a mouse, you can also highlight definition points with the [Tab] and [Space] keys. Then use the cursor keys to move the definition point and the [Return] key to place it.

Base Variables

To modify the properties of the base variable for which the linguistic variable is defined, click on the Base Variable button in the toolbar of the variable editor. This invokes the Base Variable dialog box as shown in Figure 7.12. The fields "Min:" and "Max:" let you specify the domain of the base variable. Two representations exist in *fuzzy*TECH: Shell Values and Code Values. Shell Values represent the universe of the values that are used for display in all editors and analyzers of *fuzzy*TECH. If you have selected "Double" as "Base Variable Data Type" in the Global Options dialog box (select "Options\Global Options..." to invoke this dialog box), the same values are used in the generated code.

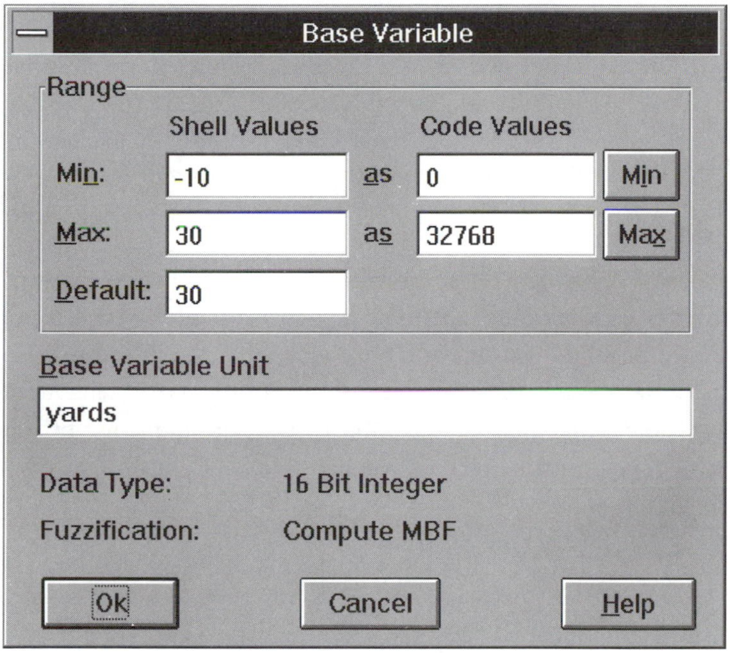

Figure 7.12   The Base Variable dialog box lets you specify the range and code value representation of a linguistic variable.

However, the use of floating point variables is of prohibitive computational effort for most microcontrollers and other real-time process controllers. Also, many compilers used with these target hardware platforms cannot provide libraries for this computation. Hence, the column "Code Values" lets you specify integer values for minimum and maximum of the variable in the generated code. The possible range for these integer values depends on the base variable data type. Assume you want to implement the crane controller on a 16-bit microcontroller. Your distance sensor delivers values from 822 to 3222 for a distance of –10 and 30 yards, respectively. If you specify 822 and 3222 as code values, *fuzzy*TECH automatically converts these values into the shell values used for display in all editors and analyzers.

The reason for this automatic range conversion is that the code generators of *fuzzy*TECH can tie in the range conversion with the fuzzification code. This saves both on conversion code as well as computing steps and makes the produced code more efficient. If you do not need this automatic range conversion, click the [Min] and [Max] buttons to achieve maximum integer resolution.

The field "Default" lets you specify a default value that is output by the fuzzy logic system if no rule for this variable fires and the variable is used in an output interface. The field "Base Variable Unit" lets you specify a unit for the base variable. This is used for display purposes only. Leave the Base Variable dialog box by clicking [Cancel] to return to the variable editor.

In the variable editor you can also hide the list box "Term" using the Term List Box button of the toolbar. This is useful to save screen space once the membership functions of the variable are defined. You may also hide the toolbar by disabling the "Variable Editor" option in the Preference dialog box. Most toolbar functions are accessible by the pop-up menu of the variable editor as well. To invoke this pop-up menu, click right somewhere in the variable editor window. To close a variable editor, double-click the system icon ▣ of the variable editor window.

Editing Linguistic Terms

To change the properties of an existing term, double-click on the term name in the list box "Term" of the variable editor. Figure 7.13 shows the Term dialog box. The term name is edited in the "Term Name" field. Note that term names may contain only alphanumeric characters and underscores because the names are used in the generated code. The button [Color...] lets you change the colors that *fuzzy*TECH automatically associates with terms.

As mentioned earlier, *fuzzy*TECH uses a pointwise definition of membership functions. Two alternatives exist in *fuzzy*TECH to connect these definition points: L-shape (linear) and S-shape. You can select between these two types using the respective radio buttons in the "shape" group. For S-shape membership function definition, you also can specify the asymmetry factor in the range from 0 to 1. Now close the Term dialog box by pressing the [Cancel] button.

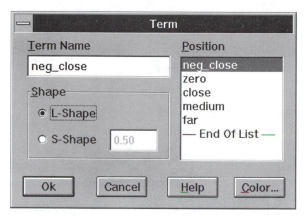

Figure 7.13 The Term dialog box lets you specify term name, position in term sequence, and membership function shape.

To create a new term, click on the New Term button or the Inverse New Term button of the variable editor's toolbar. The Inverse New Term tool creates a new term with a membership function defined as $\mu_{new} = (1-\mu_{highlighted})$. Both options open the Term dialog box.

For Standard MBFs, an expedited design alternative exists. Only define membership functions where the maximum point is at the appropriate position. Then press the Convert to Standard MBF button in the toolbar of the variable editor window, and all other definition points will be set automatically. You may press the Standard MBF button at any time to convert the current membership functions to Standard MBFs. Note that the multistage UNDO function of *fuzzy*TECH lets you take back even complex "experiments."

Editing the System Structure in the Project Editor

You define the structure of the fuzzy logic controller in the Project Editor window. Three types of objects exist in the Project Editor: Remarks, Interfaces, and Rule Blocks. Remarks are pure text objects that have no impact on the actual information processing. Interfaces contain the fuzzification and defuzzification. Rule Blocks contain the fuzzy logic rules of a system design. These three elements suffice to design even complex and hierarchical fuzzy logic systems.

All objects in the Project Editor window can be placed arbitrarily by mouse drag and drop. To fine-position the objects, keep the [Shift] key pressed. The mouse movement is then limited to the horizontal or vertical direction, depending on which direction the move started. If you do not want to use the mouse, you can highlight any object using the [Tab] key, move with the cursor keys, and place with the [Return] key. To edit the properties of an object, double-click on the object.

Double-click on the purple text "Container Crane Controller" in the Project Editor window. This invokes the Remark Attributes dialog box as shown in Figure 7.14. The text to be displayed is entered in the field "Text:." You can also specify font size (field "Size:") and text color (by pressing the [Color…] button). Leave the dialog box by pressing the [Cancel] button.

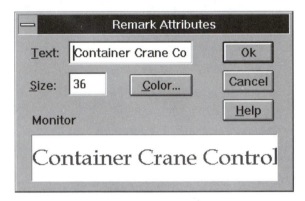

Figure 7.14   The Remark Attributes dialog box lets you specify text objects.

Now, double-click on the interface with the variable name "Angle." This invokes the Interface Options dialog box as shown in Figure 7.15. The group "Interface Type" defines the method for fuzzification or defuzzification. In the Project Editor window, each method is represented by a different icon in the interface box. The fuzzification/defuzzification choice also determines whether the interface shall act as input or output interface. In the Project Editor window, you can differentiate input and output interfaces by the location of the method icon. With input interfaces, the icon is on the left side of the interface box, with output interfaces on the right.

For input interfaces, three different fuzzification methods are supported. "Fuzzy Input" indicates that the variable is inputted into the fuzzy logic system as a "fuzzy" variable, that is, as a vector of membership degrees. This is primarily used in decision support applications where the input stems from a linguistic source. The fuzzification method "Compute MBF" is the standard

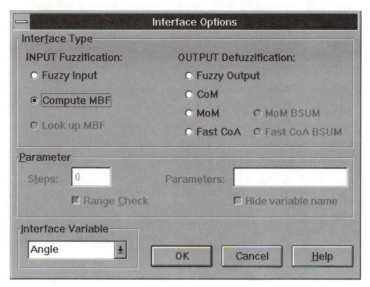

Figure 7.15   The Interface Options dialog box lets you define the properties of an interface and fuzzification/defuzzification type.

fuzzification method used in almost all applications. This method only stores the definition points of the membership functions in the generated code and computes the fuzzification at runtime. Some *fuzzy*TECH MCU Editions (that generate assembly code for microcontrollers) also support the "Look up MBF" method. This method computes the membership functions completely at compile time and stores all values in a table in the generated code. This method uses extensive code sizes and is only provided where it delivers expedited computation.

For output interfaces, different defuzzification methods exist as well. Analogous to "Fuzzy Input," "Fuzzy Output" outputs a vector of the membership degrees of the inference result. The most often used method is Center-of-Maximum ("CoM"), which delivers the best compromise of the firing rules. In contrast, the Mean-of-Maximum method ("MoM") delivers the most plausible result. Center-of-Area ("CoA") is similar to the CoM method. *fuzzy*TECH uses a modified CoA algorithm, called "Fast-CoA," which circumvents the numerical integration required by the original CoA method. The BSUM variants of CoA and MoM defuzzification use the bounded sum rather than the maximum operator to aggregate the individual area pieces. They are only used by certain fuzzy processes.

To select a variable for the interface, use the drop list "Interface Variable." Since all variables are already used in interfaces, this drop list only contains "Angle." The group "Parameter" lets you dynamically link *fuzzy*TECH variables to external variables. This is used in the process control system or PLC implementations of *fuzzy*TECH to interface the fuzzy logic system to variables and periphery. In the *fuzzy*TECH Demo Edition, the dynamic link of variables is not supported; hence, this group is disabled. Close the dialog box by clicking the [Cancel] button.

Definition of Fuzzy Logic Rules

The large block in the middle of the Project Editor window is the Rule Block. This block contains the rules of the system describing the control strategy. Double-click on the Rule Block to invoke the Spreadsheet Rule Editor shown in Figure 7.16. Each row corresponds to a single fuzzy logic rule. The leftmost column numbers each rule (gray fields). Clicking on this field highlights the rule, clicking again de-highlights it. The next two columns make up the "if-part" of the rule. Above the columns are two buttons, [Angle] and [Distance]; above them, the button [IF].

The two rightmost columns under the [THEN] button describe the "then-part" of the rules. The right column under the [Power] button denotes the result term; the columns under the [DoS] button show the individual weight of the rule. This weight (Degree-of-Support) lies in the range from zero to one.

Add and Modify Rules

To change a rule, simply click in the respective field. A pop-up list box shows all possible values for the field. To add a rule, use the last row of the table which is always empty. Once you have entered a new rule, another empty row will appear at the end of the table. Incomplete rules (i.e., rules that either have no "if-part," "then-part," or "DoS") will automatically be deleted when the Spreadsheet Rule Editor is closed. Empty fields in the "if-parts" are considered "don't care" conditions. A rule that contains an empty field is not influenced by the respective variable. Rules containing "don't care" conditions are not incomplete. In the list box that appears when you click on a field, the "don't care" condition is listed under the terms as "[…]" entry.

To delete a rule, first highlight the rule by clicking the gray left field and press the [Del] key. If you want to temporarily disable a rule, you can also set

Spreadsheet Rule Editor - RB1				
Matrix	IF		THEN	
Utilities	Angle	Distance	DoS	Power
1	zero	far	1.00	pos_mediu
2	neg_small	far	1.00	pos_high
3	neg_small	medium	1.00	pos_high
4	neg_big	medium	1.00	pos_mediu
5	pos_small	close	1.00	neg_mediu
6	zero	close	1.00	zero
7	neg_small	close	1.00	pos_mediu
8	pos_small	zero	1.00	neg_mediu
9	zero	zero	1.00	zero
10				

Figure 7.16   The Spreadsheet Rule Editor supports definition of rule sets in a table format.

the DoS to zero. Such a rule has no effect on the system but is not considered incomplete.

Now, click on the [IF] button to open the "Aggregation" dialog box as shown in Figure 7.17. In this dialog box you specify the aggregational operator. The group "Operator" lets you select the operator family; the "Parameter" scroll bar and edit field let you tune the characteristic. The closer the parameter value is to 0, the more the operator performs like a perfect AND; the closer the value is to 1, the more the operator performs like a perfect OR. The Operator Plot visualizes the transfer characteristic of the operator currently selected. The two horizontal axes denote the truth degrees of two conditions; the vertical axis is the aggregation as computed by the operator. Close the dialog box by clicking [Cancel].

To change the result aggregation, click on the [THEN] button. *fuzzy*TECH supports two methods for result aggregation, the MAX method, and the BSUM method. If more than one rule have the same result, the first method takes the maximum of the two as the final result, and the second one takes the bounded sum. Note that BSUM result aggregation is different from BSUM MoM and BSUM CoA. For more details on aggregation and result aggregation methods, refer to [116] or the online help system.

Figure 7.17   The Aggregation dialog box lets you
specify the fuzzy logic operator used for computing the
"if-part" of a rule.

To sort rules in the sequence of the terms of a certain variable, just click
on the respective button: [Angle], [Distance], or [Power]. You may also sort
rules in the sequence of their firing degree by pressing the [DoS] button. Do
not change the sequence of the rules now, as rules will be referred to later in
this chapter by their numbers.

Rule Block Utilities

Click on the button [Utilities] in the Spreadsheet Rule Editor to access
the Rule Block Utilities dialog box shown in Figure 7.18. In the group "Util-
ity" you select the function to be performed:

■ "alpha cut" deletes all rules with a DoS lower than the value specified
  in the group "Value."

■ "set all DoS" sets the rule weights to the value specified in the group
  "Value."

■ "create full rule block" deletes all existing rules and creates a new rule
  for each combination of terms. Note that for each possible
  combination of input variables to the rule block, a rule for each
  possible output variable term is generated. The weight of the
  generated rules is the one specified in the group "Value."

■ "create partial rule block" only creates a rule for each combination of input variables. You have to specify the output variable terms manually. The rules for which you do not specify an output term are incomplete and will be erased when closing the Spreadsheet Rule Editor. The weight of the generated rules is the one specified in the group "Value."

Close the dialog box by pressing the [Cancel] button.

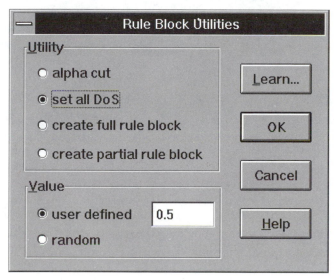

Figure 7.18   The Rule Block Utilities dialog box features a number of different functions to manipulate an entire rule block.

Matrix Rule Editor

Click the [Matrix] button to invoke the Matrix Rule Editor shown in Figure 7.19. This editor is only available for rule blocks that do not contain rules with "don't care" conditions. Many experienced fuzzy logic designers prefer the Matrix Rule Editor over the Spreadsheet Rule Editor when designing complex systems.

The lower part of the window has a list box for each input and output variable of the rule block. Each list box shows all terms that are defined for the respective variable. By highlighting a term in each list box, a single rule is addressed. The weight of this rule is shown by the scroll bar and edit field in the group "Degree of Support." Rules that are nonexistent are identical to

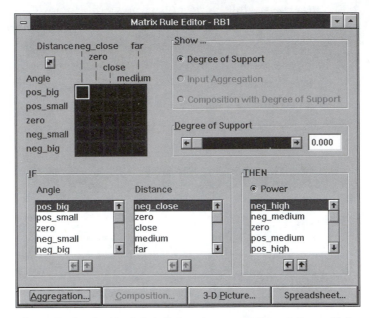

Figure 7.19 The Matrix Rule Editor shows a cut through the multidimensional rule space as a matrix.

zero-weighted rules in the Matrix Rule Editor. To add a rule in the Matrix Editor, address the rule by highlighting the respective terms in the list boxes and set the DoS to a nonzero value. To erase a rule in the Matrix Rule Editor, address it and set its DoS to zero.

To visualize the rule base, you may select two of the variables to the matrix display in the upperleft part of the window. Use the two arrow buttons underneath each list box to select variables for the matrix. The arrow buttons of the two variables currently displayed in the matrix are disabled. Use the left arrow button to select the variable as the vertical matrix variable and the up arrow button to select the variable as the horizontal matrix variable. To flip the two variables displayed in the matrix, use the double-arrow button in the upperleft corner of the window.

Now, select the linguistic variable "Power" as the horizontal variable by pressing the up arrow underneath the "Power" list box. Now highlight different terms in the list box "Distance." For each of the selected distances, the matrix shows the relation between the angle input and the power output. In the matrix, rules with a DoS of 1 are shown as white squares and rules with a DoS of 0 as well as nonexistent rules as black squares. Rules with a DoS between 0 and 1 are shown with a respective shade of gray. The matrix field that corresponds to the addressed rule is identified by a red frame. You may also address rules by clicking the respective matrix field. To toggle the DoS of a rule between 0 and 1, you can double-click the respective matrix field. This works faster than using the scroll bar.

You may also visualize the rule matrix three-dimensionally by clicking the [3-D Picture] button. The group "Show…" lets you select what the matrix should display in Debug Mode:

- Degree of Support shows the weight of the rules.
- Input Aggregation shows to what degree the condition for the rules is true.
- Composition with Degree of Support shows to what degree the output of the rule fires.

The button [Spreadsheet] lets you go back to the Spreadsheet Rule Editor. Now, close the Matrix Rule Editor with a double-click on its system icon ▬ .

If you have more than one rule block in a project, you may open a rule block editor for each block simultaneously. To differentiate between different rule block editors, the name of the rule block is shown in their title bar.

Test and Verification Using Debug Modes

Now that you have evaluated the various editors used to design a fuzzy logic system, the next development step is optimization and test. *fuzzy*TECH features numerous debug modes to support this development step. All debug modes cooperate with the editors and analyzers to expedite system verification.

When you switch from Design Mode to any of the debug modes, the entire fuzzy logic system is simulated by *fuzzy*TECH. All editors become dynamic; that is, they display information flow, fuzzification, defuzzification, and rule inference graphically. In addition, most system components may still be edited during debugging.

First, a quick overview of all debug modes.

Interactive Debug Mode

The Interactive debug mode shows the reaction of the system to input values set by yourself. All editors and analyzers of *fuzzy*TECH show the information flow graphically. When you modify any element of the fuzzy logic system, you can see the effect of this instantly. This enables quick "if-then" analyses. The Transfer Plot and the 3D Plot let you test the completeness and unambiguousness of the rule base.

DDE-Link

The DDE-Link debug mode lets you interface *fuzzy*TECH interactively with any other MS-Windows software that supports DDE (dynamic data exchange). The DDE-Link is not supported with the *fuzzy*TECH Demo Edition.

fT-Link

The fT-Link debug mode allows you to dynamically link *fuzzy*TECH to software simulations of the process to be controlled. All simulations contained with the software of this book use this interface. fT-Link uses the MS-Windows interprocess message-passing capabilities, thus supporting simulations written in any programming language. For details on how to program fT-Link, refer to [116]. A quick description is also contained in the online help system.

Serial Link

The Serial Link debug mode allows *fuzzy*TECH to operate over the serial port. The settings for the communications must be set in the Terminal dialog box you access via "Options\Terminal..." In Serial Link debug mode, *fuzzy*TECH acts as a slave to the process or simulation connected at the serial port of your PC. After activation of Serial Link debug mode, *fuzzy*TECH waits for the process or simulation to write all input values of the fuzzy logic system to the serial port. When all input values are received, *fuzzy*TECH computes the output values and writes them back to the serial port. Then *fuzzy*TECH waits for the next input. The communication format is ASCII, ASC(31) is used as delimiter between values, ASC(0) is used to indicate end of transmission. Note that the Serial Link debug mode can only be used with slow systems, as the response time for *fuzzy*TECH sending back the output values cannot be guaranteed (due to the MS-Windows operating system). For real-time applications, the more sophisticated online debug mode shall be used. For more details, refer to [116] or the online help system.

File Recorder

The File Recorder lets you use input data for the fuzzy logic system stored in files. These input data files may stem from process monitoring, the *fuzzy*TECH Pattern Generator, or real-time traces. For more details on the file formats, refer to [116] or the online help system.

Connection, Monitor, Online

The *fuzzy*TECH Online Edition supports the generation of C code that can be modified running on the target hardware remotely from the PC. The development PC is connected to the target hardware (process controller, PLC, microcontroller board) by a serial cable, a field bus, or a similar communication medium. Enabling "Connection" with *fuzzy*TECH establishes communication with the target hardware, enabling "Monitor" lets you visualize the entire information flow in the fuzzy logic system in real time, and enabling "Online" lets you also modify the running system "on-the-fly." For microcontroller implementations, the *fuzzy*TECH RTRCD Modules deliver a reduced functionality of the *fuzzy*TECH Online Edition. The *fuzzy*TECH Demo Edition does not support any of these debug modes.

System Test Using the Interactive Debug Mode

Enable the Interactive debug mode by either clicking the respective button on the main toolbar or selecting "Debug\Interactive" from the main menu. Iconize the "Debug: Interactive" window that opens. Now, open a Variable Editor window for each of the three linguistic variables of the crane controller. Open the Spreadsheet Rule Editor window for the rule block. Iconize the Project Editor and LV windows. The main window of *fuzzy*TECH should then look similar to that in Figure 7.20.

If you drag the small red arrows under the plot area of the membership functions in the Variable Editors for "Angle" and "Distance," a thin vertical line shows the fuzzification. Also, the Term list box shows the truth degree of each term after fuzzification. The firing degree of each rule is shown by small black bars on both sides of the DoS values in the Spreadsheet Rule Editor. To see the exact values, click on the bar. The defuzzification process is shown in the Variable Editor for "Power."

Now set the input variables by dragging the red arrows to the start position of the crane: "Angle" to 0 and "Distance" to 22. In the Spreadsheet Rule Editor, you see that only the first rule fires. This rule is the one stating that in start position, the crane should start with medium power. The defuzzification shown in the Variable Editor for "Power" is unequivocal: a crane connected to this controller would now start with 10 kW power.

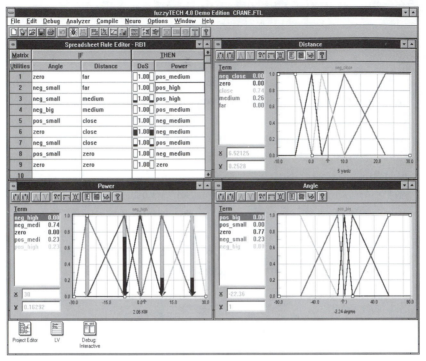

Figure 7.20   In Interactive debug mode, all editors visualize the inference graphically.

After a short time, the situation is different: because of the start, the load of the crane sways behind and the distance declines. Set "Angle" to −10 and "Distance" to 20. This is the stable situation where the crane motor should be powered up. This situation is represented by the second rule, which now completely fires. In a similar fashion, you can now test the fuzzy logic system performance for any situation. Change the "then-part" of the second rule from "pos_high" to "neg_high" and you instantly see the effects of this in the Variable Editor of "Power." In the same way, any change of a membership function or a rule weight is instantly reflected in all editors and analyzers.

Using Analyzers in Interactive Debug Mode

Open the 3D Plot by selecting "Analyzer\3D Plot…" and arrange windows similarly to Figure 7.21. By dragging the red arrows in the 3D Plot, you may also select any control operation point. All editors show fuzzification, rule inference, and defuzzification for exactly this operation point. Likewise, any change of input variable values in the Variable Editors for "Angle" and

"Distance" is reflected instantly in the 3D Plot. By enabling the tracing option in the 3D Plot window, any operation point already tested is plotted.

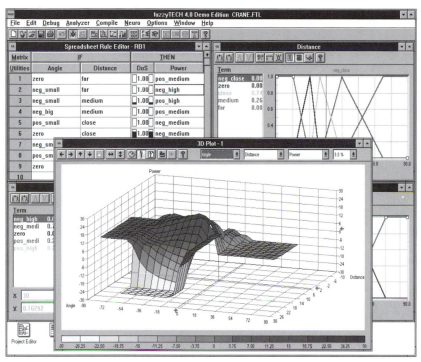

Figure 7.21   Modifications in the system become instantly visible in all editors and analyzers. If you change the "then-part" of rule 2 from "pos_high" to "neg_high," the front left part of the transfer surface flips down.

Any modification to the system is instantly visible. Change the "then-part" of the second rule from "pos_high" to "neg_high." The 3D Plot immediately shows the effect on the control surface (Figure 7.21).

In-Depth Analysis of the Crane Controller

Start the container crane simulation again by double-clicking on the crane icon in the *fuzzy*TECH Demo Edition program group of the Program Manager. Select "Debug\fT-Link" in *fuzzy*TECH without leaving the Interactive debug mode. This keeps all analyzer windows open.

Start the crane by pressing the [Fuzzy] button. Now, all editors and analyzers of *fuzzy*TECH show fuzzification, rule inference, and defuzzification while the crane is running. Does your crane operation look strange now? You may have left the "then-part" of the second rule to "neg_high." Just change it back to "pos_high;" you do not have to stop the crane for this.

Statistics Analyzer

To further examine the rule base, enable the Statistics analyzer by selecting "Analyzer\Statistics." In contrast to Time Plot, Transfer Plot, and 3D Plot, the Statistics analyzer does not have its own windows. Rather, it adds a new column in each Spreadsheet Rule Editor. In contrast to the other analyzers, you can only turn Statistics on and off by selecting "Analyzer\Statistics."

The Statistics column in the Spreadsheet Rule Editor is located at the right side of the window. You may have to widen the Spreadsheet Rule Editor window to see the Statistics column. For each rule, two bars show the minimum and maximum firing degree. The number between the bars counts how often the rule fires with a strength greater than zero. Pressing the [Statistics] button in the Spreadsheet Rule Editor invokes a configuration dialog box where you can also switch the counter to relative so that the number of rule firings is displayed in percentages. Pressing the [min-#-max] button resets the statistics.

System Modifications in Debug Mode

Note that not all modifications of the fuzzy logic system are possible in a debug mode. For example, you cannot modify the system structure in the Project Editor and you cannot create new linguistic variables or new terms. However, you can modify any existing membership function and create new definition points. Also, rules within an existing Rule Block can be added, modified, or deleted.

An analyzer similar to the 3D Plot is the Transfer Plot (Figure 7.22). A Transfer Plot is created like a 3D Plot, by selecting "Analyzer\Transfer Plot." The Transfer Plot shows a two-dimensional cut of the control surface and optionally the two cross-sections at the current operating point. The Transfer Plot also has a Trace function similar to that in the 3D Plot. Use the online help system of *fuzzy*TECH or [116] for more details.

Trace Analyzer

The Trace analyzer records the entire operation of the fuzzy logic system on file for later replay on the File Recorder. The Trace analyzer can work both on the development PC with every *fuzzy*TECH Edition as well as on the tar-

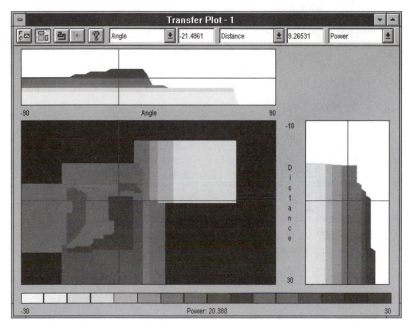

Figure 7.22   The Transfer Plot features a two-dimensional top view of the transfer surface. Optionally, the two vertical cross-section views for the current operation point are displayed too.

get hardware with the *fuzzy*TECH Online Edition or RTRCD Module. If the debug mode is Connection, Monitor, or Online/RTRCD, the Trace analyzer automatically works directly on the target hardware. If any other debug mode is active, the Trace analyzer works on the development PC.

Tracing on the Development PC

To use the Trace analyzer on the development PC, you have to first enable and configure the trace buffer. Leave debug mode and open the "Global Options" dialog box by selecting "Options\Global Options." Here, enable the check box "Trace Buffer:" in the "Trace" group and enter the value "1000" in the edit field. Then, enter fT-Link debug mode.

Select "Analyzer\Trace" to open the "Trace Control" dialog box shown in Figure 7.23. The maximum trace size of 1000 is shown in the upperright part of the dialog box. In the field "Trace Size:" you specify how much of the trace buffer you want to use for the current trace. Enter the value "100" for "Trace Size:" to store 100 records.

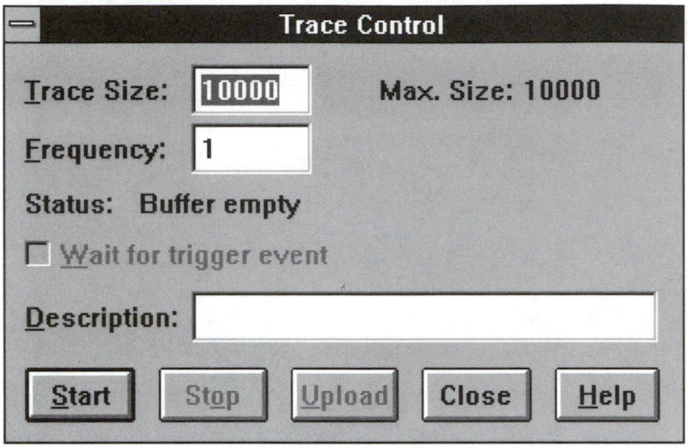

Figure 7.23   The Trace Control dialog box lets you configure traces as well as control them.

In the field "Frequency:" you specify how often the state of the fuzzy logic controller shall be recorded. Set "Frequency:" to 1, so that every single control loop will be recorded. Now, press the [Start] button. This causes the "Status:" display to move from "Buffer empty" to "Tracing in progress (0% completed)." The option "Wait for trigger event" is only active for target hardware tracing. Now, start the crane controller simulation by pressing the button [Fuzzy]. This also starts the tracing, and the Trace Control dialog box shows the progress. You can press the [Stop] button of the Trace Control dialog box any time or wait until the trace has been completed. "Status:" shows the number of steps recorded. To write the trace to a file, press the [Upload] button and accept the file name *fuzzy*TECH suggests. After completion, a dialog appears asking you whether you want to view the file just written. You can now use this file for replay with the File Recorder that is explained later. Close the Trace Control dialog box by pressing the [Close] button.

Tracing on the Target Hardware

If used on the target hardware, the Trace analyzer establishes its own trace buffer space within the generated code. Hence, you need to enable the Trace analyzer and define the maximum trace buffer size in the "Global Options" dialog box prior to code generation. Since the Trace analyzer works with its own buffer, it is not limited to the bandwidth of the serial communication between the development PC and target hardware. Thus, even the fastest processes can be recorded by the Trace analyzer, uploaded later to the development PC, and stored on disk. In later replay with the File Recorder, the Trace analyzer can give you "slow-motion" analysis of your real-time system performance. Also, very slow processes can be traced because the trace frequency can be set to a higher value, so that days of continuous operation can be uploaded at once for analysis.

Note that when you trace on the target hardware, you may also trigger the trace from the target hardware. That allows, for example, starting the trace automatically if a certain condition occurs. The development PC must not be connected while tracing. If the condition occurs at some point, you can later link to the target hardware, select "Debug/Connection," and upload the trace. Even if the communication between the development PC and the target hardware is interrupted, the trace completes automatically. After the trace is completed, you may upload it as often as you wish. If supported by the target hardware, the Trace analyzer writes a timestamp into every data record that is displayed with the File Recorder as the record name. The Trace analyzer provided with the *fuzzy*TECH Demo Edition does not support target hardware tracing.

Creating Sample Patterns

To create sample patterns that cover the control space, *fuzzy*TECH features a Pattern Generator. Select "File\Pattern Generator" to invoke the Pattern Generator dialog box as shown in Figure 7.24. The list box in the upper part of the window shows the minimum and maximum values for the pattern to be generated as well as the step width for each input variable. To change any of these values, first select the variable in the list box and then change the values in the fields "From:," "To:," and "Step:." The option "Margins: On" ensures that the minimum and maximum values will be part of the pattern in any case. *fuzzy*TECH computes the resulting number of patterns as "Number of Records" and the required disk space to save these patterns as "Disk Space." Click on the [Generate...] button to create the pattern. Accept the file name *fuzzy*TECH proposes. The suffix *.PTN indicates a pattern generated with *fuzzy*TECH. Close the Pattern Generator by pressing the [Close] button. You can view the generated pattern using the "File\View File..." option.

Now, enable the File Recorder in *fuzzy*TECH by selecting "Debug\File Recorder." This opens the "Read File From..." dialog box. Specify "Pattern Data File (*.PTN)" as "Filetype" and open the file "CRANE.PTN" you just

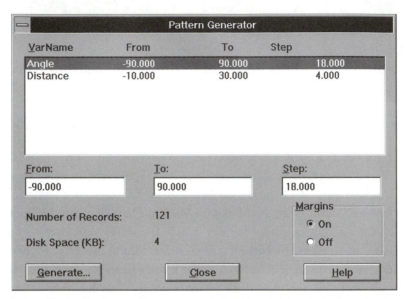

Figure 7.24   The Pattern Generator creates test input data sets for the current fuzzy logic system.

created with the Pattern Generator. Clicking the [OK] button opens the File Control dialog box (Figure 7.25).

The File Control dialog box lets you navigate through the pattern data. The File Control dialog box always sits on top of all open windows to always allow access to its controls. The group "File Information" at the upper part of this dialog box shows information about the sample data file and the current record. Open a 3D Plot, activate the Tracing in the 3D Plot, and open a Time Plot containing all input and output variables. Then press the [>>] button in the File Control dialog box. *fuzzy*TECH now processes all patterns in the files from the first record to the last. If you change the direction in which you browse through the records in the file, a vertical red line is plotted in the Time Plot. If you change anything in the fuzzy logic system, such as membership functions or rules, a vertical yellow line indicates the change in the Time Plot.

The [>] and [<] buttons step one pattern forward or back. The [■] button is the stop button. The outer buttons move the File Control to the first and last record of the file, respectively. To directly address a record, use the scroll bar. The current record name is shown as "Record:" in case a record name is specified in the file. For example, real-time traces that are uploaded

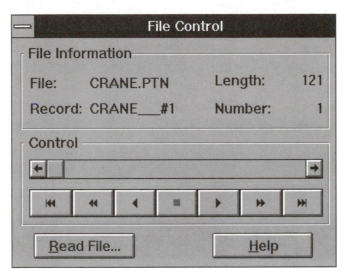

Figure 7.25   The File debug mode lets you navigate through sample data files from various sources.

from target hardware always store a timestamp as a record name. Pressing the button [Read File…] lets you change the sample data file. Now, specify "Trace Buffer File (*.TRC)" as "Filetype" and select CRANE.TRC. This lets you browse through the data you traced before.

If you want the results of the fuzzy logic inference on file, use the Batch debug mode. The Batch debug mode does not visualize the fuzzy logic inference, but generates an output file that contains the computed output values in addition to the input values. Activate the Batch debug mode by "Debug\Batch," specify the input data file "CRANE.PTN," and click [OK]. *fuzzy*TECH will suggest "CRANE.OUT" as the name for the output file. Accept this name by clicking [OK]. You can view the resulting file, "CRANE.OUT," by "File\View File…."

The FTL Format

*fuzzy*TECH uses the hardware-independent FTL format (Fuzzy Technology Language) to store a fuzzy logic system on disk. Section 3.1.3 contains a detailed description of FTL. If you manually edit an FTL file that was generated by *fuzzy*TECH, make sure to erase the line containing "SHELL = DEMO;". This forces *fuzzy*TECH to do an extended consistency check when opening the FTL file.

Data Format

*fuzzy*TECH uses the same ASCII format for input and output values for multiple purposes. The different suffixes classify the usage of the file:

*.PTN:	Files generated by the Pattern Generator
*.TRC:	Files uploaded from a target hardware trace
*.OUT:	Files generated by the Batch Mode
*.IN:	Files recorded from a real process
*.EXP:	Files for NeuroFuzzy training

In the data format, each row represents a complete record. The first and third rows of a file are reserved for comments describing the file and its origin. The second row must contain all variable names. The actual data records start with row 4. The first string in each row is interpreted as a record name. The values for all the variables in the sequence of row 2 follow, delimited by an arbitrary number of space characters. For a detailed description of the format, refer to [116] or the online help system.

Customization of the fuzzyTECH User Interface

The user interface of *fuzzy*TECH can be customized in many ways. You may, for instance, turn off individual toolbars or the status bar to save screen space on low-resolution monitors. Open the "Preferences" dialog box (Figure 7.26) by selecting "Options\Preferences..." from the main menu.

Toolbar

For each window type, you can turn the toolbar on or off.

Thick Lines

Use this option for high-resolution monitors to increase the line thickness in Variable Editors and the Time Plot.

Background Color

Use this option for screen shots of the Time Plot and the 3D Plot to turn the background color to white.

Figure 7.26   The Preferences dialog box lets you customize the user interface of *fuzzy*TECH.

Font Size

Depending on the screen size, *fuzzy*TECH has preset the font size for many windows. You can change this using the Font Size option.

Automatic Project Backup

*fuzzy*TECH periodically creates backup files from the current project. Not supported by the *fuzzy*TECH Demo Edition.

Confirm Messages

When enabled, this option ensures that a confirmation dialog box is shown any time you delete a component of the fuzzy logic system. Experienced designers should disable this option because the UNDO function of *fuzzy*TECH reverses accidental deletions.

Debug Window Iconized

The Debug window is active in any debug mode. It always displays the crisp values of all input and output variables of the system. Enabling this option always iconizes the Debug window any time you start the Debug mode. If you only have low video resolution, you can use this option to save screen space and computing time.

Show Status Line

Lets you turn the status bar on and off.

Save Window Position

By enabling this option, *fuzzy*TECH saves all window positions and all analyzer configurations together with the project. A detailed description follows.

Saving of Window and Analyzer Configurations

If the "Save Window Configuration" option in the Preferences dialog box is enabled, *fuzzy*TECH saves the positions and sizes of all windows as well as the configurations of all open analyzers in a *.CFG file whenever you save the *.FTL file. If you open an FTL file, *fuzzy*TECH searches for a *.CFG file with the same project name (the project name consists of the first eight characters of the file name). If this *.CFG file exists, it will be opened and all windows restored in size and all analyzers (once you activate a debug mode) restore in size and configuration, provided you saved your project while these windows were open. You can inspect the *.CFG file with an ASCII editor. If no *.CFG file with the same project name is found in the same directory, all windows open in default size and you have to configure analyzers manually.

The functions "Save As…" and "Open…" also let you save and open *.CFG files under a different project name. This allows you to have multiple configurations for the same FTL project. To reset the configuration to *fuzzy*TECH defaults, just erase the *.CFG with the same project name as the *.FTL file.

7.1.3   Training the XOR using the NeuroFuzzy Module

This section describes how to use the *fuzzy*TECH NeuroFuzzy Module for the exclusive or (XOR) example from Section 4.2.3. As an exercise, you can also train other logical functions (OR, AND, NOR, NAND, NOT, $\Rightarrow$) later.

Training Data

First start *fuzzy*TECH from the MS-Windows Program Manager and select "File\View File..." in the main menu, choose "Example Data File (*.EXP)" as "Filetype," and select the file "XOR.EXP." This file is located in the subdirectory "...\SAMPLES\XOR." The editor window shows the contents of the file (Figure 7.27). The first and third rows of the file contain comments while the second row specifies the names of the linguistic variables "Input_A," "Input_B," and "Output." The actual data records start with row 4. Note that the file may not contain any empty row.

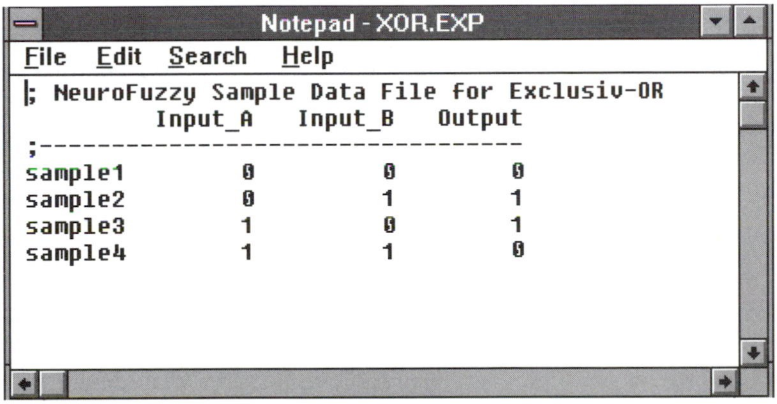

```
┌─────────────────────────────────────────────────┐
│ —              Notepad - XOR.EXP          ▼ ▲   │
├─────────────────────────────────────────────────┤
│ File   Edit   Search   Help                     │
├─────────────────────────────────────────────────┤
│ ; NeuroFuzzy Sample Data File for Exclusiv-OR  ↑│
│            Input_A    Input_B    Output         │
│ ;----------------------------------------        │
│ sample1        0          0          0          │
│ sample2        0          1          1          │
│ sample3        1          0          1          │
│ sample4        1          1          0          │
│                                                  │
│                                                 ↓│
├─────────────────────────────────────────────────┤
│ ◄                                             ► │
└─────────────────────────────────────────────────┘
```

Figure 7.27   Contents of the file XOR.EXP.

The data record rows start with the record names "sample1" through "sample4." Then the values of the two input and one output variables follow. The values must follow the IEEE format for float values. See [119] or the on-line help system for details. You may use any ASCII editor to generate a training data file. Also, most spreadsheets, databases, or data acquisition software systems can generate the training data files.

Development Steps with the NeuroFuzzy Module

To develop a solution using the *fuzzy*TECH NeuroFuzzy Module, you have to follow these steps:

1   Get training data and cluster them

2   Create an "empty" fuzzy logic system

3   Enter all existing knowledge on the solution

4   Open the components of the fuzzy logic system to be trained by the NeuroFuzzy Module

5   Configure the NeuroFuzzy Module

6   Train the sample data

7   Evaluate performance

8   Optimize manually

9   Implement the result as a "pure" fuzzy logic system

Step 1

The training data for the XOR example is easy to obtain as a decision table of the digital (Boolean) XOR. In practical applications, finding a representative set of sample data can, however, be the hardest part of the design. See [119] for details.

When you use training data that was recorded from a real process, chances are that many data sets are redundant. To use training data sets with redundant records lengthens training significantly. Even worse, if most of the data records describe the same condition they will have a much greater impact on the solution. For example, if you want to design a controller for a continuous process, 95% of your recorded training data may describe the steady state and only 5% of the data describe other conditions. Using this data will result in a controller that excels in the steady state but performs poorly in other conditions. To avoid this, training data that stems from a real process should be clustered before being used in NeuroFuzzy training.

The NeuroFuzzy Module provides a clustering function that features standard clustering methods as well as fuzzy clustering methods by selecting "Neuro/Clustering." See [119] for details on clustering training data. For the examples used with the attached software, no clustering is required. Hence, clustering will not be treated any further here. The *fuzzy*TECH Demo Edition does not support clustering features.

Step 2

The NeuroFuzzy Module can only train an existing fuzzy logic system. Hence, the "empty" structure of the fuzzy logic system must be defined before training can start. This structure consists of linguistic variables, terms, membership functions, rule blocks, rules, and interfaces. *fuzzy*TECH supports this with a Fuzzy Design Wizard.

Step 3

In this step you enter all existing knowledge on the solution into the fuzzy logic system. The NeuroFuzzy Module uses this so-called a priori knowledge as the starting point of the training. The fact that existing knowledge can easily be used is a big advantage of the NeuroFuzzy approach over a neural net solution. If no knowledge on the solution exists, you must skip step 3. The NeuroFuzzy Module must extract the necessary information solely from the sample data in this case.

Note that even if all information required to build the solution is already contained in the training data, entering existing knowledge will expedite the training. If the training data is of poor quality, using existing knowledge to help the NeuroFuzzy Module may be the only way to come up with a solution at all.

Step 4

The NeuroFuzzy Module training paradigm is highly structured. You can exactly define which components of the system shall be modified by the NeuroFuzzy Module. For linguistic variables you can open specific terms for training, and for rule blocks you can open the individual rules for training.

Use this to exclude specific rules from training. For example, you may not want the NeuroFuzzy Module to modify any of the rules that are relevant for the safe operation of a plant. You can also exclude rules that you have identified as wrong.

When using multiple sample data sets for training, you can train different parts of the fuzzy logic system with different sample data. For example, if you want to generate a controller for a continuous process, you may have data sets representing normal operation as well as data sets representing various disturbances and critical situations. If you use these data sets to train different parts of the rule base, you ensure that rules for the different operational conditions are separated.

Step 5

To configure the NeuroFuzzy Module you specify the learning method and its parameters. For details on different training methods, see [119]. For most applications, the default selections determined automatically by the NeuroFuzzy Module will be sufficient. The NeuroFuzzy Module provided with the *fuzzy*TECH Demo Edition only supports one standard learning method.

Step 6

During the actual training, the NeuroFuzzy Module continuously selects training data records to test how well the current fuzzy logic system represents this record. It then uses a modified error back propagation algorithm to determine how the fuzzy logic system shall be modified to better represent this one training data record. When reaching a predefined error threshold or a predefined number of steps, the training stops. You may start and stop the training any time to test, alter parameters, modify rules or membership functions, and select other training data sets.

Step 7

After completion of the actual training, you can test the resulting fuzzy logic system using all debug modes and analyzers of *fuzzy*TECH. If the result is not satisfactory, you can repeat some development steps.

Step 8

In contrary to neural nets, the result of NeuroFuzzy training is a fuzzy logic system that you can directly optimize by hand. How to manually optimize the system depends greatly on the application. In closed-loop control applications, often online optimization using a real process or a simulation is very efficient. In data analysis applications, a prototypical implementation of the training result and further tests show if and in what respect the solution needs further optimization.

Step 9

The result of NeuroFuzzy training is a "pure" fuzzy logic system that can be implemented using *fuzzy*TECH on microcontrollers, PCs, workstations, PLCs, or industrial controllers.

Now, back to the XOR example. The training data already exists. Hence, the next step is the creation of an "empty" fuzzy logic system using the Fuzzy Design Wizard.

The Fuzzy Design Wizard

The Fuzzy Design Wizard (FDW) supports quick generation of a system's prototype. For inexperienced designers, the FDW provides a step-by-step guide through all design steps. Experienced designers can design a system's prototype in just minutes.

With these features, the FDW is well suited to create the "empty" fuzzy logic system that the NeuroFuzzy training requires. Call the FDW by either selecting "File\Fuzzy Design Wizard..." in the main menu or clicking the respective button in the main toolbar. In the first FDW window (Figure 7.28) you specify:

■ Whether the fuzzy logic system to be created shall be added to the currently opened fuzzy logic system or whether you want to create a new system.

■ Whether a sample data file exists that can be analyzed by the FDW. The FDW uses information such as variable names as well as interval and distribution of the variable values to propose default variables in later FDW windows.

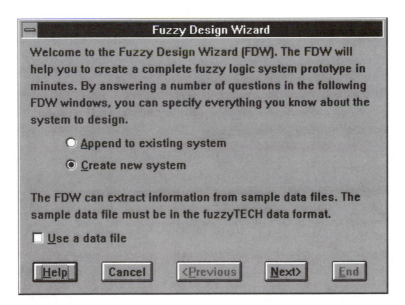

Figure 7.28   In the first Fuzzy Design Wizard window, you specify whether the new components shall be added to an existing system or shall define a new system. By specifying a sample data file, the FDW extracts design data automatically.

The buttons [Help], [Cancel], [Previous], [Next], and [End] are located at the lower part of every FDW window. The button [Next] always gets you in the next window, the button [Previous] always gets you back to the previous window. By stepping back and forth in the FDW windows, you can reverse any design decision you make.

The button [End] forces the FDW to generate the fuzzy logic system with the current specifications. Since the FDW proposes default values for every design decision, the button [End] can be pressed in every FDW window. A confirmation dialog box (Figure 7.29) appears before the actual system is generated. Do not generate the system now.

Figure 7.29   Before the Fuzzy Design Wizard generates the system, this confirmation dialog box is displayed.

The basic idea of the FDW is to propose default values for all design decisions. This minimizes the input required for generating a fuzzy logic system's prototype. If you specify a sample data file, the FDW will determine default parameters for many design decisions automatically from the data. Note that you can overwrite all of the default parameters.

Now, enable the check box "Use a data file" so that the FDW analyzes the file "XOR.EXP" which contains the training data for the XOR. When you click on the [Next] button or press the [Return] key, the FDW prompts you for the sample data file. Select "XOR.EXP" in the subdirectory "…\SAMPLES\XOR." Figure 7.30 shows the next FDW window where you specify the number of input, output, and intermediate variables as well as the number of terms. You may change the number of terms for individual linguistic variables later.

By analyzing the file "XOR.EXP," the FDW discovered that the system to be created has two input variables and one output variable. Due to the simple structure of the training data, the FDW does not propose intermediate variables. For the output variable, the FDW proposes a range from less than 0 to greater than 1. Then move to the next FDW window by clicking the [Next] button or pressing the [Return] key.

The following three FDW windows specify the three linguistic variables of the system. The first of these FDW windows (Figure 7.31) defines the first input variable. By analyzing the sample data set, the FDW has set the range

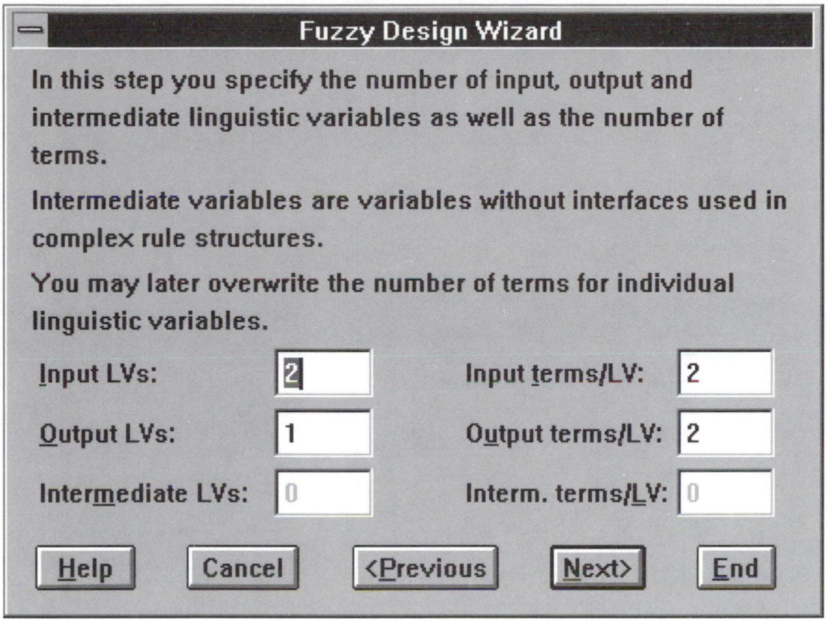

Figure 7.30   In the second FDW window you specify the number of input, output, and intermediate variables and their term numbers.

for the variable from 0 to 1. The FDW has also determined that only 0 and 1 values are specified for all variables and proposes the term names "false" and "true." You may choose other term names in the drop list box or overwrite the term number. For now, accept the default settings proposed by the FDW and step to the next FDW window.

The next FDW window defines the next input variable, "Input_B." Accept the proposed defaults and step to the next FDW window that defines the output variable. For the output variable, the FDW proposes a range larger than from 0 to 1. This is due to the consideration that a later shift of the membership functions out of the range 0 to 1 could be necessary [119]. Overwrite the range value with −0.25 and 1.25 so the analyzers will zoom the interval and step to the next FDW window.

This FDW window defines the defuzzification method for the output variable. Accept the proposed default by clicking the [Next] button or pressing the [Return] key. The next FDW window defines the rule blocks (Figure 7.32). Due to the simplicity of the training data, the FDW proposes just one rule block. Enabling the check box "Create Rule Base" lets the FDW generate

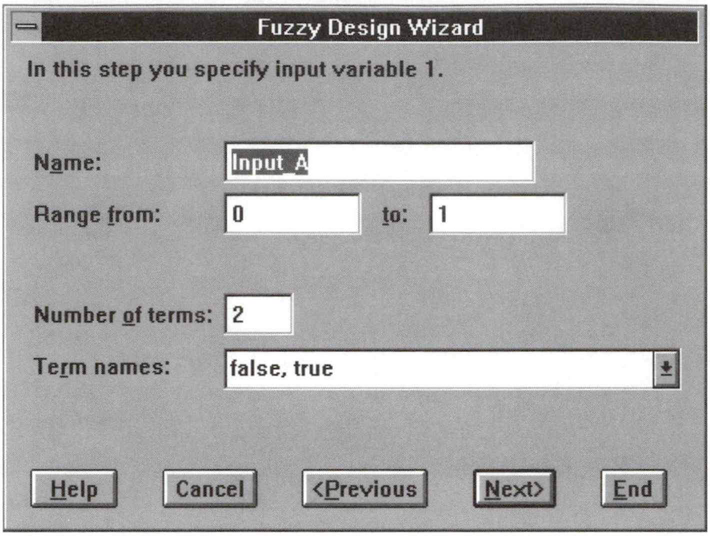

Figure 7.31   The FDW presents a variable definition window for each
variable to be defined.

a complete rule set for each rule block. For each combination of terms, a rule
is generated. As Degree-of-Support (DoS), either random values ("Random
Value") or a constant value ("User Defined Value") is assigned.

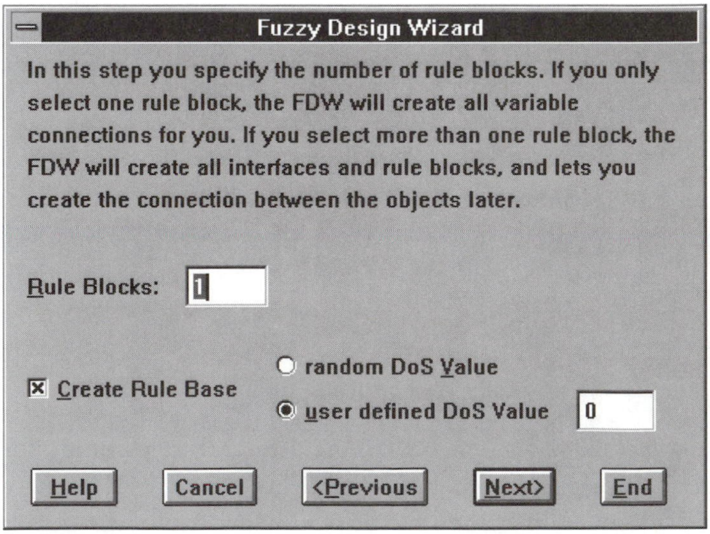

Figure 7.32   The last FDW window specifies whether and how the FDW
generates rule blocks.

The FDW proposes the generation of a rule set where all rules have a DoS of 0. Since the DoS is the degree of membership a rule has in the set of totally true rules [116], this is equivalent to a set of completely false rules. Hence, the generated rule set contains no information. The reason for creating a complete but totally false rule set is that the NeuroFuzzy training can only start with an existing rule set. Set "user defined value" to 0.5 because the 3D Plot does not display the control surface when no rule fires, and either click the [Next] button or press the [Return] key. As this is the final window of the FDW, this is equivalent to pressing the [End] button and the confirmation dialog box (Figure 7.29) appears. Confirming the dialog generates the system as shown in Figure 7.33.

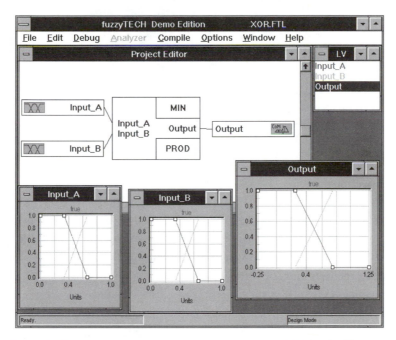

Figure 7.33 Structure of the system generated by the FDW for the file XOR.EXP.

Open Components of the Fuzzy Logic System for Learning

In this step, you open the components of the fuzzy logic system to be modified by the NeuroFuzzy training. For the XOR example, you open the output variable and all rules for training. First, open a Variable Editor window for the variable "Output" by double-clicking on the variable name in the LV window. To open all membership functions for learning, click on the "Learn all MBF" button in the toolbar of the Variable Editor. If you only want to open the membership functions partially, open the pop-up menu by clicking right somewhere in the Variable Editor and select the "Learn all MBFs..." option. This opens the dialog box shown in Figure 7.34 where you can specify the range in which the NeuroFuzzy Module may modify the membership functions. To indicate membership functions opened for learning, an "L:" appears to the left of the respective term name in the Term list box of the Variable Editor.

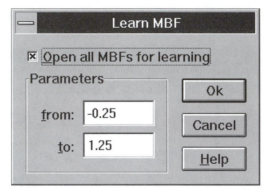

Figure 7.34   Open the membership functions for learning.

Now, open the Spreadsheet Rule Editor for the Rule Block. The Fuzzy Design Wizard already opened all rules for learning. This is indicated by the gray background of the DoS values. To open or close all rules for learning, you can use the Rule Block Utilities that you activate by clicking the [Utilities] button. Click [Learn...] in the Rule Block Utilities dialog box to invoke the Open Rules for the Learning dialog box. Here, you can enter the interval in which the NeuroFuzzy Module may alter the DoS of the rules. To open and close individual rules, click on the DoS value in the Spreadsheet Rule Editor and select [Learn...] in the pop-up list. Since the Fuzzy Design Wizard has already opened all rules for learning, you must not make any further settings here.

Configuring the NeuroFuzzy Module

In this step you specify the learn methods and set parameters for them. Open the NeuroFuzzy Configuration dialog box (Figure 7.35) by either clicking the respective button in the main toolbar or selecting "Neuro\Configuration..." in the main menu. The list box "Learn Methods:" shows all available training algorithms. The NeuroFuzzy Module of the *fuzzy*TECH Demo Edition only supports one basic training algorithm: the "Random Method." You may also develop your own training algorithm using the elements provided by the NeuroFuzzy Module [119] and list them in the "Learn Methods:" list box.

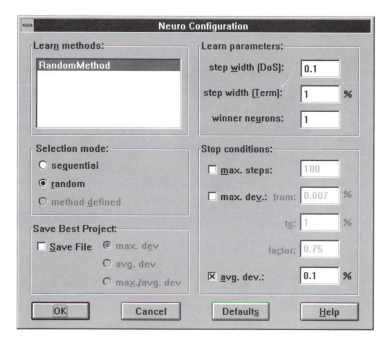

Figure 7.35   The Neuro Configuration dialog box lets you select a learning method and set parameters for it.

The group "Learn parameters:" lets you set parameters for the algorithm. Leave these parameters at the proposed default values for the training of the XOR example. The group "Stop conditions:" lets you specify when the training should automatically terminate. The three conditions are used alternatively. For instance, if you enable "max. steps:" with a value of 100 and "max. dev.:" with a value of 0.1, the training stops after 100 training cycles or when the maximum error is lower than 10%, whichever occurs first. If you do not select any stop condition, you must stop training manually.

The "Save Best Project:" group lets the NeuroFuzzy Module save the best result with minimum error automatically during training. This is useful for unsupervised training sessions because with the NeuroFuzzy paradigm, the error can increase during training to avoid being trapped in local optima.

The group "Selection mode:" lets you specify the sequence in which the samples are selected for training: "sequential" always follows the sequence in the sample data file, while "random" selects an arbitrary sequence. Whenever the sample data is sorted in some way, you should select "random." As the XOR contains sorted samples, select "random," make sure all other options are specified as shown in Figure 7.35, and leave the dialog box by clicking [OK].

Training and Analysis

All modifications the NeuroFuzzy Module carries out become visible in the *fuzzy*TECH editors and analyzers. To make the training algorithm as computationally efficient as possible, however, you may not modify any of the *fuzzy*TECH windows during training. Hence, you must configure and arrange all *fuzzy*TECH editors and analyzers before you start training. Figure 7.36 shows a window configuration that works well when training the XOR example. Activate the Interactive debug mode, iconize the Debug window, open the 3D Plot, and activate the "Repaint 3D Plot" and the "Background Paint" options in the 3D Plot. Then position the windows as in the figure.

The 3D Plot shows a flat control surface that is constant at 0.5. This is due to the fact that the rule base contains a rule for every possible combination of input and output variable terms. Each rule is valid with a degree of support of 0.5 that is as much true as false. Hence, all rules equalize each other and the result of the fuzzy logic inference is always 0.5. The following training steps will modify the degree of support of the rules and the membership functions of the output variable. Initiate the training by either clicking on the "Neuro Learning" button of the main window toolbar or by selecting "Neuro\Learning" from the main menu. Because the NeuroFuzzy Module only generates fuzzy logic systems that are easy to comprehend, it operates with Standard MBFs. Therefore, all membership functions are converted to Standard MBFs at each initiation of training. Click [OK] on the confirmation dialog for this conversion and select the file "XOR.EXP" for training. This opens the Learn Control dialog box.

Learn Control

The Learn Control dialog box lets you supervise the entire training process. While the Learn Control dialog box is open, you cannot use any other function in any window of *fuzzy*TECH. You can however, close the Learn Control dialog box any time by clicking on the "Close" button of the Learn Control

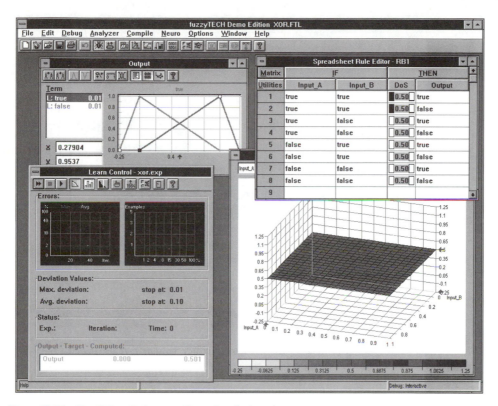

Figure 7.36   Possible window configuration for learning.

dialog box toolbar, use other *fuzzy*TECH functions, and open the Learn Control dialog box later. All of the system modifications conducted by the Neuro-Fuzzy Module will be saved.

The three left buttons on the toolbar "Start," "Stop," and "Step" let you initiate and halt the training. The next two buttons "Error Plot" and "Statistics" let you choose how the training progress is displayed in the "Errors:" group of the Learn Control dialog box. The Error Plot shows how the maximum and the average error develops over time, and Statistic displays a histogram of how many examples have been trained with a certain error. Select both buttons so Error Plot and Statistics are both displayed as in Figure 7.36.

The next button, "Error List," displays a sorted list of all examples with an error above the threshold specified in the Neuro Configuration dialog box. The next button "Perform" updates the error computation in case the training is interrupted by the "Stop" button. For computational efficiency, the Neuro-

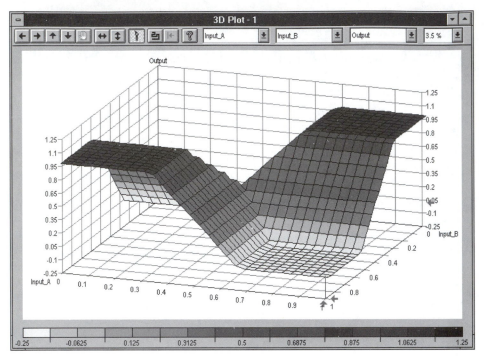

Figure 7.37   Learning result in the 3D-Plot.

Fuzzy Module automatically updates the error computation only at the start of every iteration.

The next button "Update Debug Windows" should be pressed for the XOR example. When pressed, every modification the NeuroFuzzy Module carries out is instantly reflected in all editors and analyzer windows that have been opened before the Learn Control dialog box was invoked. For details on these options and explanations of the other elements of the Learn Control dialog box, refer to the online help system.

Start Training

Now, initiate training by pressing the [Start] button. If you have followed all these steps you should now be able to monitor the training in the windows of *fuzzy*TECH. The NeuroFuzzy Module modifies the DoS of the rules and moves the membership functions of the output variable. The 3D Plot shows how this affects the transfer surface. Figure 7.37 shows the transfer surface after training. The input combinations (0,0), (0,1), (1,0), and (1,1) from the sample data file will be represented well with the trained fuzzy logic system. Between these points, the resulting fuzzy logic system performs a continuous approximation.

You may use the File debug mode to step through the samples in the "XOR.EXP" file. Try to train other logical functions as an exercise. If you want to eliminate rules that have only a small influence on the system after training, you can use the "alpha cut" function from the Rule Block Utilities.

More Functions in fuzzyTECH and the NeuroFuzzy Module

The previous sections give as much introduction to the functionality of *fuzzy*TECH and the NeuroFuzzy Module as is required to work with the other software simulations contained with this book. Other Modules, such as the DataAnalyzer Module, preconfigured links to simulation environments, spreadsheets, and databases, as well as fuzzy logic function blocks for industrial controllers and standard PLCs, are not presented here. Please ask Inform Software Corporation for more detailed information.

7.2   FTL Reference

Fuzzy Technology Language (FTL) was designed as a hardware- and vendor-independent description language for fuzzy logic systems. FTL is an ASCII format to support cross-platform porting of code. Also, the FTL format documents a fuzzy logic system. Section 7.2.1 contains a complete FTL keyword reference and Section 7.2.2 a context reference.

7.2.1   FTL Keyword Reference

Different keywords are used for objects, slots, and slot values. A section of dedicated keywords to enter values or strings as slot entries follows. All keywords are in capital letters.

KEYWORDS	
INTERFACE	defines an interface in the object section.
LVAR	section containing the definition of a linguistic variable.
MODEL	section containing the entire model definitions (variable and object section).

KEYWORDS *(Continued)*

NEUROFUZZY	section with tokens dedicated to the NeuroFuzzy module, not mandatory.
OBJECT_SECTION	contains interfaces, remarks, and ruleblock objects.
ONLINE	section containing information for online development, not part of the project section, not mandatory.
PROJECT	main section for project data.
REMARK	defines a remark in the object section.
RULEBLOCK	defines a ruleblock in the object section.
RULES	defines a fuzzy rule as part of a ruleblock object.
SHELLOPTIONS	section containing a terminal configuration dedicated to a project, not mandatory.
SYSTEM	part of the sucologic section, containing the informations concerning the hardware configuration of development system and PLC, not mandatory.
TERM	section containing the definitions of a term, part of the lvar object.
TERMINAL	section containing information concerning the terminal configuration, not part of the project section, section not mandatory.
VARIABLE_SECTION	section containing all definitions of linguistic variables.

SLOTS

AGGREGATION	= (MIN_MAXIGAMMAIMIN_AVG,PAR(fnumber));
AUTHOR	= authorstring;

SLOTS *(Continued)*	
AUTORESTART	= ONIOFF;
AVGDEVIATION	= fnumber;
BASEVAR	= stringtoken;
BAUDRATE	= inumber;
BSUM_AGGREGATION	= ONIOFF;
BTYPE	= FLOATIDOUBLEI8_BITI16_BITI32_BIT;
C_TYPE	= ANSIIKR;
CMDLINE	= cmdstring;
COLOR	= RED(inumber),GREEN(inumber),BLUE(inumber);
COMPOSITION	= (MIN_MAXIGAMMAIMIN_AVGI,PAR(fnumber));
CONDITIONS	= COLDIWARMIHOT;
CONNECT	= (stringtoken,SHOWIHIDE)
CONNECTION	= PORT1IPORT2IPORT3IPORT4IPORTNFS
CONST_MODIFIER	= ONIOFF;
CREATED	= datestring;
CYCLETIME	= inumber;
DATAREAD	= ONLINEIOFFLINE
DATASEQUENCE	= RANDOM I SEQUENTIAL;
FAST_CMBF	= ONIOFF;
FASTCOA	= ONIOFF;

SLOTS *(Continued)*

FILE CODE	= ONIOFF;
FILESIZE	= inumber KB;
FLOAT_COA	= ONIOFF;
FONTSIZE	= inumber;
HIRES_INFERENCE	= ONIOFF;
INPUT	= (varstring,FUZZYICMBFILUT, STEPS(inumber)IFCMBF);
INPUTBUFFER	= inumber;
LASTCHANGE	= datestring;
LEARNRULE	= stringtoken;
LOGFREQUENCE	= inumber;
LVRANGE	= MIN(fnumber),MAX(fnumber),MINDEF(inumber), MAXDEF(inumber),DEFAULT_OUTPUT(fnumber);
MARKERRESET	= ONIOFF;
MAXDEVIATION	= fnumber;
MAXSTEPS	= inumber;
MEMORYTEST	= ONIOFF;
NAME	= stringtoken;
NEURONS	= inumber;
ONLINE_BUFFER	= (ONIOFF,PAR(inumber));
ONLINE_CODE	= ONIOFF;

SLOTS *(Continued)*	
OUTPUT	= (varstring,COAIMOMBSUMIMOMICOMICOABSUMI FCOABSUMIFCOAINO);
OUTPUTBUFFER	= inumber;
PARAMSTR	= parameterstring;
POINTS	= (fnumber,fnumber),(fnumber,fnumber),..., (fnumber,fnumber);
POS	= inumber,inumber;
PROTOCOL	= HARDWAREINO;
PUBLIC_IO	= ONIOFF;
RANGECHECK	= ONIOFF;
RESOLUTION	= XGRID(fnumber),YGRID(fnumber), SHOWGRID(ONIOFF),SNAPTOGRID(ONIOFF);
RULE_BUFFER	= (ONIOFF,PAR(inumber));
SCALE_MBF	= ONIOFF;
SCALE_MEMBERSHIP	= ONIOFF;
SHAPE	= LINEARIS_SHAPE,PAR(inumber);
SHELL	= stringtoken;
STEPWIDTHDOS	= fnumber;
STEPWIDTHTERM	= fnumber;
STOPBITS	= inumber;
TARGET	= F166IPCII196;
TERMNAME	= stringtoken;

SLOTS *(Continued)*	
TIMESTAMP	= timestampstring;
TRACE_BUFFER	= (ONIOFF,PAR(inumber));
UPDATEDBGWIN	= ONIOFF;

FUZZY RULES	
IF	varstring=termstring
AND	varstring=termstring
THEN	varstring=termstring
WITH	fnumber
:OPEN	(fnumber,fnumber);

SLOT VALUE KEYWORDS		
16_BIT	COLD	FCOABSUM
32_BIT	COLD	FLOAT
8_BIT	COM	FUZZY
AND	CRISP	GAMMA
ANSI	DEFAULT_OUTPUT	GREEN
BLUE	DOUBLE	HARDWARE
CMBF	F166	HIDE
COA	FCMBF	HOT
COABSUM	FCOA	HOT

SLOT VALUE KEYWORDS *(Continued)*

I196	NO	RANDOM
IF	NOMBF	RED
KB	OFF	S_SHAPE
KR	OFFLINE	SEQUENTIAL
LINEAR	ON	SHOW
LUT	ONLINE	SHOWGRID
MAX	OPEN	SNAPTOGRID
MAX_PROD	PAR	STEPS
MAXDEF	PC	THEN
MIN	PORT1	WARM
MIN_AVG	PORT2	WARM
MIN_MAX	PORT3	WITH
MINDEF	PORT4	XGRID
MOM	PORTRPC	YGRID
MOMBSUM	POS	

SLOT VALUES

authorstring	string of max 255 characters terminated by semicolon
awlstring	string terminated by }
cmdstring	string of max 255 characters terminated by semicolon
commentstring	string of max 255 characters terminated by }

SLOT VALUES *(Continued)*	
dateformat	format for datestring using the characters: "Y" (year), "M" (month), or "D" (day)
	Examples: >> YYYY.MM.DD << (U.S. format)
	>> DD.MM.YYYY << (International format)
datestring	date in specified format up to 4 plus 2 plus 2 digits seperated by "."
	Examples: >> 1992.10.06 << (U.S. format)
	>> 06.10.1992 << (International format)
fnumber	floating point number using digits, ".", "e", or "E", and "+" or "−" behind the ".", a digit is expected, exponential notation is possible Examples: >> 0.56 <<, >> −5.4e−1 <<
inumber	integer number of max 5 digits with leading +/− (not mandatory) Examples: >> 6 << >> −5 <<
parameterstring	string of max 255 characters terminated by semicolon
stringtoken	sequence of characters (letters, digits, set of symbols of maximum length of 16 terminated by semicolon. Feasable symbols are !_$%&\[\]\?\.\−
termstring	string of max 16 characters terminated by a blank and checks whether the name matches to one of the terms of the variable specified before
textstring	string of max 39 characters terminated by semicolon
timestampstring	sequence of 16 digits
varstring	string of max 16 characters terminated by blank

7.2.2   FTL Context Reference

The context of FTL is expressed by the keywords, a set of separators (brackets, commas, semicolons, and equal signs), and sequencing rules. Comments, as with C, are marked by /*..*/ brackets and typed in italics. In several rules, the comment /*NULL*/ occurs. Here, an empty section will be accepted; no keyword, sign, or other entry is necessary.

Separators

Separators directly used in FTL are denoted in quotation marks; the complete set of separators is:

"{"   "}"   "("   ")"   ","   ";"   "="

Sequences

"{ " and "}" brackets are used if a given sequence is mandatory for a list of objects. Values and arrays of values are put into "(".. ")" brackets, values of an array are separated by commas. The "=" equal sign allocates values, arrays, or a slot keyword to an object keyword. A semicolon ";" ends every section and command. Separators denoted without quotation marks are used for the syntax of rules; the set of these separators is colon, slash, back slash, semicolon, and comment signs:

: | \   ;   /*comments*/

Sequencing Rules

Sequencing rules are used for allocating a structure to keywords, separators, and slot entries. A rule starts with the name (here denoted in small letters) and a colon; the end of the rule is marked by a semicolon. Of course, a rule can contain other rules and itself—as with a recursive function call. The names of the rules do not occur in the FTL files. Every project in FTL must be globally seen as the first referenced rule:

program

| —An Exclusive OR

The "|" sign is a logical construct. It must be used as a logical OR for selecting one out of different alternatives (e.g.: ON | OFF). The | sign does not occur in the FTL files.

\ —A Nonexclusive OR

Sometimes, more than one alternative of a rule or more than one section classified by a different keyword can be used. Here, no special sequence of the sections or slots is recommended.

```
program:
        PROJECT    projectspec
    \   ONLINE     online
    \   TERMINAL   terminalspec
    \   NEUROFUZZY neurofuzzy
    |   /* NULL */ ;

projectspec:
        "{"
        namespec
        optionspec
        defaultspec
        modelspec
        "}";

namespec:
        NAME "=" stringtoken ";"
        COMMENTSTRING "}"
    \   AUTHOR = authorstring";"
    \   LASTCHANGE "=" DATESTRING ";"
    \   DATEFORMAT ";"
    \   CREATED "=" DATESTRING ";"
    \   SHELL "=" stringtoken ";"
    |   /* NULL */;

optionspec:
        SHELLOPTIONS
        "{" shelloptions "}"
    |   /* NULL */;

shelloptions:
        BAUDRATE "=" inumber ";"
    \   PROTOCOL "=" ptype ";"
    \   BTYPE "=" btype ";"
    \   C_TYPE "=" ctype ";"
    \   ONLINE_CODE "=" onoff ";"
    \   TRACE_BUFFER "=" "(" onoff ","PAR "(" inumber ")" ")" ";"
    \   RULE_BUFFER "=" "(" onoff "," PAR "(" inumber ")" ")" ";"
    \   ONLINE_BUFFER "=" "(" onoff "," PAR "(" inumber ")" ")" ";"
    \   CONST_MODIFIER "=" onoff     ";"
    \   BSUM_AGGREGATION "=" onoff    ";"
    \   PUBLIC_IO "=" onoff      ";"
    \   FAST_CMBF "=" onoff       ";"
    \   FLOAT_COA "=" onoff       ";"
    \   FAST_COA "=" onoff       ";"
    \   SCALE_MBF "=" onoff       ";"
    \   FILE_CODE "=" onoff       ";"
    \   HIRES_INFERENCE "=" onoff ";"
    \   CMDLINE "=" cmdstring; ";"
    |   /* NULL */;
```

```
onoff:      ON | OFF
btype:      DOUBLE | 8_BIT | 16_BIT | 32_BIT ;
ctype:      ANSI | KR ;
ptype:      HARDWARE | NO ;


defaultspec:
        MODELDEFAULTS
        "{" modeldefaults "}"
    |      /* NULL */


modeldefaults:
  TARGET "=" target ";"
    \     LVRANGE "=" MIN "(" fnumber ")" "," MAX "(" fnumber ")" ","
          MINDEF "(" inumber ")" "," MAXDEF "(" inumber ")" ","
          DEFAULT_OUTPUT  "(" fnumber ")" ";"
    \     AGGREGATION "=" "(" aggrtype ","PAR "(" fnumber ")"")"";"
    \     COMPOSITION "=" "(" comptype ","PAR "(" fnumber ")" ")" ";"
    \     RESOLUTION "=" XGRID "(" fnumber ")" "," YGRID "(" fnumber ")"
          "," SHOWGRID  "(" onoff ")" "," SNAPTOGRID "(" onoff ")" ";"
    \     STEPS "=" inumber ";"
    \     SHAPE "=" shapetype ";"
    \     FONTSIZE "=" inumber ";"
    \     /* NULL */;
target: F166 | I196 | PC ;
ctype: ANSI | KR ;
aggrtype: MIN_MAX | GAMMA | MIN_AVG ;
comptype: MIN_MAX | GAMMA | MIN_AVG;
deffuzzyfcmode: CMBF | FAST_CMBF | FUZZY | LUT | NOMBF;
defbtype: FLOAT | DOUBLE | 8_BIT | 16_BIT | 32_BIT;
defdefuzzmode: COA | MOM | COM | FCOA | NO | error;
shapetype: "(" S_SHAPE "," PAR "("fnumber ")" ")" | LINEAR;


/* Specification of projects */


modelspec:
        MODEL
        "{" variablespec objectheader "}"
    |    /* NULL */;


variablespec:
        VARIABLE_SECTION
        "{" lvar "}"
    |    /* NULL */;


lvar:
        LVAR
        "{" lvspec "}"
    |    /*NULL*/;
```

```
lvspec: NAME "=" stringtoken ";"
        BASEVAR "=" stringtoken ";"
   \    LVRANGE "=" MIN "(" fnumber ")" "," MAX "(" fnumber ")"
                 "," MINDEF "(" inumber ")" "," MAXDEF "(" inumber ")"
                 "," DEFAULT_OUTPUT "(" fnumber ")" ";"
   \    RESOLUTION "=" XGRID "(" fnumber ")" ","
                      YGRID "(" fnumber ")" "," SHOWGRID "(" onoff ")"
                      "," SNAPTOGRID "(" onoff ")" ";"
   \    COMMENTSTRING  "}"
   \    termspec
   |    /* NULL */;


termspec: TERM "{" termoptions "}";


termoptions:
        TERMNAME "=" stringtoken ";"
   \    POINTS  "=" pointcount ";"
   \    SHAPE   "=" shapetype ";"
   \    COLOR "=" RED "("inumber")" "," GREEN "("inumber")" "," BLUE
"("inumber")" ";"
   \    COMMENTSTRING "}"
   |    /* NULL */;


pointcount:
        "(" fnumber "," fnumber ")" "," pointcount
   |    "(" fnumber "," fnumber ")" ":" OPEN "(" fnumber "," fnumber
")";
   |    "(" fnumber "," fnumber ")";


shapetype:
        "(" S_SHAPE "," PAR "("fnumber ")" ")"
   |    LINEAR;


objectheader:
        OBJECT_SECTION
        "{" objectspec "}"
   |     /* NULL */;


objectspec:
        RULEBLOCK "{" rulevars rulespec "}"
   \    INTERFACE "{" interfacespec "}"
   \    REMARK "{" remarkspec "}"
   |     /* NULL */;


rulevars:
        INPUT "=" varstring varlist
        OUTPUT "=" varstring varlist
   \     /* NULL */;


varlist:"," varstring varlist
   \     ";"
```

```
rulespec:
       AGGREGATION "=" "(" aggrtype "," PAR  "(" fnumber ")" ")" ";"
   \   COMPOSITION "=" "(" comptype "," PAR  "(" fnumber ")" ")" ";"
   \   POS "=" inumber "," inumber ";"
   \   COLOR "=" RED "("inumber")" "," GREEN "("inumber")"
            "," BLUE  "("inumber")" ";"
   \   COMMENTSTRING "}"
   |   RULES "{" rules "}"
        /* Rules must be  the last entry in the list */
   |    /* NULL */;


aggrtype: MIN_MAX | GAMMA | MIN_AVG;
comptype: MIN_MAX | GAMMA | MIN_AVG;


rules:   IF one_rule rules | /* NULL */;
one_rule: varstring "=" termstring rule_cont;
rule_cont:AND  one_rule | THEN rule_conc;
rule_conc:
     varstring "=" termstring WITH fnumber ":"
                 OPEN "(" fnumber";"fnumber ")" AND rule_conc;
   | varstring "=" termstring WITH fnumber ":"
                 OPEN "(" fnumber";"fnumber ")" ";" ;
   | varstring "=" termstring WITH fnumber AND rule_conc;
   | varstring "=" termstring WITH fnumber ";" ;


interfacespec:
       INPUT  "=" "(" stringtoken "," fuzzmode ")" ";"
   |   OUTPUT "=" "(" stringtoken "," defuzzmode ")" ";"
   \   RANGECHECK "=" onoff ";"
   \   COMMENTSTRING "}"
   \   POS   "=" inumber "," inumber ";"
   \   COLOR "=" RED "("inumber")" ","GREEN "("inumber")"
            ","BLUE "("inumber")" ";"
   \   PARAMSTR "=" "(" visible "," parameterstring ")" ";"
   \   /* NULL */;


fuzzmode:
   |   FUZZY
   |   CMBF
   |   LUT "," STEPS "(" inumber ")"
   |   FCMBF;


defuzzmode:
       COA "," STEPS "(" inumber ")"
   |   MOMBSUM "," STEPS "(" inumber ")"
   |   MOM
   |   COM
   |   COABSUM   "," STEPS "(" inumber ")"
   |   FCOABSUM   "," STEPS "(" inumber ")"
   |   FCOA   "," STEPS "(" inumber ")"
   |   NO;
```

```
visible:    SHOW | HIDE;


remarkspec:
        TEXTSTRING ";"
   \    POS "=" inumber "," inumber ";"
   \    FONTSIZE "=" inumber ";"
   \    COLOR "=" RED "("inumber")" "," GREEN "("inumber")"
               "," BLUE  "("inumber")" ";"
   \    COMMENTSTRING "}"
   |    /* NULL */;


terminalspec:"{" terminal "}";


terminal:
        BAUDRATE "=" inumber ";"
   \    STOPBITS "=" inumber ";"
   \    PROTOCOL "=" ptype ";"
   \    CONNECTION "="  connect ";"
   \    INPUTBUFFER "="  inumber ";"
   \    OUTPUTBUFFER "="  inumber ";"
   \    PARAMSTR "=" parameterstring ";"
   |    /*NULL*/;


ptype:      HARDWARE | NO;
connect:    PORT1 | PORT2 | PORT3 | PORT4 | PORTRPC;


online:     "{" onlinesec "}";


onlinesec:  TIMESTAMP "=" timestampstring ";" ;


systemspec:
        CYCLETIME "=" inumber ";"
   \    MEMORYTEST "="onoff ";"c
   \    MARKERRESET "="onoff ";"
   \    AUTORESTART "="onoff ";"
   \    CONDITIONS "="syscon ";"
   \    DATAREAD "="  dataread ";"
   |    /* NULL */;


dataread:   ONLINE | OFFLINE;
syscon:     COLD | WARM | HOT;


foxboro:    "{" foxborosec "}";


foxborosec:
        CONNECT "(" stringtoken "," visible "," ")" ";" foxborosec
   |    /* NULL */;


neurofuzzy "{" neurosec "}";
```

```
neurosec:
        LEARNRULE "=" stringtoken ";"
    \   STEPWIDTHDOS "=" fnumber ";"
    \   STEPWIDTHTERM "=" fnumber ";"
    \   FILESIZE "=" inumber KB ";"
    \   MAXDEVIATION "=" fnumber  ";"
    \   AVGDEVIATION "=" fnumber ";"
    \   NEURONS "=" inumber ";"
    \   UPDATEDBGWIN "=" onoff ";"
    \   DATASEQUENCE "=" learnsequence ";"
    \   MAXSTEPS  "=" inumber ";"
    \   LOGFREQUENCE "=" inumber ";"
    |   /* NULL*/;
```

8

Fuzzy Logic vs.
Conventional Control

The question of what fuzzy logic brings to the party has been hotly debated over the past several years and will continue to be controversial for some time. The primary reason for this is that the ultimate universal proof of why a fuzzy logic solution is "better" than a conventional one (for whatever reason) does not exist. First of all, this is because fuzzy logic does not replace conventional control techniques. Instead, fuzzy logic renders possible new solutions that were not feasible to implement before. Hence, a direct comparison between a fuzzy logic solution and a conventional one rarely exists. Even when a conventional solution for comparison exists, the advantages of the fuzzy logic solution depend very much on the type of application. Thus, it is impossible to quantify the "benefits in general" of using fuzzy logic.

For these reasons, I did not attempt to prove any "benefits in general" in this book. Rather, I showed case studies of successful fuzzy logic applications in many technical areas. Whenever possible, I quantified the results. When I was unable to quantify results, I presented solutions to suggest how fuzzy logic can be used. I was a member of the design team in only a portion of the projects mentioned in this book. Thus, I often had to rely on published information. In publications, authors often do not quantify the performance of the fuzzy logic solution. Most authors claim competitive reasons for this. Some even publish only results achieved with a prototype rather than the full-blown solution, again for competitive reasons. So, if you want to find out for sure what fuzzy logic can do for your application, you have to roll up your sleeves and try it yourself. Many others already have, and their results were promising.

Sound publications of commercial fuzzy logic solutions are generally rare. Let me illustrate the reasons with an example. In 1992, a major German car manufacturer completed prototypes of six different control systems for a car. Four of them showed great potential for a fuzzy logic solution, and three of them are in preproduction now and due to hit the market in 1996. None of these fuzzy logic solutions has ever been published or will be. It is unlikely that the company will even mention the fact that fuzzy logic was used as a design technique in the product announcement. "Our customers buy our cars because "X" is the best car in the world and not because it uses fuzzy logic," their VP of Marketing once told me. This is why most publications about fuzzy logic systems stem from a research background rather than from commercial products.

When you do your own research on publications, you will find papers that make wild claims of the miraculous advantages of fuzzy logic and at the same time give very little information about the actual system they designed or the conventional system they used for comparison. I have left out all such publications from this book and the bibliography, and I can only encourage you to disregard such papers. Unfortunately, these papers give critics of fuzzy logic a target to bash. Fortunately, most recent papers are of much better quality.

Some critics of fuzzy logic claim that "the successful fuzzy logic applications are successful because of factors other than the use of fuzzy logic." When I look back at the more than 300 fuzzy logic applications my engineering team has supported in the last decade, I have to agree with this [191]. These applications did benefit from either exploiting information from additional sensors, better exploited information from existing sensors, or simply the ease of integrating engineering experience. So in a sense, these benefits do not directly stem from the use of fuzzy logic. However, I cannot think of even one of these applications that could have been solved as nicely as they were without fuzzy logic.

References

More than 30,000 scientific papers on fuzzy logic have appeared since 1965. The vast majority of these papers deals with the mathematical implications of relaxing classical logic to fuzzy logic. For an overview, refer to [221]. This textbook is also an excellent introduction to fuzzy set theory, the background of fuzzy logic. The following literature references either cover applications cited in this book or have strong relevance for practitioners. For a list of journals in the area, refer to the end of this section.

[1]   Adcock, T., "DSP + Fuzzy Logic: A Whole New Level of Performance," *Computer Design Conference on Fuzzy Logic* in San Diego (1994).

[2]   Aihara, K., "Philosophic Aspects of Uncertainty—Deterministic Dynamics and Predictability in Chaotic Systems," *Joint Japanese-European Symposium on Fuzzy Systems in Berlin*, Publications of the Japanese-German Center, Berlin, Volume 8 (1994), ISSN 0937-3799.

[3]   Akahoshi, K., "SLR Camera 'a-7xi': Using Fuzzy Logic in AF, AE, AZ," *Proceedings of IFES '91* (1991).

[4]   Akaiwa, E. et al., "Hardware and Software of Fuzzy Logic Controlled Cardiac Pacemaker," *Proc. of the Int'l. Conf. on Fuzzy Logic & Neural Networks*, IIZUKA, Japan (1990), pp. 549–552.

[5]   Altnether, J., "Increasing Intelligence Quotients of Microcontrollers with Fuzzy Logic," *Computer Design Fuzzy Logic '94 Conference* in San Diego (1994), pp. 59–66.

[6]   Altnether, J., "Fuzzy Logic ABS System," *Computer Design Fuzzy Logic '94 Conference* in San Diego (1994), pp. 495–500.

[7]   Anderson, J. A. and Rosenfeld, E. (Ed.), *Neurocomputing*, Boston/London (1988).

[8]   Aoki, P. and Kawachi, P., "Application of Fuzzy Control for Dead-Time Processes in a Glass Melting Furnace," *Fuzzy Sets and Systems* 38 (1990), pp. 251–256.

[9]   Arita, P. and Tsutsui, T., "Fuzzy Logic Control of Blood Pressure Through Inhalational Anesthesia," *Proc. of the Int'l. Conf. on Fuzzy Logic & Neural Networks*, IIZUKA, Japan (1990), pp. 545–547.

[10]   Arita, P., "Development of an Ultrasonographic Cancer Diagnosis System Using Fuzzy Theory," *Japanese Journal of Fuzzy Theory and Systems*, Vol. 3, No. 3 (1991), ISSN 1058-7349, pp. 215–230.

[11]   Åström, K. J., Anton, J. J., and Årzen, K.-E., "Expert Control," *Automatica*, Vol. 22, No. 3 (1986), pp. 277–286.

[12]   Assilian, P., "Artificial Intelligence in the Control of Real Dynamical Systems," Ph.D. dissertation, London University (1974).

[13]   Assilian, P. and Mamdani, E. H., "An Experiment in Linguistic Synthesis with a Fuzzy Logic Controller," *International Journal of Man-Machine Studies* 7 (1975), pp. 1–13.

[14]   Aurrand-Lions, J.-P., des Saint Blancard, M., and Jarri, P., "Autonomous Intelligent Cruise Control with Fuzzy Logic," *EUFIT '93– First European Congress on Fuzzy and Intelligent Technologies* in Aachen (1993), pp. 1–7.

[15]   Auzas, E., "Handwritten Recognition Using Fuzzy Methods," *Computer Design Fuzzy Logic '94 Conference* in San Diego (1994), pp. 321–347.

[16]   Badami, V. et al., "Fuzzy Logic Supervisory Control For Steam Turbine Prewarming Automation," *Third IEEE International Conference on Fuzzy Systems* (1994), ISBN 0-7803-1896-X, pp. 1045–1050.

[17]   Becker, K., Käsmacher, H., Rau, G., Kalff, G., and Zimmermann, H.-J., "A Fuzzy Logic Approach to Intelligent Alarms in Cardioanesthesia," *Third IEEE Conference on Fuzzy Logic* (1994), pp. 2072–2076.

[18]   Bellon, C., Bosc, P. and Prade, H., "Fuzzy Boom in Japan," *International Journal of Intelligent Systems,* Vol. 7 (1992), pp. 293–316.

[19]   Bennett, G. and Adcock, T., "DSP and Fuzzy Logic: A Whole New Level of Performance," *Computer Design Fuzzy Logic '94 Conference in San Diego* (1994), pp. 365–380.

[20]   Berrie, P.G., "Fuzzy Logic Elements in Ultrasonic Level Measurement," *EUFIT' 93–First European Congress on Fuzzy and Intelligent Technologies* in Aachen (1993), pp. 181–187.

[21]   Bezdek, J. C., Tsao, E. C.-K., and Pal, N. R., "Fuzzy Kohonen Clustering Networks," *FUZZ-IEEE Conference* (1992), pp. 1035-1043.

[22]   Bien, Z., Hwang, D.-H., Lee, J. H., and Ryu, H.-K., "An Automatic Start-Up and Shut-Down Control of a Drum-Type Boiler Using Fuzzy Logic," *2nd Int'l. Conference on Fuzzy Logic and Neural Networks Proceedings,* IIZUKA, Japan (1992), ISBN 4-938717-01-8, pp. 465–468.

[23]   Blöchl, B., "Vision Guided Path Tracking Using Fuzzy Control," *EUFIT '93—First European Congress on Fuzzy and Intelligent Technologies* in Aachen (1993), pp. 1043–1047.

[24]   Böning, D., "Methodical Tool Based Design of a Fuzzy Controller for a Granulated Medium Refining Machine," *EUFIT '93—First European Congress on Fuzzy and Intelligent Technologies* in Aachen (1993), pp. 1016–1022.

[25]   Boverie, S. and Titli, A., "Different Applications of Fuzzy Logic Control in the Context of Automotive Systems," *26th International Symposium on Automotive Technology and Automation ISATA* (1993), pp. 451–458.

[26]   Chen, H., Mitzumoto, M., and Ling, Y.-F., "Automatic Control of Sewerage Pumpstation by Using Fuzzy Controls and Neural Networks," *2nd Int'l. Conference on Fuzzy Logic and Neural Networks Proceedings,* IIZUKA, Japan (1992), ISBN 4-938717-01-8, pp. 91–94.

[27]   Christian, P., "Fuzzy Logic Control of a Hypervelocity Interceptor," *Second IEEE International Conference on Fuzzy Systems* (1993), ISBN 0-7803-0615-5, pp. 877–882.

[28]   Chui, S. et al., "Fuzzy Logic for Control of Roll and Moment for a Flexible Wing Aircraft," *IEEE Control Systems Magazine* (1991), 11 (4), pp. 42–48.

[29] Cleland, J., "Fuzzy Logic Motor Control," *EUFIT '93—First European Congress on Fuzzy and Intelligent Technologies* in Aachen (1993), pp. 112–116.

[30] Corbin, J., "Fuzzy Logic-Based Financial Transaction Card Security System," *Embedded Systems Conference* in Santa Clara (1994).

[31] Davis, L. I. et al., "Fuzzy Logic for Vehicle Climate Control," *Third IEEE International Conference on Fuzzy Systems* (1994), ISBN 0-7803-1896-X, pp. 530–534.

[32] Doehm, C., "Case Study for the Implementation of a Fuzzy Logic Controller to Control the Quality Characteristics Moisture and Color of Biscuits," *MARS*, Viersen (1992).

[33] Dote, Y., "Adaptive Grasping Force Control for Manipulator Hand Using Fuzzy Set Theory," *Proc. of the Int'l. Workshop in Intelligent Robots and Systems*, Tokyo (1988).

[34] Douglass, B.P., "Application of Fuzzy Logic to Alarm Integration on Anesthesia Workstations," *Computer Design Fuzzy Logic '94 Conference* in San Diego (1994), pp. 147–167.

[35] Duckstein, L., "Fuzzy Modeling of Patient State: Distance-Based Versus Rule-Based Approach," *Second IEEE International Conference on Fuzzy Systems*, ISBN 0-7803-0615-5, pp. 1033–1038.

[36] Elting, D., "Fuzzy Control of an ABS System Using Intel's 8XC196KX," *Computer Design Fuzzy Logic '94 Conference* in San Diego (1994).

[37] Egusa, Y., Akahori, H., Morimura, A., and Wakami, N., "An Electronic Video Camera Image Stabilizer Operated on Fuzzy Theory," *IEEE Conference on Fuzzy Systems* (1992), ISBN 0-7803-0237-0, pp. 851–858.

[38] Erens, F., "Process Control of a Cement Kiln with Fuzzy Logic," *EUFIT '93—First European Congress on Fuzzy and Intelligent Technologies* in Aachen (1993), pp. 1667–1678.

[39] Evans, G. W., Karowski, W., and Wilhelm, M. R., "Application of Fuzzy Set Methodologies in Industrial Engineering," Amsterdam, Oxford, New York, Tokyo (1989).

[40] Feldkamp, L. and Puskorius, G., "Trainable Fuzzy and Neural-Fuzzy Systems for Idle-Speed Control," *Second IEEE International Conference on Fuzzy Systems*, ISBN 0-7803-0615-5, pp. 45–51.

[41] Fennich, M., "Voice Input Calculating Instrument using Fuzzy Logic," *Computer Design Fuzzy Logic '94 Conference* in San Diego (1994), pp. 31–57.

[42] Fujimoto, J., Nakatani, T., and Yoneyama, M., "Speaker-Independent Word Recognition Using Fuzzy Pattern Matching," *Fuzzy Sets and Systems* 32 (1989), pp. 181–191.

[43] Fujiwara, Y. et al., "Image Processing Using Fuzzy Logic for Video Print Systems," *IFES '91—Fuzzy Engineering toward Human Friendly Systems*, pp. 1003–1012.

[44] Fujiyoshi, M. and Shiraki, T., "A Fuzzy Automatic-Combustion-Control-System of Refuse Incineration Plant," *2nd Int'l. Conf. on Fuzzy Logic and Neural Networks Proceedings*, IIZUKA, Japan (1992), ISBN 4-938717-01-8, pp. 469–472.

[45] Galichet, S. et al., "Fuzzy Logic Control of a Floating Level in a Refinery Tank," *Third IEEE International Conference on Fuzzy Systems* (1994), ISBN 0-7803-1896-X, pp. 1538–1542.

[46] Gebhardt, J., "Application of Fuzzy Logic to the Control of a Wind Energy Converter," *EUFIT '93—First European Congress on Fuzzy and Intelligent Technologies* in Aachen (1993), pp. 692–698.

[47] Guillemin, P., "Universal Motor Control with Fuzzy Logic," *Fuzzy Sets and Systems*, Volume 63 (1994), pp. 339–348.

[48] Gwaltney, D. and Humphreys, G., "Fuzzy Logic Control of Wind Tunnel Temperature Processes," *Third IEEE International Conference on Fuzzy Systems* (1994), ISBN 0-7803-1896-X, pp. 825–830.

[49] Hakata, T. and Masuda, J., "Fuzzy Control of Cooling System Utilizing Heat Storage," *Proc. of the Int'l. Conf. on Fuzzy Logic & Neural Networks*, IIZUKA, Japan (1990), pp. 77–80.

[50] Hale, C. and Nguyen, C. Q., "Using Fuzzy Logic Based Digital Filters for Voice Command Recognition," *Computer Design Fuzzy Logic '94 Conference* in San Diego (1994), pp. 279–298.

[51] Hanakuma, Y. et al., "Ethylen e Plant Distillation Column Bottom Temperature Control," *Keisi,* Vol. 32, No. 8 (1989), pp. 28–39.

[52] Hebb, D., *The Organization of Behavior*, New York (1947).

[53] Hecht-Nielsen, R., *Neurocomputing*, Boston (1989).

[54] Hintz, G. W. and Zimmermann, H.-J., "A Method to Control Flexible Manufacturing Systems," *European Journal of Operations Research* (1989), pp. 321–334.

[55] Hiroyuki, N. and Hakata, T., "Development of Fuzzy Control to Daily Load Follow Operation for PWR Plants," *Proceedings of the 3rd IFSA Congress* (1989), pp. 254–257.

[56] Hishida, N. et al., "Development of the Operator Support System Applying Fuzzy Algorithms for Glass Tube Molding Equipment," *2nd Int'l. Conference on Fuzzy Logic and Neural Networks Proceedings*, IIZUKA, Japan (1992), ISBN 4-938717-01-8, pp. 1097–1100.

[57] Hiyama, T. and Sameshima, T, "Fuzzy Logic Control Scheme for On-Line Stabilization of Multi-Machine Power Systems," *Fuzzy Sets and Systems* 39 (1991), pp. 181–194.

[58] Hofbauer, P., Arend, H.-O., and Pfannstiel, D., "New Heating System Control Based on the Use of Fuzzy Logic," *EUFIT '93—First European Congress on Fuzzy and Intelligent Technologies* in Aachen (1993), pp. 1036–1042.

[59] Hofmann, W. and Krause, M., "Fuzzy Rules for Regulation of Torque in AC-Drives," *EUFIT '93—First European Congress on Fuzzy and Intelligent Technologies* in Aachen (1993), pp. 1059–1065.

[60] Högener, J., "Fuzzy-PLC: A Connection with a Future," *EUFIT '93—First European Congress on Fuzzy and Intelligent Technologies* in Aachen (1993), pp. 688–691.

[61] Hou, R. and Lauer, L., "A Fuzzy Feedback Controller and Its Application to the Sewage Treatment Process," *EUFIT '93—First European Congress on Fuzzy and Intelligent Technologies* in Aachen (1993), pp. 275–277.

[62] Hoyer, R. and Jumar, U., "Fuzzy Control of Traffic Lights," *Third IEEE International Conference on Fuzzy Systems* (1994), ISBN 0-7803-1896-X, pp. 1526–1531.

[63] Hsia, R.-W. and Chen, Y.-Y., "Fuzzy Control of Jet Engines," *EUFIT '93—First European Congress on Fuzzy and Intelligent Technologies* in Aachen (1993), pp. 1182–1188.

[64] Ichihashi, H., "Fuzzy Systems—Optimization by Neuro-like Fuzzy Model," *Japanese-European Symposium on Fuzzy Systems* (1992).

[65] Ikeda, H. et al., "An Intelligent Automatic Transmission Control Using a One-Chip Fuzzy Inference Engine," *Proceedings of the International Fuzzy Systems and Intelligent Control Conference* in Louisville (1992), pp. 44–50.

[66]   Imaizumi, M. et al., "Advanced Auto Alignment System Using Approximate Reasoning," *Proc. of the Int'l. Conf. on Fuzzy Logic & Neural Networks*, IIZUKA, Japan (1990), pp. 119–122.

[67]   Imasaki, N. et al., "A Fuzzy Neural Network and Its Application to Elevator Group Control," *IFES '91—Fuzzy Engineering toward Human Friendly Systems*, pp. 1126–1127.

[68]   Ishibuchi, H., Tanaka, H., and Fukuoka, N., "Discriminant Analysis of Fuzzy Data and Its Application to a Gas Sensor System," *Japanese Journal of Fuzzy Theory and Systems*, Vol. 1, No. 1 (1989), ISSN 1058-7349, pp. 27–46.

[69]   Ishii, K. et al., "Application of Artificial Intelligence for Blast Furnace Operation," *Proc. of NAFIPS '90 Conference*, Toronto (1990), pp. 235–238.

[70]   Iwasaki, T. and Morita, A., "Fuzzy Auto-Tuning for PID Controller with Model Classification," *Proc. of NAFIPS '90 Conference*, Toronto (1990), pp. 90–93.

[71]   Kamada, H. and Yoshida, M., "A Visual Control System Using Image Processing and Fuzzy Theory," *Proc. of the Int'l. Conf. on Fuzzy Logic & Neural Networks*, IIZUKA, Japan (1990), pp. 409–412.

[72]   Kandel, A., *Fuzzy Techniques in Pattern Recognition*, New York (1982).

[73]   Kageyama, S. et al., "Blood Glucose Control by a Fuzzy Control System," *Proc. of the Int'l. Conf. on Fuzzy Logic & Neural Networks*, IIZUKA, Japan (1990), pp. 557–560.

[74]   Katayama, R., "Neuro, Fuzzy and Chaos Technology and Its Application to (Sanyo) Consumer Electronics," *Japanese-European Symposium on Fuzzy Systems* (1992).

[75]   Kawai, H. et al., "Engine Control System," *Proc. of the Int'l. Conf. on Fuzzy Logic & Neural Networks*, IIZUKA, Japan (1990), pp. 929–937.

[76]   Kickert, W. and van Nauta Lemke, H. R., "The Application of Fuzzy Theory to Warm Water Process," *Automatica*, Volume 12, No. 4 (1976), pp. 301–308.

[77]   King, R. E. and Karonis, F. C., "Multi-Level Expert Control of a Large-Scale Industrial Process," in Gupta and Yamakawa (Ed.), *Fuzzy Computing Theory, Hardware, and Applications*, Amsterdam, New York, Oxford, Tokyo (1988) pp. 323–340.

[78]   Kipersztok, O., "Active Control of Broadband Noise Using Fuzzy Logic," *Second IEEE International Conference on Fuzzy Systems*, ISBN 0-7803-0615-5, pp. 906–911.

[79]   Kipersztok, O., "Fuzzy Active Control of a Distributed Broadband Noise Source," *Third IEEE International Conference on Fuzzy Systems* (1994), ISBN 0-7803-1896-X, pp. 1342–1347.

[80]   Kishi, M. et al., "Fuzzy Control System for Automatic Transmission," United States Patent No. 4841815 by Nissan Corporation (1989).

[81]   Kitamura, T., "Design of Intelligent Support System for Artificial Heart Control," *Japanese Journal of Fuzzy Theory and Systems*, Vol. 3, No. 3 (1991), ISSN 1058-7349, pp. 231–240.

[82]   Kitamura, T. and Komori, M., "Stability Analysis of a Fuzzy Control System of a Superconducting Actuator," *2nd Int'l. Conference on Fuzzy Logic and Neural Networks Proceedings*, IIZUKA, Japan (1992), ISBN 4-938717-01-8, pp. 461–464.

[83]   Koskinen, H., "A Fuzzy PID-Controller for Active Magnetic Bearings," *EUFIT '93—First European Congress on Fuzzy and Intelligent Technologies* in Aachen (1993), pp. 1169–1174.

[84]   Kosko, B., *Neural Networks and Fuzzy Systems* (1992), Englewood Cliffs, New Jersey.

[85]   Kumar, S. R. and Majumder, D. D., "Fuzzy Logic Control of a Multivariable Steam Generating Unit Using Decoupling Theory," *IEEE Transactions on Systems, Man, and Cybernetics*, Volume 15, No. 4 (1985), pp. 539–558.

[86]   Kummert, A., "Fuzzy Logic in der Auswertung von Akustischen Sensorsignalen," in v. Altrock, Zimmermann (Eds.), *Fuzzy Logic—Anwendungen*, Munich (1993) ISBN 3-486-22677-0.

[87]   Kuwahara, H. et al., "Application of Fuzzy Theory to the Control of Shield Tunneling," *Proceedings of the 3rd IFSA Congress* (1989), pp. 250–253.

[88]   Layne, J. R., Passino, K. M., and Yurkovich, S., "Fuzzy Learning Control for Anti-Skid Braking Systems," *IEEE Control Systems Magazine* (1993), 1 (2), pp. 122–129.

[89]   Layne, J. R. and Passino, K. M., "Fuzzy Model Reference Learning Control for Cargo Ship Steering," *IEEE Control Systems Magazine* (1993), 13 (6), pp. 23–34.

[90]   Lee, K.-C., Min, P.-P., Song, J.-W., and Cho, K.-B., "An Adaptive Fuzzy Current Controller with Neural Network for Field-Oriented Controlled Induction Machine," *2nd Int'l. Conference on Fuzzy Logic and Neural Networks Proceedings*, IIZUKA, Japan (1992), ISBN 4-938717-01-8, pp. 449–452.

[91]   Leonetti, M.C., "Classification of Underwater Acoustic Contacts Using Fuzzy Sets," *Computer Design Fuzzy Logic '94 Conference* in San Diego (1994), pp. 189–199.

[92]   Li, Y. and Yonezawa, Y., "Stability Analysis of a Fuzzy Control System by the Hyperstability Theorem," *Japanese Journal of Fuzzy Theory and Systems*," Vol. 3, No. 2 (1991), ISSN 1058-7349, pp. 209–214.

[93]   Liaw, C.-M. and Wang, J.-B., "Design and Implementation of a Fuzzy Controller for a High Performance Induction Motor Drive," *IEEE Transactions on Systems, Man, and Cybernetics*, Vol. 21,. No. 4 (1991), pp. 921–929.

[94]   Lippmann, R.P., "An Introduction to Computing with Neural Nets," *IEEE ASSP Magazine* 4, (1987), pp. 4–22.

[95]   Maeda, M. and Murakami, P., "Stability Analysis of Fuzzy Control Systems Using Phase Planes," *Japanese Journal of Fuzzy Theory and Systems*, Vol. 3, No. 2 (1991), ISSN 1058-7349, pp. 149–160.

[96]   Mamdani, E. H., "Application of Fuzzy Logic to Approximate Reasoning Using Linguistic Synthesis," *IEEE Transactions on Computers*, Vol. C-26, No. 12 (1977), pp. 1182–1191.

[97]   Mamdani, E. H., "Twenty Years of Fuzzy Control: Experiences Gained and Lessons Learned," *Second IEEE International Conference on Fuzzy Systems*, ISBN 0-7803-0615-5, pp. 339–344.

[98]   Maron, C. and Burgert, K., "Adaptive pH Value Control in a Neutralization Plant," *EUFIT '93—First European Congress on Fuzzy and Intelligent Technologies* in Aachen (1993), pp. 279–289.

[99]   Matsumoto, N. et. at., "Expert Antiskid System," *IEEE IECON '87* (1987), pp. 810–816.

[100]   McNeill, D. and Freiberger, P., *Fuzzy Logic*, (1993), ISBN 0-671-73843-7.

[101]   Meier, R., Nieuwland, J., Hacisalihzade, S. S., and Zbinden, A. M., "Fuzzy Control of Blood Pressure During Anesthesia," *IEEE Control Systems* 12 (1992), pp. 12–17.

[102]   Mitzumoto, M. and Zimmermann, H.-J., "Comparison of Fuzzy Reasoning Methods," *Fuzzy Sets and Systems* 8 (1982), pp. 253–283.

[103]   Mündemann, F., "Estimating the Behavior of Other Drivers on a Highway Using an Internal World Model Based on Fuzzy Concepts," *EUFIT '93—First European Congress on Fuzzy and Intelligent Technologies* in Aachen (1993), pp. 1048–1054.

[104]   Murayama, Y. et al., "Optimizing Control of a Diesel Engine," in Sugeno (Ed.) *Industrial Applications of Fuzzy Control* (1985), pp. 63–72, Amsterdam, New York.

[105]   Murakami, P. et al., "Weld-Line Tracking Control of Arc Welding Robot Using Fuzzy Logic Controller," *Fuzzy Sets and Systems* 32 (1989), pp. 221–237.

[106]   N.N., "CreditExpert—ASK," INFORM GmbH Aachen (1988).

[107]   N.N., "FELIS User Manual," INFORM GmbH Aachen (1989).

[108]   N.N., "E5AF Manual," OMRON Corp. Osaka (1990).

[109]   N.N., "Fuzzy Theory Control of Cold Strip Mill," *Techno Japan,* Vol. 23, No. 3 (1990), pp. 33–38.

[110]   N.N., "Special Issue on Applications of Fuzzy Logic," *Sanyo Technical Review*, Vol. 23, No. 2 (1991).

[111]   N.N., "FUZZY-166 Quick Reference Manual," INFORM GmbH Aachen (1992).

[112]   N.N., "Expert Fuzzy CNC EDM," Sodick Corporation, Ltd. (1992), Yokohama, Japan.

[113]   N.N., "Benchmark Suites for Fuzzy Logic," Working Group Protocol VDI/VDE GMA (German Association of Mechanical and Electrical Engineers) UA-4.5.1 (1994).

[114]   N.N., "*fuzzy*TECH 4.0 MCU Edition Manual," INFORM GmbH Aachen /Inform Software Corp., Chicago (1995).

[115]   N.N., "*fuzzy*TECH 4.0 RTRCD Module Manual," INFORM GmbH Aachen /Inform Software Corp., Chicago (1995).

[116]   N.N., "*fuzzy*TECH 4.0 Online Edition Manual," INFORM GmbH Aachen/Inform Software Corp., Chicago (1995).

[117]   N.N., "*fuzzy*TECH 4.0 PLC Edition Manual," INFORM GmbH Aachen /Inform Software Corp., Chicago (1995).

[118] N.N., "*fuzzy*TECH 4.0 IAS Edition Manual," INFORM GmbH Aachen /Inform Software Corp., Chicago (1995).

[119] N.N., "*fuzzy*TECH 4.0 NeuroFuzzy Module Manual," INFORM GmbH Aachen /Inform Software Corp., Chicago (1995).

[120] N.N., "*fuzzy*TECH 4.0 DataAnalyzer Module Manual," INFORM GmbH Aachen /Inform Software Corp., Chicago (1995).

[121] Norita, T., "Engineering Application of Fuzzy Systems—Applications of Image Processing and Understanding with Fuzzy Theory (Minolta, LIFE)," *Japanese-European Symposium on Fuzzy Systems* (1992).

[122] Novak, V., "Fuzzy Sets and Their Applications," Adam Hilger, (1989).

[123] Nowottnick, A. and Lange, R., "Fuzzy-Control Support Operator at Hanling of a Two Chamber Ball Mill in the Cement Industry," *EU-FIT'93—First European Congress on Fuzzy and Intelligent Technologies* in Aachen (1993), pp. 1659–1666.

[124] Ohnishi, T., "A Self-Learning Fuzzy Control System for an Urban Refuse Incineration Plant," *Japanese Journal of Fuzzy Theory and Systems*," Vol. 3, No. 2 (1991), ISSN 1058-7349, pp. 187–200.

[125] Oishi, K. et. at., "Application of Fuzzy Logic Control Theory to the Sake Brewing Process," *Journal of Fermentation and Bioengineering* (1991), 72 (2), pp. 115–121.

[126] Okey, Ch., Foslien, W., and Kesselring, J., "Fuzzy Logic Controls for the EPRI Microwave Clothes Dryer," *Third IEEE International Conference on Fuzzy Systems* (1994), ISBN 0-7803-1896-X, pp. 1348–1353.

[127] Ono, H., Ohnishi, T., and Terada, Y., "Combustion Control of Refuse Incineration Plant by Fuzzy Logic," *Fuzzy Sets and Systems* 32 (1989), pp. 193–206.

[128] Opris, I. E. and Kovacs, T. A., "An Analog Voltage-Mode Fuzzy Logic Controller," *Computer Design Fuzzy Logic '94 Conference* in San Diego (1994), pp. 475–485.

[129] Østergaard, J.-J., "Fuzzy Control of Cement Klins—A Retrospective Summary," *EUFIT '93—First European Congress on Fuzzy and Intelligent Technologies* in Aachen (1993), pp. 552–558.

[130] Otani, M. et al., "2-Phase Stepping Motor Driver Based on Fuzzy-Logic Control," *IFES '91—Fuzzy Engineering toward Human Friendly Systems*, p. 1130.

[131]   Parisi, D. M. and Sturzenbecker, M. C., "Application of Fuzzy In-
        ferencing Techniques to Automated Classification of Defects in
        Semiconductor Wafers," *Computer Design Fuzzy Logic '94 Conference*
        in San Diego (1994), pp. 351–363.

[132]   Pedrycz, W., "Fuzzy Control and Fuzzy Systems," John Wiley &
        Sons (1989).

[133]   Qin, Y. and Du, S. S., "A Practical and Low-Cost PWM Battery
        Charger Using Fuzzy Logic Controllers for UPS Application,"
        Computer Design Fuzzy Logic '94 Conference in San Diego (1994),
        pp. 223–232.

[134]   Ramaswamy, P., Edwards, R. M., and Lee, K. Y., "An Automatic Tun-
        ing Method of a Fuzzy Logic Controller for Nuclear Reactors," *IEEE
        Transactions on Nuclear Science* (1993), 40 (4), pp. 1253–1262.

[135]   Roffel, B. and Chin, P. A., "Fuzzy Control of a Polymerization Re-
        actor," *Hydrocarbon Processing*, June (1991), pp. 47–50.

[136]   Ruspini, E., Saffiotti, A., and Konolige, K., "Blending Reactivity and
        Goal-Directedness in a Fuzzy Controller," *Second IEEE International
        Conference on Fuzzy Systems*, ISBN 0-7803-0615-5, pp. 134–139.

[137]   Russ, R., "Designing a Fuzzy Logic Traction Control System," *Pro-
        ceedings of the Embedded Systems Conference* (1994), Vol. 2, ISBN 0-
        87930-356-5, pp. 183–196.

[138]   Rummelhart, D. E., Hinton, G. E., and Williams, R. J., "Learning
        Representations by Back-Propagating Errors," *Nature* 323 (1986)
        pp. 533–536.

[139]   S. D., Ullah, Z., and Khan, N., "Development of a Fast Charger
        for Secondary Batteries by using NeuFuz Neural-Fuzzy Technolo-
        gy," *Computer Design Fuzzy Logic '94 Conference* in San Diego
        (1994), pp. 79–84.

[140]   Saito, Y. and Ishida, T., "Fuzzy PID Hybrid Control—An Applica-
        tion to Burner Control," *Proc. of the Int'l. Conf. on Fuzzy Logic &
        Neural Networks*, IIZUKA, Japan (1990), pp. 65–69.

[141]   Sakaguchi, P. et al., "Application of Fuzzy Logic to Shift Scheduling Method for Automatic Transmission," *Second IEEE International Conference on Fuzzy Systems*, ISBN 0-7803-0615-5, pp. 52–58.

[142]   Sasaki, T. and Akiyama, T., "Traffic Control Process of Expressway by Fuzzy Logic," *Fuzzy Sets and Systems* 26 (1988), pp. 165–178.

[143]   Sato, M. et al., "Fuzzy Logic Based Banknote Transfer Control," *Second IEEE International Conference on Fuzzy Systems* (1993), ISBN 0-7803-0615-5, pp. 279–284.

[144]   Sibigtroth, J. M., "Creating Fuzzy Micros," *Embedded Systems* 12, Vol. 4, (1991).

[145]   Shimizu, H. et al., "Application of Fuzzy Control to a Yeast Fed-Batch Culture," *IFES '91—Fuzzy Engineering toward Human Friendly Systems*, pp. 824–835.

[146]   Shear, D., "The Fuzzification of DSP—Texas Instruments and Inform Software Team Up," *EDN* 12/9/1994, pp. 145.

[147]   Shimojima, K. et al., "Sensor Integration Utilizing Fuzzy Inference with LED Displacement Sensor and Vision System," *Second IEEE International Conference on Fuzzy Systems*, ISBN 0-7803-0615-5, pp. 59–64.

[148]   Shingu, T. et al., "Fuzzy-Based Automatic Focusing System for Compact Camera," *Proceedings of the 3rd IFSA Congress* (1989), pp. 436–439.

[149]   Smith, P., "Application of Fuzzy Logic to the Control of an Autonomous Underwater Vehicle," *Second IEEE International Conference on Fuzzy Systems*, ISBN 0-7803-0615-5, pp. 1099–1105.

[150]   Steinberg, M., "Development and Simulation of an F/A-18 Fuzzy Logic Automatic Carrier Landing System," *Second IEEE International Conference on Fuzzy Systems* (1993), ISBN 0-7803-0615-5, pp. 797–802.

[151]   Steinmüller, H. and Wick, O., "Fuzzy and NeuroFuzzy Applications in European Washing Machines," *EUFIT '93—First European Congress on Fuzzy and Intelligent Technologies* in Aachen (1993), pp. 1031–1035.

[152]   Stumpf, H. and Lux, F. H., "Extraction of Subjective Assessments of Tyres for Handling, Comfort and Noise, Based on Laboratory Tests by Use of Fuzzy Logic," *26th International Symposium on Automotive Technology and Automation* (1993), pp. 415–424.

[153] Sugeno, M. (Ed.), *Industrial Application of Fuzzy Control,* North-Holland (1985).

[154] Sugeno, M. and Kang, G. T., "Fuzzy Modeling and Control of a Multilayer Incinerator," *Fuzzy Sets and Systems,* Volume 18 (1986), pp. 329–346.

[155] Sugeno, M., "Philosophic Aspects of Uncertainty—Categories of Uncertainty and Their Modalities," *Japanese-European Symposium on Fuzzy Systems* (1992).

[156] Sugiura, T. et al., "Fuzzy Control of a Rate-Adaptive Cardiac Pacemaker with Multiple Indicators," *Japanese Journal of Fuzzy Theory and Systems,* Vol. 3, No. 3 (1991), ISSN 1058-7349, pp. 241–249.

[157] Suzuki, K. et al., "Fuzzy Multi-Model Control of a High-Purity Distillation System," *IFES '91—Fuzzy Engineering toward Human Friendly Systems,* pp. 684–693.

[158] Takahashi, H., Ikeura, K., and Yamamori, T., "5-Speed Automatic Transmission Installed Fuzzy Reasoning," *IFES '91—Fuzzy Engineering toward Human Friendly Systems,* pp. 1136–1137.

[159] Takahashi, M. et al., "Biomedical Applications of Fuzzy Logic Controllers," *Proc. of the Int'l. Conf. on Fuzzy Logic & Neural Networks,* IIZUKA, Japan (1990), pp. 553–556.

[160] Takayama, A., "Automatic Cruising System Using Fuzzy Logic Control," *Journal of Japan Society for Fuzzy Theory and Systems,* Volume 3, No. 2 (1991), pp. 168–169.

[161] Tanaka, K. and Sugeno, M., "Stability Analysis of Fuzzy Systems Using Lyapunov's Direct Method," *Proc. of NAFIPS '90 Conference,* Toronto (1990), pp. 133–136.

[162] Tanaka, K. and Sano, M., "Concept of Stability Margin for Fuzzy Systems and Design of Robust Controllers," *Second IEEE International Conference on Fuzzy Systems,* ISBN 0-7803-0615-5, pp. 29–34.

[163] Tani, T., Utashiro, M., Umano, M., and Tanaka, K., "Application of Practical Fuzzy-PID Hybrid Control System to Petrochemical Plant," *Third IEEE International Conference on Fuzzy Systems* (1994), ISBN 0-7803-1896-X, pp. 1211–1216.

[164] Takata, K., "Signature Identification System Using a Fuzzy Template," *IFES '91—Fuzzy Engineering toward Human Friendly Systems,* pp. 1124–1125.

[165] Terai, H. et al., "Application of Fuzzy Logic Technology to Home Appliances," *IFES '91—Fuzzy Engineering toward Human Friendly Systems*, pp. 1118–1119.

[166] Terano, T., "Image Understanding by Fuzzy Logic," *Japanese-European Symposium on Fuzzy Systems* (1992).

[167] Tews, V., Wehhofer, J., and Werner, H., "Suppression of Interferences in Differential Distribution Weighting Means," *EUFIT '93— First European Congress on Fuzzy and Intelligent Technologies* in Aachen (1993), pp. 708–713.

[168] Thuillard, M., "The Development of Algorithms for a Smoke Detector with NeuroFuzzy Logic," forthcoming in *Fuzzy Sets and System* (1994).

[169] Thurm, V. M., Schaefer, P., and Schielen, W., "Fuzzy Control of a Speed Limiter," *ISATA Conference* (1993).

[170] Tobi, T. and Hanafusa, T., "A Practical Application of Fuzzy Control for an Air-Conditioning System," *International Journal of Approximate Reasoning* 5 (1991), pp. 331–348.

[171] Tobi, T. et al., "The Application of Fuzzy Control to a Coke Oven Gas Cooling Plant," *Fuzzy Sets and Systems* 46 (1992), pp. 373–381.

[172] Tobi, T. and Anbe, J., "A Practical Application of Fuzzy Theory to an Auto-Regulated System for Extra-Corporal Circulation," *2nd Int'l. Conference on Fuzzy Logic and Neural Networks Proceedings*, II-ZUKA, Japan (1992), ISBN 4-938717-01-8, pp. 995–1001.

[173] Tong, R. M., "Analysis of Fuzzy Control Algorithms Using the Relation Matrix," *International Journal of Man-Machines Studies*, 8 (1976), pp. 679–686.

[174] Tong, R. M., "A Retrospective View of Fuzzy Control Systems," *Fuzzy Sets and Systems* 14 (1984), pp. 199–210.

[175] Tong, R. M. and Bonissone, P.P., "Linguistic Solutions to Fuzzy Decision Problems," in Zimmermann, H.-J., Zadeh, L.A. and Gaines, B.R. (Ed.), "Fuzzy Sets and Decision Analysis," Amsterdam, New York, Oxford (1984), pp. 323–334.

[176] Tozawa, Y., "Progress of Ethylene Production Plants," *MOL* 10 (1990), pp. 73–91.

[177] Ueki, K. and Fujieda, H., "Application of Fuzzy Logic Control to an Electronic Mixing Unit," *Proceedings of the 3rd IFSA Congress* (1989), pp. 216–219.

[178]   Uomori, K. et al., "Automatic Image Stabilizing System by Full-Digital Signal Processing," *IEEE Transactions on Consumer Electronics*, Vol. 36, No. 3 (1990), pp. 510–519.

[179]   Uriuhara, M., Hattori, T., and Moride, S., "Development of Automatic Cruising using Fuzzy Control Systems," *Journal of the Society of Automotive Engineers of Japan*, Volume 42, No. 2 (1988), pp. 224–229.

[180]   von Altrock, C., Krause, B., and Zimmermann, H.-J. "Advanced Fuzzy Logic Control of a Model Car in Extreme Situations," *Fuzzy Sets and Systems*, Vol. 48, No. 1 (1992), pp. 41–52.

[181]   von Altrock, C. and Krause, B., "On-Line-Development Tools for Fuzzy Knowledge-Base Systems of Higher Order," *2nd Int'l. Conference on Fuzzy Logic and Neural Networks Proceedings*, IIZUKA, Japan (1992), ISBN 4-938717-01-8.

[182]   von Altrock, C., Krause, B. and Zimmermann, H.-J., "Advanced Fuzzy Logic Control Technologies in Automotive Applications," *IEEE Conference on Fuzzy Systems* (1992), ISBN 0-7803-0237-0, pp. 831-842.

[183]   von Altrock, C., "Fuzzy Logic Technologies in Automotive Engineering," *Proceedings of the Embedded Systems Conference* (1994), Vol. 2, ISBN 0-87930-356-5, pp. 407–422.

[184]   von Altrock, C. and D'Souza, S., "Fuzzy Logic and NeuroFuzzy Technologies in Appliances," *Proceedings of the Embedded Systems Conference* (1994), Vol. 2, ISBN 0-87930-356-5, pp. 423–444.

[185]   von Altrock, C., Franke, S., and Froese, T., "Optimization of a Water-Treatment System with Fuzzy Logic Control," *Computer Design Fuzzy Logic '94 Conference* in San Diego (1994).

[186]   von Altrock, C., "NeuroFuzzy Technologies," *Computer Design Magazine* 6/94 (1994), pp. 82–83.

[187]   von Altrock, C., Krause, B., Limper, K., and Schäfers, W., "Optimization of a Waste Incineration Plant Using Fuzzy Logic," *EUFIT '94 Conference* in Aachen (1994).

[188]   von Altrock, C., Arend, H.-O., Krause, B., Steffens, C., and Behrens-Rommler, E., "Customer-Adaptive Fuzzy Control of Home Heating System," *IEEE Conference on Fuzzy Systems* in Orlando (1994).

[189] von Altrock, C., "Enhanced Fuzzy Systems Using Data Analysis Techniques and Neural Networks," *Computer Design Fuzzy Logic Conference*, San Diego (1994).

[190] von Altrock, C. and Krause, B., "Multi-Criteria Decision Making in German Automotive Industry Using Fuzzy Logic," *Fuzzy Sets and Systems* 63 (1994), pp. 375–380.

[191] von Altrock, C., "Fuzzy Logic Applications in Europe," in Yen, Langari, Zadeh (Eds.), *Industrial Applications of Fuzzy Logic and Intelligent Systems,* IEEE Press 1995.

[192] Vossiek, M. et al., "Intelligente Signalverarbeitung durch Kombination von Fuzzy Logic und klassischer Signalvorverarbeitung am Beispiel eines Luftultraschallsystems zur Platinenbestückungskontrolle," *VDE-Fachtagung Technische Anwendungen von Fuzzy-Systemen* (1992), pp. 71–80.

[193] Wakami, N. "Engineering Application of Fuzzy Systems—Fuzzy Control and Neural Networks: Applications for (Matsushita) Home Appliances," *Joint Japanese-European Symposium on Fuzzy Systems* in Berlin, Publications of the Japanese-German Center Berlin, Volume 8 (1994), ISSN 0937-3799.

[194] Wal, A. J. van der, and Mattaar, T. C., "Performance Finetuning of a PID Controller by Fuzzy Logic," *Japanese-European Symposium on Fuzzy Systems* (1992).

[195] Wassermann, P. D., *Neuro Computing: Theory and Practice*, New York (1989).

[196] Watada, V., "Methods for Fuzzy Classification," *Japanese Journal of Fuzzy Theory and Systems* 4 (1992), pp. 149-163.

[197] Watanabe, T. et al., "AI and Fuzzy–Based Tunnel Ventilation Control System," *Proc. of the Int'l. Conf. on Fuzzy Logic & Neural Networks*, IIZUKA, Japan (1990), pp. 71–75.

[198] Watanabe, T. and Ichihashi, H., "Iterative Fuzzy Modeling Using Membership Function of Degree n and Its Application to Crane Control," *Japanese Journal of Fuzzy Theory and Systems*, Vol. 3, No. 2 (1991), ISSN 1058-7349, pp. 173–186.

[199] Wegmann, H. and Prehn, E., "Fuzzy Logic mit SPS Standardkomponenten zur PH-Neutralisation Chemischer Abwässer," *Swiss Fuzzy Logic Conference '92* , Baden (1992).

[200] Weil, H.-G., Probst, G., and Graf, F., "Fuzzy Shift Logic For an Automatic Transmission System," *EUFIT '93—First European Congress on Fuzzy and Intelligent Technologies* in Aachen (1993), pp. 15–23.

[201] Williams, T., "Alliances to Speed Acceptance of Fuzzy Logic Technology—Intel and Inform Software Team Up for 16-bit MCUs," *Computer Design* 12 (1992), pp. 52–56.

[202] Williams, T., von Altrock, C., Banks, W., Xu, W., and Yani, Y., "Fuzzy Logic Benchmark Panel Discussion," *Computer Design Fuzzy Logic '94 Conference* in San Francisco (1993).

[203] Yager, R., "Implementing Fuzzy Logic Controllers Using a Neural Network Framework," *Fuzzy Sets and Systems* 48 (1992) pp. 53–64.

[204] Yagishita, O., Itoh, O., and Sugeno, M., "Application of Fuzzy Reasoning to the Water Purification Process," in Sugeno (Ed.) *Industrial Applications of Fuzzy Control* (1985), pp. 19–40, Amsterdam, New York.

[205] Yamakawa, T., Shirai, Y. and Ueno, F., "Implementation of Fuzzy Logic Hardware Systems," *Transactions of the IEEE*, Vol. C-63 (1980), pp. 720–725 and pp. 861–862.

[206] Yamakawa, T. and Miki, T., "The Current Mode Fuzzy Logic Integrated Circuits Fabricated by Standard CMOS Process," *IEEE Transactions on Computers*, Vol. C-35, No. 2 (1986), pp. 161–167.

[207] Yamashita, R. and Yamakawa, T., "Application of Fuzzy Control to a Localized Cleanroom," *2nd Int'l. Conference on Fuzzy Logic and Neural Networks Proceedings*, IIZUKA, Japan (1992), ISBN 4-938717-01-8, pp. 1101–1102.

[208] Yasunobu, P. and Miamoto, P., "Automatic Train Operation by Predictive Fuzzy Control" in Sugeno (Ed.) *Industrial Applications of Fuzzy Control* (1985), pp. 1–18, Amsterdam, New York.

[209] Yen, J.-Y., Lin, C.-P., Li, D.-H. and Chen, Y.-Y., "Servo Controller for an Optical Disk Drive Using Fuzzy Control Algorithm," *IEEE Conference on Fuzzy Systems* (1992), ISBN 0-7803-0237-0, pp. 989–995.

[210] Yen, J., Langari, R., and Zadeh, L., "Industrial Applications of Fuzzy Logic and Intelligent Systems," *IEEE Press* (1994), ISBN 0-7803-1048-9.

[211] Ying, H. and Sheppard, L. C., "Real-Time Expert-System-Based Fuzzy Control of Mean Arterial Pressure in Pigs with Sodium Nitro-prusside Infusion," *Medical Programming Technology* (1990), pp. 69–76.

[212] Yoshida, S. and Wakabayashi, N., "A Fuzzy Logic Controller for a Rigid Disk Drive," *IEEE Control Systems* (June 1992), pp. 65–70.

[213] Yu, C., Cao, Z., and Kandel, A., "Application of Fuzzy Reasoning to the Control of an Activated Sludge Plant," *Fuzzy Sets and Systems* 38 (1990), pp. 1–14.

[214] Zadeh, L. A., "Fuzzy Sets," *Information and Control*, Vol. 8 (1965), pp. 338–353.

[215] Zadeh, L. A., "Outline of a New Approach to the Analysis of Complex Systems and Decision Processes," *IEEE Trans. Systems, Man, Cybernet*, 3 (1) (1973), pp. 8–44.

[216] Ziegler, J. G. and Nichols, N. B., "Optimum Settings for Automatic Controllers," *ASME Trans.*, Vol. 64, No. 8 (1942), pp. 759–768.

[217] Zimmermann, H.-J. and Thole, U., "On the Suitability of Minimum and Product Operators for the Intersection of Fuzzy Sets," *Fuzzy Sets and Systems*, 2, pp. 173-186.

[218] Zimmermann, H.-J. and Zysno, P. "Latent Connectives in Human Decision Making," *Fuzzy Sets and Systems* 4 (1980), pp. 37–51.

[219] Zimmermann, H.-J. and Zysno, P. "Decision Analysis and Evaluations by Hierarchical Aggregation of Information," *Fuzzy Sets and Systems* 10 (1983), pp. 243–266.

[220] Zimmermann, H.-J., *Fuzzy Sets, Decision Making, and Expert Systems* (1987), Boston, Dordrecht, London, ISBN 0-89838-149-5.

[221] Zimmermann, H.-J., *Fuzzy Set Theory—and Its Applications*, Second Revised Edition (1991), Boston, Dordrecht, London, ISBN 0-7923-9075-X.

[222] Zimmermann, H.-J. and von Altrock, C. (Hrsg.), "Fuzzy Logic–Band 2: Die Anwendungen," Munich: Oldenburg, (1993), ISBN 3-486-22677-0.

Most journals in the area of fuzzy logic cover research areas. However, some of the journals (for example, FSS) do issue so-called applicational issues that concentrate on practical papers. Here is a list of the major journals:

Name (Abbreviation)	Year of Publication	Country of Editor/ Publisher	Volume No. (as of December 1993)
Fuzzy Sets and Systems (FSS)	1978	Germany/ Netherlands	60
BUSEFAL	1980	France	56
Intelligent Systems (IS)	1986	U.S.A.	8
Approximate Reasoning (AR)	1987	U.S.A.	9
Japanese Journal on Soft Computing, Engl. Ed. (SOFT)	1988	Japan/U.S.A.	5
Fuzzy Sets and Artificial Intelligence (FSAI)	1992	Romania	2
IEEE Transactions on Fuzzy Systems	1993	U.S.A.	1
International Journal of Uncertainty, Fuzziness and Knowledge Based Systems	1993	Singapore/France	1
Journal of Intelligent and Fuzzy Systems	1993	U.S.A.	1
Journal of Fuzzy Mathematics	1993	U.S.A.	1

Name (Abbreviation)	Year of Publication	Country of Editor/ Publisher	Volume No. (as of December 1993)
Journal of Fuzzy Logic and Intelligent Systems	1993	Korea	1

Other journals that publish a considerable number of papers about fuzzy logic are:

IEEE Transactions on Systems, Man and Cybernetics (IEEE)

International Journal of General Systems (Gordon & Breach)

International Journal of Man-Machine Studies (Academic Press)

Information Sciences (Elsevier-North Holland)

Journal of Mathematical Analysis and Applications (Academic Press)

Index